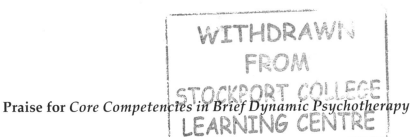

Praise for *Core Competencies in Brief Dynamic Psychotherapy*

"Drs. Jeffrey L. Binder and Ephi J. Betan are not only experts in brief dynamic psychotherapy, they are experts in clinical training, having many years experience in the education and training of doctoral students in clinical psychology."

> —Philinda Smith Hutchings, PhD, ABPP, Professor and Director of Clinical Training, Clinical Psychology Program, Midwestern University, Illinois

"This book is exceptionally clear and sophisticated in conveying the subtle interplay of theory and practice in brief dynamic psychotherapy. Based in current studies and concepts of expertise and competence, it constitutes a superb training guide for novice and experienced clinicians who wish to learn how to conduct this essential mode of psychotherapy."

> —Stanley B. Messer, PhD, Dean and Professor II, Graduate School of Applied and Professional Psychology, Rutgers University, New Jersey

"In this volume, *Core Competencies in Brief Dynamic Psychotherapy*, Jeffrey L. Binder and Ephi J. Betan offer the reader a compendium of knowledge, methods, and therapeutic frameworks necessary for conducting effective brief dynamic psychotherapy. This is a must read for students, as well as advanced practitioners who want an up-to-date resource. The volume includes abundant case material, which gives the reader intimate insight into the therapeutic process revealing the power of focal dynamic psychotherapy. Binder and Betan integrate the latest findings in clinical science and demonstrate the process of effective brief dynamic psychotherapy."

> —Jeffrey J. Magnavita, PhD, ABPP, Previous President of the Division of Psychotherapy of the American Psychological Association, Fellow, American Psychological Association

D1145609

Core Competencies in Brief Dynamic Psychotherapy

This book addresses the essential clinical competencies required to conduct brief dynamic therapy. Authors Jeffrey L. Binder and Ephi J. Betan discuss the conceptual foundation of their treatment model, and the application of this framework in forming and maintaining a therapeutic alliance, assessment, case formulation, implementing a treatment plan, termination, and treatment evaluation. All topics include a multicultural perspective and sensitivity to ethical issues. Binder and Betan attempt to bridge practice and research by consistently incorporating relevant research findings. Graduate students in the mental health fields and beginning therapists will find in this text the basic concepts and principles of brief dynamic psychotherapy presented in a clear and straightforward style, with many clinical examples drawn from detailed patient and therapist interchanges. Seasoned psychotherapists will find in Binder and Betan's discussions of case formulation and therapeutic discourse a fresh treatment of classic ideas about the therapeutic value of constructing personal narratives. At all times, the authors explicitly tie the components of their approach to the competencies required of the brief dynamic therapist. In the current environment of accountability for results, attention is given to the ongoing assessment of therapeutic progress and ultimate outcomes. This text is a scholarly yet practical guide to the evidence-based practice of brief dynamic psychotherapy.

Jeffrey L. Binder, PhD, ABPP is Professor of Psychology at the Georgia School of Professional Psychology, Argosy University. Dr. Binder has extensively published and presented on the topics of brief psychotherapy practice, training, and research, and the nature and development of clinical expertise.

Ephi J. Betan, PhD is Professor of Psychology at the Georgia School of Professional Psychology, Argosy University. Dr. Betan has published and presented in the areas of professional ethics, multicultural competence, countertransference, relational psychoanalysis, clinical expertise in psychotherapy, and psychotherapy training.

Core Competencies in Psychotherapy Series

SERIES EDITOR
Len Sperry
Florida Atlantic University, Medical College of Wisconsin

Competency represents a paradigm shift in the training and practice of psychotherapy that is already challenging much of what is familiar and comfortable. This series addresses the core competencies common to highly effective psychotherapeutic practice, and includes individual volumes for the most commonly practiced approaches today: cognitive behavior, brief dynamic, and solution-focused therapies, and others.

VOLUMES IN THIS SERIES

Highly Effective Therapy: Developing Essential Clinical Competencies in Counseling and Psychotherapy
Len Sperry

Core Competencies in Counseling and Psychotherapy: Becoming a Highly Competent and Effective Therapist
Len Sperry

Core Competencies in the Solution-Focused and Strategic Therapies: Becoming a Highly Competent Solution-Focused and Strategic Therapist
Ellen K. Quick

Case Conceptualization: Mastering this Competency with Ease and Confidence
Len Sperry and Jonathan Sperry

Core Competencies in Cognitive-Behavioral Therapy: Becoming a Highly Effective and Competent Cognitive-Behavioral Therapist
Cory F. Newman

Core Competencies in Brief Dynamic Psychotherapy: Becoming a Highly Effective and Competent Brief Dynamic Psychotherapist
Jeffrey L. Binder and Ephi J. Betan

Core Competencies in Brief Dynamic Psychotherapy

Becoming a Highly Effective and Competent Brief Dynamic Psychotherapist

JEFFREY L. BINDER
EPHI J. BETAN

Routledge
Taylor & Francis Group

NEW YORK AND LONDON

First published 2013
by Routledge
711 Third Avenue, New York, NY 10017

Simultaneously published in the UK
by Routledge
27 Church Road, Hove, East Sussex BN3 2FA

Routledge is an imprint of the Taylor & Francis Group, an informa business

Library of Congress Cataloging in Publication Data
Binder, Jeffrey L.
    Core competencies in brief dynamic psychotherapy : becoming a highly effective and competent brief dynamic psychotherapist / by Jeffrey L. Binder and Ephi J. Betan.
    p. cm.
    Includes bibliographical references and index.
    ISBN 978-0-415-63776-3 (hardback : alk. paper) — ISBN 978-0-415-88599-7 (pbk. : alk. paper) 1. Psychodynamic psychotherapy. 2. Brief psychotherapy. 3. Core competencies. I. Betan, Ephi J. II. Title.
    RC489.P72B53 2012
    616.89'147—dc23
    2012016330

ISBN: 978-0-415-63776-3 (hbk)
ISBN: 978-0-415-88599-7 (pbk)
ISBN: 978-0-203-83741-2 (ebk)

Typeset in Palatino
by EvS Communication Networx, Inc.

SUSTAINABLE
FORESTRY
INITIATIVE

Certified Sourcing
www.sfiprogram.org
SFI-00555
The SFI label applies to the text stock.

Printed and bound in the United States of America by Walsworth Publishing Company, Marceline, MO.

CONTENTS

CONTENTS

FOREWORD

The evolving *zeitgeist* within the mental health disciplines increasingly places a competency-based framework squarely at the center of contemporary professional education and practice. This trend extends to the field of psychotherapy, where the dialogue on core competencies is just beginning to unfold. It is within this context that Drs. Jeffrey L. Binder and Ephi J. Betan lend their considerable expertise as clinicians, scholars, and educators to provide a timely and incisive perspective on the application of a competency-based model in the practice of psychotherapy.

In this formative period for the articulation of core psychotherapy competencies, including the constellation of knowledge, skills, and attitudes required for effective psychotherapy practice, theory-based approaches can yield key insights into the essences of what competency-based psychotherapy should look like. This is precisely what Drs. Binder and Betan accomplish in this highly lucid and comprehensive account of core competencies required for the effective conduct of brief dynamic psychotherapy. The conceptual and clinical foundations of the model they describe are derived from Time-Limited Dynamic Psychotherapy (TLDP), a seminal research-based relational psychodynamic and interpersonal approach developed in the 1980s at Vanderbilt University by Dr. Binder in collaboration with his distinguished colleague Dr. Hans Strupp. As a descendant of TLDP, Drs. Binder and Betan's brief dynamic psychotherapy model is anchored theoretically by relational psychodynamic principles and thoroughly informed by the extant evidence base. It also incorporates an integrative dimension that, in its current evolution, draws upon concepts from cognitive science and cognitive psychotherapy. As such, the competency-based framework described is pertinent to emerging innovations in psychotherapy integration.

Guided by their overarching conceptual vision of brief dynamic psychotherapy, Drs. Binder and Betan synthesize the relevant theoretical, empirical, and clinical strands of the psychotherapy literature to yield a seamless and elegantly coherent account of the specific core competencies required for effective psychotherapy practice from start to finish. These competency domains include grounding in the requisite conceptual knowledge base needed to frame the work of psychotherapy, facility in establishing and sustaining a working alliance, proficiency in clinical assessment/case formulation along with intervention planning and implementation, expertise in the evaluation of psychotherapy process and outcome, and skill in navigating the exigencies of psychotherapy termination. The importance of a cultural and ethical responsiveness that threads these respective competency domains also is highlighted.

Psychotherapists in training will find the presentation to be a conceptually nuanced and yet accessible inquiry into the core principles of effective psychotherapeutic practice. The extensive use of case material is especially effective in bringing to life key concepts and illustrating how they may be expressed in the context of real world psychotherapy. The discussion of how to construct and track a narrative cyclical maladaptive pattern is particularly vivid, providing an invaluable template for novice psychotherapists seeking to learn core competencies in psychotherapy assessment, case formulation, planning, and intervention. Advanced psychotherapists will appreciate the conceptual richness and clarity with which Drs. Binder and Betan characterize the mutual influences of theory, practice principles, and clinical research in informing their brief dynamic psychotherapy model. Practitioners familiar with brief dynamic psychotherapy will recognize points of discussion illustrative of the ongoing evolution of the model. For instance, a new element is added to the cyclical maladaptive pattern case formulation method in order to capture explicitly the self-protective interpersonal behaviors by which an individual may unwittingly sustain maladaptive relational patterns. In addition, recent empirical research is characterized as a basis for informing further reformulation of the role of transference-focused intervention strategies.

The question of what constitutes a high level of psychotherapist competency and effectiveness is an intriguing one. What are the characteristics that define psychotherapeutic expertise? Acknowledging the complexity and uniqueness of any given psychotherapeutic context, Drs. Binder and Betan conclude that competency in psychotherapy is a dynamic and not a static construct. They suggest that highly competent brief dynamic psychotherapy practitioners not only are possessed of the requisite knowledge, skills, and attitudes for effective practice, but also are flexible, relying on the disciplined use of intuition and improvisation to ensure that they respond meaningfully and substantively to the uniqueness of each client and clinical circumstance. In this sense, Drs. Binder and Betan evoke a narrative of psychotherapy as not solely a technical enterprise, but a creative one as well. Highly competent psychotherapists are defined by a capacity to combine theoretical and empirical knowledge, technical skill, *and* creativity in guiding psychotherapeutic discourse in accordance with the unique experiential world and relational narrative of a given client. Whether experienced practitioners, clinician-educators, clinical researchers, or students, readers will undoubtedly find in this characterization of psychotherapy competency a fertile context for reflection and dialogue on the dimensions that constitute clinical expertise in 21st century psychotherapy practice.

Eugene W. Farber, PhD, ABPP
Associate Professor of Psychiatry & Behavioral Sciences
Emory University School of Medicine

ABOUT THE AUTHORS

Jeffrey L. Binder, PhD, ABPP is Professor of Psychology at the Georgia School of Professional Psychology, Argosy University. Previously he was the Chair of the Clinical Psychology Program at GSPP, and he has taught psychotherapy at the University of Michigan, the University of Virginia, and Vanderbilt University, where he also conducted psychotherapy training research. Dr. Binder also has directed an outpatient clinic and inpatient adolescent and adult mental health programs. In 1984 he co-authored with Hans H. Strupp the seminal work, *Psychotherapy in a New Key: A Guide to Time-Limited Dynamic Psychotherapy* and in 2004 he authored *Key Competencies in Brief Dynamic Psychotherapy: Clinical Practice Beyond the Manual.* Dr. Binder has extensively published and presented on the topics of brief psychotherapy practice, training, and research, and the nature and development of clinical expertise. He is a Fellow of the American Psychological Association, Division 29 of the APA, the Georgia Psychological Association, and the Academy of Clinical Psychology.

Ephi J. Betan, PhD is Professor of Psychology at the Georgia School of Professional Psychology, Argosy University. Dr. Betan completed her postdoctoral fellowship at the Menninger Hospital in Topeka, Kansas, as well as the Course of Study in the Theory of Psychoanalysis at the Emory University Psychoanalytic Institute. Dr. Betan has published and presented in the areas of professional ethics, multicultural competence, countertransference, relational psychoanalysis, clinical expertise in psychotherapy, and psychotherapy training.

1

Introducing the Clinical Competencies of Brief Dynamic Psychotherapy

Brief dynamic psychotherapy (BDP) is a time sensitive version of the psychodynamic approach to individual psychotherapy with adults. It is one of the products of a diverse and evolving theory of personality, psychopathology, and psychotherapy, which originated with the works of Sigmund Freud (Breuer & Freud, 1893–1895/1955). Freud always focused on modifying and elaborating his theories of personality and psychopathology, derived from systematic and keen observations made during the course of his clinical work. Given the paucity of his writings on the topic, Freud seemed to have given short shrift to the topic of therapy technique. Most of his thoughts on technique appeared in papers written between 1912 and 1915. In his autobiography, he states that the essence of psychoanalysis is "the art of interpretation" and that this skill is "not hard to acquire" (cited in Ehrenwald, 1991, p. 285).

During most of the 20th century, the literature on psychoanalysis and psychodynamic theory reflected Freud's focus on theories of personality and psychopathology to the relative neglect of studies of therapeutic technique and its development. The conduct of psychodynamic therapy continued to be viewed as an "art," and the therapist's "artistic" talent was acquired through supervisory relationships not unlike a master–apprentice relationship. The pedagogy of psychodynamic psychotherapy

1

training rested on the successful resolution through personal therapy of the therapist's neurotic impediments to empathy and objectivity. The implication was that good therapy technique would develop relatively easily once the novice therapist had the requisite mind-set. One of the most influential 20th century books on psychodynamic therapy supervision was based on the idea that the primary task of the therapy supervisor was to identify the way in which the novice therapist's neurotic entanglements with his patient was impacting the supervisory relationship and interfering with the supervisee's receptivity to learning (Eckstein & Wallerstein, 1972). In the same vein, a common assumption among teachers of short-term psychodynamic therapies has been that if the novice therapist does not have a bias against time-limited approaches, acquiring the skill to conduct them is relatively straightforward.

Beginning in the latter part of the 20th century, the confluence of a variety of forces has led ultimately to a focus on therapist competency in the mental health disciplines. From the perspective of the delivery of mental health services, increasing concerns with the escalating cost of health care has led to a focus on provider accountability. The pressure to demonstrate effective practices, in turn, has made clinical training programs in the mental health disciplines more sensitive to the quality of their training. In order to evaluate training outcomes, it is necessary to have a clear understanding of the nature of the skills that trainees are expected to acquire. Indeed, for clinical training programs to receive government and professional association accreditations, program learning outcomes must be spelled out and empirically assessed. There also is societal pressure for professionals to explain exactly what is it that they do for the consumers of their services (Borden & McIlvried, 2010). In order to obtain funding from the National Institute of Mental Health (NIMH) for their projects, psychotherapy researchers also have to articulate what is distinctive about therapist performance in the treatments to be studied and evaluated. The methods prescribed for a particular model of therapy have to be spelled out in a "treatment manual." The original manuals focused on therapist technical adherence, but the need to also articulate what characterized the competent use of techniques became evident. Several of the early treatment manuals provided detailed guidance for the conduct of different forms of short-term psychodynamic therapies (Horowitz, 1986; Luborsky, 1984; Strupp & Binder, 1984; Weiss, Sampson, & Mt. Zion Psychotherapy Research Group, 1986). In recent years additional manuals on brief dynamic therapy have appeared (e.g., Binder, 2004; H. Levenson, 2010).

For the mental health disciplines, we are in an epoch in which professional survival requires that the nature of the competencies associated with being an effective psychotherapist must be articulated and methods for evaluating these competencies must be developed. These realities have led to a major shift in clinical training programs from content-based curricula (in which certain content areas must be covered to satisfy graduation requirements) to competence-based curricula (in which specific competencies must be acquired and their acquisition must be empirically demonstrated; Kenkel & Peterson, 2010). Of course, the foundation of the competency movement in the mental health disciplines is a clear definition of "competency."

DEFINITION OF COMPETENCIES
AND THEIR COMPONENTS

In the broadest sense, a "competency" has been defined as the demonstrated achievement of a sufficient level of quality of performance in a given domain relative to some external standard or training requirements (Sperry, 2010a). As applied to clinical competencies, Sperry (2010b) has provided the following definition:

> Competency is the capacity to integrate knowledge, skills, and attitudes reflected in the quality of clinical practice that benefits others, which can be evaluated by professional standards and be developed and enhanced through professional training and reflection. (p. 5)

It should be noted that in this context "competency" refers to a cluster of capacities comprising a complex performance in a specific domain of professional activity. This definition should not be confused with the more common definition of "competence" as a level of performance sufficient for a situation or that meets minimal level of standards as determined by an external agency, such as a licensing board. In fact, the two definitions have some overlap.

A "competency" is composed of three components: (a) knowledge, (b) skills, and (c) attitudes. In the broadest sense, knowledge refers to comprehension of a domain topic, including both an understanding of content and an understanding of when and how to apply this content. For our purposes the term *clinical knowledge* usually refers to the conceptual

3

foundation for the conduct of psychotherapy. Cognitive scientists call this type of understanding, declarative knowledge, which includes facts, general propositional concepts, principles, and rules. It makes up the content of the "cognitive map" which a therapist uses to identify and focus on those aspects of an immediate therapeutic environment that are relevant to the pursuit of his or her selected goals (Binder, 1999). Declarative knowledge is acquired through reading, course work, and study. It provides the conceptual foundation for clinical practice. Skills, or therapeutic procedures, involve the application of declarative knowledge in real practice situations. Skillful behavior reflects a complementary form of knowledge, which cognitive scientists call *procedural knowledge* (Binder, 1999). This term refers to largely tacit understanding (Polanyi, 1967) that automatically guides the clinician in applying his or her declarative knowledge in the appropriate contexts and in the most effective ways. Schön (1983) described procedural knowledge as "knowing-in-action." Skills are acquired through watching the work of more experienced therapists, ideally "master therapists," and practice with feedback from a teacher or supervisor. The attitudes associated with a clinical competency are those beliefs, dispositions, motivations, and values that support the acquisition and progressive enhancement of the knowledge and skills associated with a competency, as well as its use to improve the well-being of one's patients. One chooses to become a psychotherapist because of certain long-held attitudes, such as a belief in the importance of psychological health for the overall well-being of the individual. During the course of training, attitudes are acquired that are associated with the development of a professional identity, such as the importance of self-reflection and self-monitoring as part of the conduct of psychotherapy.

The conduct of psychotherapy comprises a set of integrated complex performances and, therefore, the progressive development from novice to expert therapist involves a variety of knowledge organizations and levels of skill complexity. The most basic facet of therapist performance development, however, may be the transformation of therapeutically relevant declarative knowledge into usable procedural knowledge. Without this basic developmental step, the therapist may be a fund of knowledge—a superb "locker room" player—but this declarative knowledge does not provide guidance about when and how to implement theories, concepts, principles, and rules. In the words of the British mathematician and philosopher, Alfred North Whitehead (1929) the knowledge remains "inert." Any doubts about this observation are easily dispelled when observing a novice therapist fumbling around in an attempt to develop an understanding of a new patient and to do something therapeutically helpful with this person. All of the therapist's book knowledge appears to have departed his or her head.

Procedural knowledge represents the integration of declarative knowledge, ideally organized in a coherent conceptual framework, with skills associated with the timely and appropriate application of this knowledge in real-world situations.

> Procedural knowledge is the gradually accumulated product of experiences with applying theoretical concepts, principles, and technical prescriptions in real practice contexts. It consists of the pairing of propositions and concrete experiences with action strategies and rules, as well as appraisals of the consequences. It is in the form of condition–action sequences. (Binder, 1999, p. 711)

In other words, a therapist's competencies progressively develop when he or she learns from clinical experiences. Early in a therapist's development, supervised learning experiences are crucial. Learners need usable feedback on the quality of their performance, in order to make error-correcting changes. Memorizing a golf instructional book by a renowned golf professional will not prepare the novice golfer to play a solid round of golf. On the other hand, the cumulative experiences of repeatedly playing rounds of golf without ever reading about swing technique or getting lessons is unlikely to produce a skilled golfer.

ESSENTIAL CLINICAL COMPETENCIES

The pictures of clinical training and practice are rapidly being redone in the language of competencies. The various mental health disciplines have begun the task of compiling and organizing descriptive lists of knowledge, skills, and attitudes, including such lists for characterizing the practice of psychotherapy. Within disciplines, various workgroups have been formed with the task of articulating the competencies associated with the various types of clinical work, as well as their respective components (Kenkel & Peterson, 2010). In his ongoing review of the clinical competency literature, Sperry (2010b) has enumerated six core competencies and 20 essential clinical competencies required for therapy to be effective. The six core competencies are: (a) conceptual foundation, (b) relationship building and maintenance, (c) intervention planning, (d) intervention implementation, (e) intervention evaluation and termination, and (f) culturally and ethically sensitive practice.

There are several major schools of psychotherapy practiced today, including: psychodynamic; cognitive-behavioral; systemic; person-centered, and emotional-focused. This book elaborates on these core competencies characterize highly effective work in brief psychodynamic therapies.

DEVELOPMENTAL STAGES OF COMPETENCY

As we mentioned above, competency refers both to a cluster of capacities composed of knowledge, skills, and attitudes and to a level of performance. A competent therapist represents a midlevel point in professional development. The seminal work on the progressive development of generic complex performances was written by two brothers, one of whom was a computer scientist and the other a philosopher (Dreyfus & Dreyfus, 1986). Their "stage model" is a conceptual framework widely used in various forms by cognitive scientists who study the nature and development of expertise. This developmental model has five stages, with those beyond the first or novice stage achieved through practice and experience.

Novice therapists operate entirely on the basis of declarative knowledge acquired through coursework and reading. They have been taught to recognize certain situational elements and rules for determining how to manage these elements, but they have not learned how to comprehend what they see within the immediate context nor have they integrated current actions with longer term goals. For example, novice psychodynamic therapists will know the concept of "transference" and can appreciate idiosyncratic behavior, but lacking experience with patients, they will not usually be able to identify transference patterns within the interpersonal context of which they are a part. They also will tend to confuse the idea that "transference" refers to context-relevant explanations of behavior rather than descriptions of specific types of behavior. Consequently, it is not uncommon to hear novice therapists talk about the "amount" of transference in a therapy session. Through practical experiences coping with real situations, advanced beginners are more skillful at recognizing relevant aspects of a situation as well as beginning to develop a meaningful conception of the situation itself. At this stage of development novice therapists are becoming more skillful at recognizing patient attitudes and behavior that can meaningfully be viewed as expressions of transference. They are also beginning to see how they may be playing a role in evoking and influencing the form of the transference behavior; that is, they are becoming aware of their "countertransference."

With more experience—especially with good mentoring, in order to make these experiences productive learning episodes—declarative knowledge is transformed into procedural knowledge. Consequently, the person engaged in a complex performance is able to independently comprehend a problem situation in terms of selecting what factors are relevant in working toward a specific goal. A given competency is associated with a specific domain of performance. Within a domain, certain kinds of situations tend to recur and become more or less routine. Competent performers automatically recognize in routine situations similarities from one time to the next. This is the stage of competence in which performers begin to see meaningful patterns rather than discrete situational elements, and their goal-directed actions are dictated by the patterns they see. They have accumulated sufficient practical experience so that their reasoning processes are shifting from rule-based to case-based or "analogical reasoning" (Buchanan, Davis, & Feigenbaum, 2006). In this type of reasoning, new problem situations are automatically compared with similar, previously managed past situations that have been stored in memory. This reasoning process facilitates pattern recognition and evokes previously successful action-consequence sequences of behavior. Furthermore, these cognitive and behavioral processes are increasingly tacit and automatic (Sternberg & Horvath, 1999). Thus, the competent performer's behavior tends to appear smooth and purposeful.

Within a session, competent therapists can construe a patient's problematic behavior toward them as a manifestation of transference. They compare the patient's behavior with memories of similar interactions with the same or other patients, in order to help them attach narrative meaning to the behavior. In addition, they automatically embed the immediate interpersonal experience in a conceptual framework of psychoanalytic principles. These principles might include the superimposition on current interpersonal situations of scenarios from the patient's childhood, the defensive function of action substituted for remembering, and the interpretive linking of transference to other similarly enacted transactions in other relationships. Therapists with an interpersonal orientation may also reflect on their countertransference contribution based on the interpersonal principle that transference and countertransference enactments are ineluctably intertwined.

In the fourth stage of the development of a competency, proficient performers will have continued to expand their memory store of relevant problem situations and the behavior strategies that successfully managed them. Consequently, their capacity to utilize analogical reasoning to comprehend and successfully deal with immediate situations has become more extensive and automatic. Their grasp of situations appears intuitive, especially those problem situations that have come to be experienced as more or less routine. Their management of these situations is increasingly smooth and appears effortless. Proficient psychodynamic therapists' ability to automatically manage many routine therapeutic situations allows them to remain alert to even very subtle interactions between themselves and their patients that have transference implications. The tacit nature of the therapists routine actions also allow them to be more alert to how their personal reactions to the patient influence their behavior, and how their actions contribute to the specifics of the patient's transference enactments.

Within their performance domains, experts operate in routine situations with a speed, fluidity, and efficiency that is unparalleled in any earlier stage of competency development. The expert comprehends and acts in one seamless motion. For example, the chess master is not able to plan moves significantly further along than a less accomplished player; rather, he or she "knows" the right move. It is estimated that a chess master has a memory store of at least 50,000 board positions, and the one that best fits the current situation influences his or her perception of the current configuration of pieces and what would be the most advantageous move (Dreyfus & Dreyfus, 1986). But, it is not the routine situation that distinguishes experts from those in earlier stages of competency development. Within his or her domain, the expert sees elements and patterns within the immediate situation with a precision, clarity, and depth of understanding that is unique. World class athletes describe being "in the groove," when their perceptions of the ball field slow down, allowing them to refine their actions and to anticipate and make adjustments to changing contextual circumstances (Binder, 2004; Ericsson & Charness, 1999). Experts have an enhanced pattern recognition capacity and extensive store of procedural knowledge that makes it possible for them to rapidly respond in ambiguous and unique situations. The psychotherapy relationship is often an ambiguous even unique setting. It is what Schön (1983) has called an "indeterminate zone." Researchers who have studied master therapists have observed that one characteristic of these therapists is that they did not "go by the book" as much as nonexpert therapists do, even if the former wrote the books (Goldfried, Raue, & Castonguay, 1996). In relatively routine circumstances, expert therapists' characteristic mode of engaging a patient and their accompanying technical actions are so seamless a part of who they are that they are largely unaware of their actions and interpersonal style (Dreyfus & Dreyfus, 1986). The base of automatic interpersonal actions allows expert therapists to remain keenly attuned to changing interpersonal circumstances. Expert therapists are continuously able to "reflect-in-action" (Schön, 1983); that is, while they are interacting with the patient, they are simultaneously able to monitor what is happening and modify their understanding and actions accordingly—they are able to "improvise." It is this capacity to improvise when called for that distinguishes experts (Binder, 2004; Ericsson, 1996; Sternberg & Horvath, 1999). For example, expert therapists always monitor the affective nuances of the patient–therapist interchange, detect their own personal reactions and responses that appear to be part of an unfolding interpersonal scenario having the characteristics of the patient's salient transference theme. In those circumstances, therapists are able to "freeze the action" and engage the patient in a productive discussion of what has been transpiring between them.

BECOMING AN EFFECTIVE PSYCHOTHERAPIST

It could be argued that effective psychotherapists acquire their competence despite their training, because the formal structure of graduate training programs that teach psychotherapy do not typically incorporate principles and procedures that have been found to facilitate the development of complex performances (Binder, 1993, 1999). For example, the abrupt transition from course work to conducting supervised therapy with actual patients in real-world settings tends to maintain declarative knowledge about psychotherapy processes and procedures in an "inert" state (Binder, 1999). Experience alone will not necessarily produce increments in therapeutic competence (Ericsson, 2006). On the other hand, there is substantial evidence that for learning complex performances like conducting psychotherapy, structured, progressively more challenging practice sessions, in which components of the complex performance are mastered in a planned sequence are most effective (Binder, 1999, 2004; Ericsson, 2006). Structured sessions like this allow for immediate error-correcting feedback by a trainer, and the opportunity to incorporate this feedback into subsequent practice performance. This form of training is called deliberate practice (Ericsson, 2006). In his text spelling out the essential elements of well-conducted, effective psychotherapy, Sperry (2010b) provides the content for deliberate practice as well as some proposals on how to implement its principles. We will return to this subject in chapter 11.

COMPETENCIES IN BRIEF DYNAMIC PSYCHOTHERAPY

This book addresses the specific knowledge, skills, and attitudes that comprise competency in the brief dynamic psychotherapies. Its structure and content are guided by the six competencies and 20 clinical skills described by Sperry (2010b), elaborating on how they are actualized in brief dynamic therapy. The book aims to provide a picture of how the brief dynamic therapist integrates relevant knowledge, skills, and attitudes in the process of conducting treatment and in the process of striving to develop from a competent psychotherapist to a proficient or expert clinician.

Chapter 2 introduces the "conceptual map" that is the foundation for understanding people and guiding the conduct of brief dynamic psychotherapy. This "map" is comprised of integrated theories of personality development and functioning, psychopathology, and therapy. The personality theory combines core psychoanalytic principles with contemporary attachment theory, and object relations and interpersonal theories. A person's personality is formed through the internalization of perceived interactions with childhood caretakers (usually parents). These internalizations form a template that constitutes personality structure associated with characteristic patterns of interpersonal relating. Psychological health is characterized by an acceptance of one's feelings and needs, an optimistic attitude about the anticipated actions of others, a wide diversity of modes of interpersonal relating, and a flexible capacity for accommodating and learning from new experiences. By contrast, psychopathology is characterized by a disavowal of aspects of one's personality that were considered unacceptable to parental figures, a pessimistic attitude about the anticipated actions of others, a constricted range of interpersonal patterns of relating, and a rigidity in the face of new experiences. Brief dynamic therapy is based on establishing a trusting and collaborative alliance with a patient, in the process of identifying a content focus for the work. This content focus is articulated in the form of a maladaptive personal story line; that is, a chronic issue or conflict in the form of a personal narrative. This story line is collaboratively explored in order to expand the patient's self-awareness and, in the process, provide a "corrective interpersonal experience" in the context of the therapeutic relationship. It is posited that the combination of insight and this corrective relational experience produce positive psychological and behavioral change.

In order for any form of psychotherapy to benefit a patient, a collaborative working relationship must be established based on mutual trust between therapist and patient. This essential facet of the therapeutic relationship is referred to as the "therapeutic alliance" (Horvath, Del Re, Flückiger, & Symonds, 2011). Chapter 3 discusses the therapist and patient factors determining whether or not an alliance is formed. While both parties affect the nature of the therapeutic alliance, a combination of therapist interpersonal and intervention skills plays a critical role in the establishment of an alliance regardless of the patient's personality characteristics. These therapist skills will be addressed in detail. Once a therapeutic alliance is established, the therapist must ensure that it is maintained throughout the course of therapy. Chapter 4 reviews the challenges to the alliance created by various types of alliance "ruptures" that can occur. In order to resolve these disruptions in the working relationship between therapist and patient, the therapist must be able to flexibly respond to the particular context in which these alliance ruptures occur. He or she, also, must be able to face and constructively manage the negative affects that inevitably arise during these difficult periods.

The first task initiated when beginning a BDP is to conduct a broad diagnostic assessment of the nature and severity of the patient's psychopathology. This task corresponds to the first diagnostic decision that the clinician makes: Is BDP the most suitable intervention for this patient or does she require something else (e.g., hospitalization) or something in addition to psychotherapy (e.g., a medication evaluation) or another form of treatment (e.g., exposure and desensitization for a specific phobia)? If the patient is judged to potentially benefit from psychotherapy, another early diagnostic question concerns the specific adjustments to the therapist's interpersonal stance and technical strategy that are likely to be necessary to engage this particular patient in a productive therapeutic relationship. These questions are part of the initial integrative assessment that is discussed in chapter 5. This chapter focuses on the three major aims of an integrative BDP assessment: (a) evaluating the type and severity of the patient's problems; (b) generating initial hypotheses about the specific psychological and interpersonal struggles associated with the patient's presenting problems, and (c) establishing a therapeutic alliance. Consistent with the change mechanisms and processes posited to operate in BDP, three personality dimensions receive particular attention during the assessment phase: (a) the patient's emotional experiences, including their range, intensity, and management; (b) the patient's self-perceptions and self-experiences, including an assessment of how successfully these experiences are integrated (e.g., their consistency and coherence over time); and (c) the patient's characteristic patterns of interpersonal relating. In order to aid the therapist in assessing these personality dimensions, chapter 5 enumerates questions to be asked by the therapist that facilitate exploration of the respective dimensions. Along with the questions are discussions of issues associated with the respective dimensions of personality. The chapter concludes with a discussion of when and how to be relatively supportive or exploratory and probing while conducting an initial assessment.

The heart of a BDP assessment is the construction of an individualized case formulation, which articulates the content focus of the treatment. Time-limited therapy inherently requires a circumscribed area for the therapeutic work. Consequently, it is particularly important to clearly identify the distinctive features of that area. Chapter 6 addresses the nature of the structured case formulation model that is associated with BDP and the procedures used to construct an individualized case formulation that will guide the content of the therapist's interventions. The structured case formulation model is called the cyclical maladaptive pattern (CMP), which is a narrative format that guides the organization of relevant clinical material into a chronic, rigid pattern of construing interpersonal relationships and acting within them. The conceptual elements of a CMP are described in chapter 6, along with guidelines for the BDP therapist to use in conducting an inquiry that encourages a patient to provide clinical information relevant to the construction of a CMP. The chapter also provides guidelines for organizing clinical material into a

CMP. The first step is to identify a prepotent psychological theme (e.g., emotional neglect) that occurs as a subtext in the patient's descriptions of interpersonal interactions and in relationships dating back to childhood. Then, this theme is elaborated into a salient maladaptive interpersonal pattern that commonly reoccurs in current and past relationships. Case material is used throughout the chapter to illustrate major concepts and procedures. Chapter 6 ends with a discussion of treatment planning based on the integrative assessment and case formulation.

The heart of BDP is the collaborative exploration of how the salient issues that brought the patient to treatment (formulated as a therapeutic focus in the CMP) are manifested throughout his or her life. The therapeutic discourse is examined in chapter 7 and is conceptualized in two phases: the first phase is the inquiry in which the CMP begins to be elaborated into a personal narrative, termed the *maladaptive personal story line*; the second phase is the dialogue in which the personal story line is further elaborated in sufficient detail to begin identifying the dysfunctions associated with this way of living. In the dialogue phase of treatment, the therapist searches for hypothetical origins for the patient's maladaptive ways of living in recollections from his or her past. These two phases of therapeutic discourse compose the middle stage of treatment, in which the two fundamental mechanisms of change are facilitated: expansion of self-understanding and implementation of new and healthier emotional/ interpersonal experiences.

A competency area that recently has assumed great importance is the monitoring and evaluating of treatment outcomes. Chapter 8 discusses the reasons this endeavor has become an important part of the professional practice of psychotherapy. The chapter also reviews strategies for the continuous assessment of treatment progress and enumerates the most widely used assessment tools for achieving this goal.

An inherent component of any brief therapy is the consideration of a planned termination from the outset of treatment. Chapter 9 examines the subject of termination in BDP as well as strategies for maintaining treatment gains and minimizing the likelihood of relapse. In an era of increasing cultural diversity, an essential competency for any clinician to possess is cultural sensitivity, which includes knowledge about and sensitivity to the cultural background of any patient that is seen. This subject is discussed in chapter 10. In this chapter, ethically competent practice also is described and discussed. Finally, chapter 11 discusses the process of becoming a highly competent therapist and enhancing knowledge, skills, and attitudes through training. Highly competent therapists are able to use their knowledge, skills, and attitudes in an intuitive, flexible manner to respond to unique treatment contexts. The ability to adapt in new clinical situations depends on what we call *metabolizing theory*, the process of assimilating, synthesizing, and transforming knowledge so that it becomes intuitive and automatic in one's work. We end with several recommendations for using pedagogic strategies that can facilitate the metabolization of theory and therapeutic procedures. We have found them very helpful in our own teaching of psychotherapy to graduate students.

2

Understanding the Conceptual Basis of Brief Dynamic Psychotherapy

Initially, the patient presents with a welter of information and, thus, begins an encounter that involves complex communications having multiple meanings and multifaceted interpersonal dynamics: this is psychotherapy. Under these circumstances, it is very important to have sufficient grasp of a clinical theory to help process and make sense of what the patient presents and to help plan a therapeutic strategy that will foster psychological change. BDP involves first clearly understanding a patient's troubles and then intervening in intentional ways that help the patient expand realistically positive beliefs about one's self and the attitudes and intentions of others. A solid theoretical foundation, or a "conceptual map" (Binder, 2004) helps guide what we pay attention to in our patient's interpersonal narratives in order to foster a productive therapeutic inquiry that increases a patient's insight into her struggles.

COMPETENCY IN APPLYING A CONCEPTUAL FOUNDATION

This essential clinical competency of applying a conceptual foundation involves developing a coherent conceptual framework for understanding personality development, psychopathology, and the therapeutic process. It also involves the ability to adapt theoretical knowledge to understand the unique patient, plan treatment interventions, and direct the therapeutic process.

The competent therapist is capable of adapting theoretical knowledge in a way that is meaningful to each patient who brings a unique mix of internal struggles, interpersonal needs, and modes of relating. Theoretical knowledge that cannot be made relevant to the specific person's suffering is not likely to be helpful. Competence in using theory to help generate a relevant narrative of a patient's core difficulties requires a coherent conceptual framework. This chapter offers such a conceptual framework that is comprised of the key elements of a useful theory: (a) personality development, (b) psychopathology, and (c) the therapeutic process. Theory serves as a guide for understanding a patient, constructing a case conceptualization, and planning an intervention strategy.

BDP draws on relational approaches, including psychodynamic and interpersonal theories that offer a rich conceptual foundation for understanding personality development and psychopathology. With a predominantly relational focus, we emphasize that ways of relating to others are at the root of difficulties in a patient's sense of self, psychological functioning, and quality of life. We organize case conceptualization around identifying a patient's cyclical maladaptive pattern (CMP), which is an individualized, experience-near narrative of a patient's core assumptions about relationships, as well as typical ways of interacting interpersonally. The CMP is a narrative structure that is used to explain how the patient's difficulties in life are perpetuated. Therefore, we pay particular attention to what occurs in the patient's relationships, past and present (including immediately with the therapist), with an eye toward identifying the patient's potentially maladaptive modes of relating. We begin with a theoretical understanding of how early relational experiences contribute to personality development in general. We move then to understanding how adverse early experiences lead to repetitive interpersonal disturbances that may contribute to a patient's emotional and behavioral struggles. Knowledge of personality development and psychopathology greatly enhances a clinician's capacity to construct a patient's interpersonal narrative in a therapeutically meaningful way.

A CONCEPTUAL MODEL OF
PERSONALITY DEVELOPMENT

Personality refers to enduring patterns of feeling, thinking, and behaving that are generally consistent across context and time. One's characteristic ways of being in, responding to, and thinking about the world emerge prominently in one's style of interpersonal relating. We conceptualize personality in terms of two key domains that encompass the primary capacities necessary for healthy, adaptive functioning, as well as the roots of many symptomatic, subjective, and interpersonal difficulties that bring patients to treatment: interpersonal relating and self-functioning. Many theorists from diverse orientations identify self- and interpersonal functioning as key elements in personality development and dysfunction (e.g., Anchin & Pincus, 2010; Benjamin, 2005; Blatt, 2006; Clarkin, Lenzenweger, Yemans, Levy, & Kernberg, 2007; Livesley, 2003; Meyer & Pilkonis, 2005; Pretzer & Beck, 2005).

Domains of Personality Functioning
Interpersonal Relating

Mature interpersonal relating is marked by (a) trust in benign motives and desires on the part of others; (b) realistic appraisals of others' intentions and motivations; (c) capacities to create positive, supportive, intimate interactions with others; (d) capacities for empathy and perspective taking; (e) capacities to see others and self as multidimensional and separate; and (f) capacities for flexibility and collaboration.

Self-Functioning

Adaptive functioning depends on (a) a coherent and realistically positive sense of self that is stable over time, and (b) capacities for self-regulation including emotional regulation and coping, impulse control, and motivation.

Dual Motivational Strivings: Attachment and / ˙ ˉ ⁿ ᵒmy

We start with a core premise that early relational exp both domains of interpersonal relating and self-funct

17

into account developmental experiences related to both attachment and autonomy/self-definition. The pull toward attachment is innate, because a close physical and emotional connection to a primary caregiver is key to a baby's survival. As such, we seek out other people, and we are profoundly affected by experiences, disturbances, and disruptions in relationships with significant others. Concurrently, there is a universal human striving for autonomy and personal agency (Blatt, 2008; Safran & Muran, 2000). The drive toward individuality fosters the emergence of a positive sense of self that is differentiated from others, as well as one's initiative to pursue interests and desires.

Psychodynamic theory has long recognized that human beings are always negotiating the opposing pulls for closeness with others on the one hand and, on the other hand, strivings toward personal agency and power. Conflict between these two motivational strivings is a universal human experience. Attachment and autonomy are not mutually exclusive and are best understood in dialectical relationship, whereby each striving is reciprocally influenced by the other. For example, a person typically wishes to be recognized by others for her independence and abilities. Similarly, one may express autonomous strivings in the context of a relationship; for example, taking care of another person can be an act of self-agency and determination. The capacity to connect with others must be harmonized with one's desires for independence (Blatt, 2006). Mutuality and intimacy in a relationship depend on both genuine regard for the other and a clear sense of self. We see problems for those individuals who function at the extreme of one or the other dimension or who use one motivational striving to defend against the other (e.g., avoiding relationships in the name of individuality in order to ward off fears of closeness).

How caregivers respond to and facilitate both attachment needs and independence strivings early in childhood will influence the child's development of adaptive capacities and the activation of innate personality potentialities. A caregiver's ability to foster a child's autonomy is, paradoxically, a positive indicator of the quality of the attachment. Furthermore, a sense of basic trust is necessary for a child to feel secure enough to venture away from the parent and assert her independence (Blatt, 2006). In this regard, the quality of attachment between child and caregiver early in life sets the stage for the child's personality and psychological development.

Internalization of Early Relational Experiences

A core principle of psychoanalytic developmental theory is that early relationships influence interpersonal functioning and self-development throughout life. The child internalizes, or takes in, interactions with parents, and they become part of the child's mind as mental representations: that is, evocative memories, images, sounds, and sensations associated with earlier relational experiences. Referred to as "internalized object relations," these representations include the perceived self and other as a dyad linked by an emotion and a belief or expectation about what occurs between two people (Gabbard, 2005). An internalized self-object relationship is not based on a discrete incident but, rather, it is a composite of many interactions that share a common theme. For example, a child who consistently experiences her mother as attentive and responsive will internalize a self-representation as one who is cared for and an other-representation who is benevolent and available; self and other are linked together by feelings of love.

Carried throughout life, such representations of self and other *in relationship* become "working models" (Bowlby, 1969) that capture dominant interpersonal themes that have emerged over repeated relational experiences. They become the schemas or templates for subsequent interpersonal interactions and have an enduring impact on the adult's characteristic feelings, beliefs, and behaviors in relationships. In BDP, we attend very closely to how these longstanding interpersonal themes influence one's ways of relating to others and how they may account for one's core difficulties.

It is important to keep in mind that self–other representations capture relational experiences as a unit. One does not internalize separate sets of self-schemas and other schemas, but rather schemas of self and other *in a relationship.* That is, we internalize possibilities for relating, possibilities for how one may behave and feel in relationships. Therefore, a person may identify with and actualize any aspect of this relational template, *taking on either role.* This accounts for how a child who has been abused may in turn become one who abuses, or how a therapist may experience a patient as alternately passive and needy on the one hand and domineering and rejecting on the other. As a relationship schema is activated, roles may be exchanged. We expect to be treated as we have experienced others treat us early in life. In turn, we also treat ourselves and others as we have been treated. This is significant to keep in mind as we discuss maladaptive relational patterns.

Internalization and Self-Development

In addition to influencing the way an individual perceives and relates to others, internalization of earlier experiences with significant others is also at the root of self-experience and capacities for self-regulation. With regard to self-development, the child learns about herself and develops a sense of self as a result of the responses from others. To see oneself depends on being seen by another, and this is one function of the parent's early mirroring of the baby's gestures and coos (Stern, 2002; Winnicott, 1975, 1992). Later, as a toddler, parents' mirroring and labeling of emotions help the child learn to recognize her feelings, needs, and desires. With such empathy from caregivers, a child can come to know herself as one who feels angry, sad, scared, happy, or loving, and she can begin to distinguish these feelings and learn to modulate her reactions and seek comfort. How caregivers respond to the child is at the root of the child's developing capacities to self-soothe; that is, to name and reflect on feelings, regulate behavioral impulses, and relate to others. A parent's attunement and responsiveness help a child learn to be attuned to and responsive to herself and to others as well, thereby fostering the capacities for empathy and relatedness. A parent's recognition of the child's individuality and evolving interests and desires, in turn, fosters the child's growing sense of self.

The way a parent reacts and behaves toward a child profoundly influences the child's appraisal of self-worth and self-concept. A loving, supportive response from a caregiver not only facilitates a child's growth, but also conveys a message that the child is lovable and worthy. One who internalizes repeated experiences with loving and interested others is more likely to sustain positive images of self. Although others' responses impact one's sense of self throughout life, they have the most profound influence on the nascent self. A young child is the most vulnerable to perceiving how another repeatedly treats her as an indication of who she is and her self-worth. For example, a child may take on a caregiver's anger and see herself as bad as a result. Or, a child may come to feel undeserving and overly needy in response to a parent's impatience. Or, as a result of a parent's hostile criticism, a patient may have become vulnerable to self-hatred and unrelenting self-criticism, unable to find self-acceptance or pleasure in her achievements. Negative self-schemas formed in early childhood are apt to negatively influence one's sense of self and core emotional experiences throughout life. In consequence, early relationships come to have a lasting impact on an individual's sense of self, expectations of others, and ways of moving through the world and approaching life's possibilities.

In this theory, the fundamental building blocks of healthy personality development involve secure, stable, predictable, loving, and supportive relationships with parents early in life. In order to set the stage for a child's positive adaptation, secure sense of self, and mature interpersonal relating, parents must respond empathically to a child's subjective experiences, needs, and desires (Beebe & Lachman, 1988; Fonagy, Gergely, Jurist, & Target, 2002; Slade, Grienenberger, Bernbach, Levy, & Locker, 2005; Stern, 2002) and remain consistent and available (Bowlby, 1969). Out of this basic sketch of our relational theory of personality development, we can begin to look at how development goes awry, leading to dysfunction in interpersonal relating and self-pathology.

A CONCEPTUAL MODEL OF PSYCHOPATHOLOGY: SELF-PROTECTION AND MALADAPTIVE RELATIONAL FUNCTIONING

The emotional quality of early childhood experiences and subsequently internalized representations of these experiences are key in understanding both adaptive and maladaptive functioning. A patient's difficulties are ultimately the consequence of disturbances in early attachments. Strained, unpredictable, neglectful, or abusive early relationships are associated with later difficulties in self-concept and interpersonal relating that may revolve around issues such as self-devaluation, abandonment, mistrust, or victimization. Adverse experiences can also leave a child vulnerable to developing core deficits in emotional regulation and cognitive functioning (such as distortions in perceptual and conceptual processing), which in turn may impact self and interpersonal functioning.

To survive, children exposed to painful, frightening, neglectful, or confusing relational experiences must learn to cope with and accommodate such emotional trauma. *They become invested in self-protection, as well as the preservation of major attachments.* Underlying this self-protective pull is the child's profound dependency on caregivers for both physical and psychological needs. Attachment to others is a matter of survival and its motivating influence cannot be underestimated. The need for a sense of security and predictability is equally powerful. Together, these needs motivate the child to find ways to maintain connection to the caregiver while also avoiding harm. Unfortunately, these efforts tend to disrupt autonomous strivings along with possibilities for adaptive relationships.

We highlight two major means of self-protection that contribute to later difficulties in self-experience and interpersonal relating that bring patients to treatment: (a) restricting awareness and expression of desires and subjective experience in order to accommodate caregivers; (b) rigidity in interpersonal relating.

Self-Protection via Restricting Self-Awareness and Self-Expression

Restricting one's self-awareness and self-expression in an effort to accommodate the emotional needs of caregivers can result in significant disruption in the organic development of a child's healthy sense of self. Children arrive in the world not as blank slates, but rather genetically and biologically wired with innate capacities and motivations, as well as core personality traits. From a psychological perspective, these are the seeds of a coherent identity (including the capacity to recognize one's subjective experience and feeling states) and self-confidence in dealing with the world. To actualize their potentials and achieve a coherent sense of self, children need space to discover and express their desires and capacities. They also need interest and patience from parents who celebrate the child's expressions, as well as the safety that comes from their limit setting and guidance.

There is always some degree to which a child restricts self-expression and conforms to parents' expectations. Parents have a significant role in shaping the child's behavior, as well as influencing the developing child's mind, capacities, and sense of self. Furthermore, it is natural for children to pay close attention to their parents' reactions and desires. However, if a child does not have a sufficient sense of safety for self-expression, she may become overly concerned with preserving connection by accommodating caregivers at the expense of self-awareness and self-confidence. As a result, a child may come to shut down self-expression (Winnicott, 1965) and dampen her desires and strivings toward autonomy. This often involves restricting feelings, needs, desires, and awareness of one's experiences and surroundings. Restricting self-expression may manifest in limiting or distorting emotional experiences, or alternatively, through reacting and acting impetuously to escape awareness of feelings and desires. Avoidance or suppression of emotions can lead to significant disruptions in one's capacities to experience genuine feelings, as well as problems in emotional regulation. Likewise, avoiding certain thoughts and defensively narrowing one's awareness of what is happening can create disruptions in thinking including potential problems in learning (Winnicott, 1975), diminished capacities for mentalization (Fonagy et al., 2002), and faulty or distorted reasoning regarding experiences (Wachtel, 1993).

Case Example: Renee

When Renee was a child, her mother was often emotionally unavailable as a result of chronic major depression. Renee's father was rarely home and, when present, paid little attention to her. Renee experienced her mother as profoundly withdrawn when she would fall into periods of sadness and hopelessness. At other times, her mother would become acutely irritable and yell at Renee for making noise when playing or for seeking her mother's attention or help. Her mother would then sequester herself in her bedroom, leaving Renee alone for hours on end. Renee relished the rare times when her mother seemed responsive and energetic enough to sit with Renee during meals or take her out on errands. In time, Renee became acutely sensitive to her mother's moods, trying to prolong her mother's attention or avoid her mother's irritation. Renee concealed her growing feelings of sadness and anxiety, made sure to play quietly, took care of her needs by feeding and clothing herself, and pretended she was happy when her mother noticed her. In short, Renee learned to shut down her feelings and needs. Later as an adult, Renee rarely enjoyed herself, felt as though she didn't deserve anything from material items to another person's affection, and kept others from knowing her needs. Although Renee seemed jovial and outgoing on the surface, underneath she suffered chronic dysphoria and loneliness as a result of her early experiences. Renee invested great energy in keeping up her façade so she was often exhausted as well as confused about what she felt and wanted in life.

As can be seen in this case, a child's attempts at self-protection can lead to disturbances in self-concept and ways of relating. A child may turn against herself with self-blame and criticism, in order to preserve perceived acceptance by the significant other. A child also may behave in ways that invite punishment, both as a means of proving to herself that she deserves the parent's aggression and also as a means of eliciting attention (as a path toward connection, albeit a painful one). Finally, a child may come to define her needs and wishes based on others' concerns in order to protect against the threat of rejection or attack. In contrast, in the face of an intrusive caregiver who interferes with a child's emerging sense of autonomy, the child may attempt to preserve her sense of self by disavowing her need for connection with others, which is equally restrictive. These protective mechanisms all result in stunted development, poor self-regard, fluctuations in self-esteem, and thwarted relationships.

Case Example: Alan

Alan grew up with a volatile, erratic father who was a frightening and desired figure for a young child who was longing for connection with this undeniably important attachment figure. The father's emotional absence and unpredictable anger threatened Alan's sense of security in profound ways, while also leaving him longing for his father's affection. Although a considerate, loving child who enjoyed music and art, as he grew up, Alan eventually pursued competitive sports and bullied other kids in ways that mimicked his father's aggression. Through this identification with his father, Alan sought to gain his father's attention by behaving in ways he believed his father would approve. Bullying also became a means to express his anger, reflecting a struggle to cope with his profound disappointment in his father as well as his resulting self-hatred. Unfortunately, in disavowing his natural inclinations toward sensitivity and compassion, Alan had little chance of developing an authentic sense of self and genuine way of relating with others. Instead, he was often very lonely, agitated, and mistrusting of others. In turn, others withdrew from him, becoming frightened or annoyed by his hostility.

Self-Protection via Rigidity in Interpersonal Relating

Stressful or traumatic childhood relationships with parental figures can result in distorted perceptions of relationships that, in turn, can cause constricted and maladaptive patterns of relating to others. Well-entrenched and enduring representations have a profound influence on how an individual perceives and responds to others. Furthermore, negative, painful schemas from childhood are more likely to be reinforced, rather than be changed or tempered by subsequent experiences. Motivated to protect herself and preserve what attachments she does have, an individual works to avoid interpersonal harm and awareness of long-restricted feelings and desires. As a result, she tends to repeat early modes of relating in current relationships, including identifications with significant attachment figures. Such repetition based on an ingrained relational schema can result in rigid patterns of relating that inhibit new ways of engaging in relationships.

With a secure base, a child can take risks interpersonally, generally expecting positive responses from others. Trustworthy, loving relationships foster many possibilities for the child's sense of self and ways of relating. Therefore, in the face of a negative response from another, a child secure in attachment is more likely to have the capacity to reflect on her own and another's intentions and roles in the interaction. As such, her interpretations are more nuanced and complex (Blatt, Auerbach, & Levy, 1997).

In contrast, a child with insecure and damaging early relationships is apt to anticipate exactly the kind of negative response from others that he experienced early in life. Possibilities for positive, meaningful, loving interactions with others are restricted by virtue of the individual's continuing need to protect himself against the hurt he has learned to anticipate. No matter how different a current interpersonal interaction is from early experiences, the individual is inclined to misperceive the interaction in terms of prior emotionally stressful or traumatic relationships. The current relationship comes to mirror what the person has known because that is what he is primed to perceive. In simplistic form, the individual misses the positive cues; by reacting as though the other's intentions or responses are negative, the individual unwittingly re-creates that negative experience all over again. Primed for the worst in interpersonal encounters, the individual ironically acts in ways that evoke reactions from others that can be misperceived to confirm what has been expected and feared. This is at the core of our model of conceptualization, the Cyclical Maladaptive Pattern, initially developed by Strupp and Binder (1984). This dynamic is also captured in the core conflict relationship theme (Book, 1998; Luborsky, 1984) and by Wachtel (1993) in his concept of cyclical psychodynamics.

We characterize psychopathology in terms of (a) *rigidity* of interpersonal schema, (b) *repetition* of early modes of relating in current relationships that leads to a *constricted* range of possibilities for interacting, and an unwitting proclivity to evoke a restricted range of reactions from others, and (c) *chronic distress* or failure. A person's interpersonal interactions become rigidly scripted with limited capacity for adaptation and flexibility in response to what may be unique to a current situation. We elaborate each of these areas.

a. *Interpersonal Schema*: Expectations of others' responses and perceptions of others' behaviors are based on early experiences, and the more malignant those experiences were, the more likely they are to rigidly influence current interpersonal expectations because of the greater need to protect against further harm. For example, one who has been emotionally overwhelmed by a parent's criticism generally will expect all others to be judgmental and disparaging. Experiences of rejection early in life lead one to anticipate that others will not be interested, or will turn away, withdraw, or disappear. Expectations are bound to color one's interpretations of the intentions behind another's behaviors, as well. These expectations and interpretations of others can be significantly distorted by rigid schemas, *re-creating past scenarios in current interactions*.

b. *Constricted Interpersonal Repertoire*: Behavioral responses become inflexible and limited in adaptability as a result of rigid interpersonal expectations. Rigidity in interpersonal relating produces behavior that, paradoxically, invites a response from others that is similar to what one anticipated and hoped to avoid. For example, Lionel repeatedly shuts down and becomes reserved, timid, constrained, or guarded in his interactions because he expects and attributes disapproval or rejection from others (regardless of the actual circumstances). In turn, others are turned off by Lionel's guardedness and they withdraw, leaving him feeling rejected. Alternatively, Amy is often aggressive, demanding, or pushy in her interactions, believing that others will always misunderstand, ignore, or exploit her if she doesn't stand up for herself. By pushing others away with her antagonistic and unpleasant behavior, Amy avoids the rejection she assumes will occur anyway; however, she perpetually feels misunderstood. In another illustration, Eric is socially affable and very likeable, having learned to please others and keep peace. Constantly overused, however, Eric's compliant behavior occurs at the cost of closeness in relationships because it stifles true intimacy.

c. *Chronic Distress* is a sign of rigidity: For example, a person chronically vulnerable to anxiety, sadness, despair, agitation, or hatred displays constricted emotional experiences and disturbances in affect regulation that may emerge from efforts to accommodate painful experiences and preserve attachments.

A Caveat: Preserving Empathy and Understanding

There is a risk of overpathologizing when using terms such as *pathology, disturbance, maladaptive,* or *distortions.* It is quite important to keep in mind that what we are describing is, to some extent, a natural aspect of development. That is, there always will be some degree of incongruity or mismatch between what a parent has to give and what a child needs. To the extent that every child is significantly dependent on adults, every child learns to accommodate the caregiver and restrict or alter her own needs and expression. Wachtel (1993) has noted that there are natural developmental needs and limitations that contribute to some "neurosis" or conflict in most everyone. However, when combined with a child's unique sensitivities or unfortunate exposure to adversity early in life, chances for significant disruptions and constrictions in psychological functioning increase.

In order for a therapist to temper a judgmental attitude, as well impatience and aversion, in the face of a patient's repetitive difficulties, it is important to remember that self-protection is a key unconscious motivating factor in rigidly maintaining negative, painful modes of relating. Empathy with the patient's predicament allows for perspective in the face of the patient's "resistance" to achieving more adaptive ways of functioning, including how she relates to the therapist (Schlesinger, 1982). Behaviors and beliefs once adaptive in childhood are no longer necessary or adaptive in adulthood. However, having experienced pain and confusion early in life with significant caregivers, the risk is too great to experiment with new ways of relating. This points to a key role of the therapist: helping the patient attempt new ways of thinking about and relating to others by offering a safety net of concern and commitment.

CONCEPTUALIZING THERAPEUTIC
DISCOURSE IN BDP

At the heart of BDP is an approach to therapeutic discourse that is both a means of obtaining information and a therapeutic intervention. BDP is specifically geared toward increasing insight by identifying, examining, questioning, and challenging the maladaptive modes of relating that interfere with living a satisfying, fulfilling, and productive life. We emphasize a systematic process of therapeutic inquiry that focuses on getting a clear picture of the patient's desires, expectations, and reactions in primary relationships. Using the Cyclical Maladaptive Pattern (CMP) as the framework for this inquiry, therapist and patient collaborate in constructing a cohesive narrative that captures the patient's most currently influential interpersonal schemas and the painful emotions associated with them. In doing so, the patient gains insight into how he may unwittingly constrict possibilities for positive interactions by routinely reacting to new interpersonal situations as though they are inevitably bound to be the same as earlier painful relationships. Insight brings about the changes in feelings, thoughts, and reactions. Patients may change in nuanced, gradual ways in the process of gaining insight; for example, becoming less brittle and more open in treatment, asking a friend for help, going out more, taking pride in one's accomplishments for the first time, or toning down self-criticism. The process of reflection and achieving insight facilitates, for the patient, new ways of relating and also awareness of previously disowned aspects of self. Insight is therapeutic only when the growing awareness results in changes in the patient's sense of self and typical ways of relating.

From a relational perspective, therapy depends on there being something reparative in the relationship that develops between patient and therapist. What transpires in this relationship is sometimes a vital and fruitful source of information for understanding the patient's struggles and reoccurring patterns in relationships. Elements of the patient's key difficulties in relating may be present with the therapist, typically referred to as transference-countertransference enactments. Understanding how a patient's maladaptive modes of relating may impact the treatment becomes imperative to establishing a working relationship and to maintaining a therapeutic alliance in the face of strains in the relationship. This situation is most likely to occur with patients having significant personality pathology. The therapist's relational stance—how she engages patients and conveys a wish to understand—is a key ingredient in establishing

a process that opens up possibilities for change in the patient's ways of relating to self and others. The opportunity to develop new understanding through a collaborative dialogue with the therapist is a new experience in and of itself. As such, we prioritize the therapeutic relationship and believe that something quite reparative does occur in the relationship between therapist and patient, sometimes quite overtly, sometimes in working through enactments of transferences, and sometimes quietly and subtly but nonetheless with a powerful effect.

3

Forming an Effective Therapeutic Alliance

How do we begin psychotherapy effectively? In short, we invite the patient to share her story and we convey interest and compassion in a manner that fosters the patient's trust in our capacity to be of help. We do this by starting an inquiry in which the patient feels listened to, understood, and provided with helpful questions and ideas that she had not thought of before. In doing so, we engage in a collaborative process of exploration in which patient and therapist are both committed to seeing change for the better in the patient's quality of life. Such an alliance between therapist and patient is highly influential in determining the effectiveness, progress, and outcome of a treatment (Castonguay, Constantino, & Holtforth, 2006; Pachankis & Goldfried, 2007; Safran & Muran, 2006; Safran, Muran, & Eubanks-Carter, 2011). The therapeutic alliance has long been regarded as a common principle of change in psychotherapy (Pachankis & Goldfried, 2007) and is the therapeutic process variable that has received the most consistent empirical support across the major therapeutic approaches (Horvath, Del Re, Flückiger, & Symonds, 2011). This chapter focuses on establishing an alliance with the patient that serves as the bedrock foundation of treatment. While all major approaches to psychotherapy recognize the importance of a strong therapeutic alliance, we will highlight key factors specifically relevant to brief dynamic psychotherapy.

As our approach emphasizes interpersonal relating and relational factors in understanding and addressing patients' difficulties, the therapeutic alliance takes center stage; that is, the quality and tenor of the ways in which therapist and patient work together and the emotional/relational bond they share. In our view, the alliance refers to a positive, viable, and meaningful attachment between therapist and patient that makes possible a productive dialogue and interventions that promote an effective therapeutic process. Such therapeutic work can be potentially difficult or threatening for the patient; a positive alliance between patient and therapist supports the patient as she grapples with taking the risk of knowing something new or trying out new behavior. Meissner (2006) speaks of a "therapeutic pact." From a pantheoretical perspective, Bordin (1979) set the definition of the therapeutic alliance as a collaboration on tasks and goals in the context of an "affective bond" (Castonguay, Constantino, & Holtforth, 2006; Gelso & Hayes, 1998). Most conceptions of alliance convey a sense of patient and therapist "in it together," working together toward a mutual goal. Mutuality, something shared, and a relational bond are all significant in the conceptions of the alliance. A therapeutic alliance that has been solidly established can carry the therapy dyad through difficult times when understanding and collaboration are strained or broken (Safran & Muran, 2006).

A strong therapeutic alliance established early in the therapeutic relationship is essential to the viability and success of the treatment (Castonguay, Constantino, & Holtforth, 2006; Constantino, Castonguay, & Schut, 2002). Fostering the alliance and addressing barriers to engaging or collaborating with the patient in the first moments of contact and throughout the treatment may be the difference between effective and ineffective treatments. A healthy alliance makes possible the key goals of BDP: (a) to draw out the patient's narratives and encourage dialogue through respecting, listening, and conveying empathy and understanding; (b) to foster a patient's agency, self-reflection, and involvement in the therapeutic inquiry through questions and observations; and (c) to create possibilities for changing dysfunctional cognitive/affective processes and corresponding maladaptive modes of relating. The specific nature of a therapeutic alliance depends on the roles of patient and therapist in a particular form of therapy and the tools required to implement the treatment. For the establishment of a strong therapeutic alliance, most forms of therapy require the therapist to help the patient feel understood and respected, as well as facilitate a process of change with attention to the patient's relevant needs and goals.

ESTABLISHING AN EFFECTIVE
THERAPEUTIC RELATIONSHIP IN BDP

There are two essential clinical competencies associated with establishing an effective therapeutic relationship in BDP, namely, the therapist's stance and accommodating the patient's relational needs and concerns. The therapist's stance is an essential competency and refers to a therapist's attitudes and ways of engaging that help the patient feel understood and respected, foster a positive connection, and facilitate the therapeutic process. Key clinical skills of listening, empathy, curiosity, and reciprocity are at the center of building and maintaining an alliance with a patient.

Accommodating the patient's relational needs and concerns is an essential competency that involves adapting in ways that are responsive to the patient's relational needs and concerns so the patient is more likely to engage in treatment. Such responsivity to a patient's relational needs involves *attending to the patient's immediate experience in session, flexibility in one's approach*, and *addressing relationship problems* in the treatment in ways that show compassion, understanding, and openness to the patient's experiences.

THE THERAPIST'S STANCE: HOW
THERAPISTS INFLUENCE THE ALLIANCE

We return to a concept of the *therapist's stance* introduced by Strupp and Binder (1984). This term captures the essence of a therapist's attitudes and ways of approaching a patient that foster a positive connection and facilitate the therapeutic process. How the therapist enters into relationships and engages interpersonally are no doubt relevant to the quality and potential of the alliance. Not surprisingly, a positive alliance is present with therapists who convey warmth, interest in the patient's subjective experiences, respect, empathy, trustworthiness, flexibility, confidence, and clarity in communication (Ackerman & Hilsenroth, 2003; Jungbluth & Shirk, 2009). In addition, a therapist's efforts toward collaboration, attending to interpersonal themes, emotional exploration, and supportive techniques are positively related to the alliance (Ackerman & Hilsenroth, 2003) and the patient's evaluation of how expert and trustworthy the therapist seems to be (Kivlighan, 2010). In turn, therapists' rigidity, tendency toward being critical, and inappropriate self-disclosures hold a negative association with development of an alliance (Ackerman & Hilsenroth, 2001).

In building an alliance with the patient, it is not so much *what* the therapist must do, but rather *how the therapist is* with a patient. Being with and following a patient's lead, listening to a patient's narrative as she wishes or needs to tell it, being willing to enter into a patient's experience, and responding empathically all convey a wish to genuinely and deeply understand the patient. The therapist is a "privileged participant in the life of another person who has turned to the therapist for help" (Strupp & Binder, 1984, p. 40). As therapists, we carry a profound responsibility to respect and recognize the patient as she lets us into her world. In early sessions, we emphasize attending to the patient's experience, getting to know her and her world, and educating her about the process of therapy. This approach promotes greater involvement on the part of the patient (Jungbluth & Shirk, 2009; Patterson & Forgatch, 1985), a stronger alliance (Castonguay, Goldfried, Wiser, Raue, & Hayes, 1996), and greater trust in the therapist (Kivlighan, 2010). In later sessions, dialogue and reciprocity reflect the strength of the alliance, a give-and-take in which patient and therapist together are pursuing a meaningful understanding of the patient's struggles.

Listening, Empathy, Curiosity, and Reciprocity: Making a Connection

In initial meetings with a patient, we are gathering information, but we are also establishing a relationship and setting the foundation for collaborative discourse and exploration. The patient reveals information and gradually questions long-held assumptions, only after she has developed a sense of trust in the therapist and the process. To foster this trust, the highest priority is to convey interest, respect, and a genuine commitment to understand and to help. Therefore, *listening, empathy, curiosity, and reciprocity* are at the center of building and maintaining an alliance with a patient.

Listening

Listening is a key to drawing out a patient's current and past experiences, as well as hopes, dreams, and fears. The therapist listens actively until she begins to gain a clear understanding of what the patient is telling her (Strupp & Binder, 1984). Listening is often taken as a given by psychotherapists, but with the increasing pressure toward showing measurable results as quickly as possible (i.e., to be accountable to society for one's work), clinicians often feel pressured to do something for the patient, with the patient, or to the patient. The problem lies in trying to do something without first understanding not only what is wrong, but who the person is that you are working with. Simply being receptive to learning from the patient and attuned to what the patient needs to communicate is often underestimated, and yet, it is probably the most powerful means of deeply understanding the patient's struggles. Listening is also the most powerful means of conveying respect, entering into a patient's world, and establishing a commitment to work together to help the patient find new possibilities.

At the start of treatment, the main goal is to help the patient tell her story in her own way. The therapist starts with an *open-ended inquiry* and follows the patient's lead. In doing this, the therapist shows that he recognizes the patient's capacity to collaborate in the therapy, which is a key ingredient of an alliance. The therapist also is less likely to truncate the narrative with premature assumptions, to foreclose exploration, and to convey that he "know" the patient without the patient's active participation in the process. In this way, the patient can appreciate that her own curiosity about her story, actions, and desires will be an important aspect of personal growth.

An open-ended inquiry does not by any means imply a passive and nonengaged therapist. Rather, building an alliance and deepening a therapeutic process depend on finding a balance between following the patient's lead and directing the conversation toward pertinent information. The therapist very much wants to hear how the patient uniquely experiences and thinks about her life and her relationships, and he needs to help her explore these crucial domains. The therapist also must help the patient represent her experience; that is, find words for and ways of describing it. The therapist's willingness to hear the patient's story and his ability to convey somehow that he "gets it" creates that sense of working together that is so essential to the alliance.

Empathy

Empathy and listening go hand in hand. As Strupp and Binder (1984) describe, "Listening means immersing oneself in the world of another human being; allowing oneself to resonate to the spoken, and, more important, the unspoken messages; and being aware of one's own feelings, images, fantasies and associations" (p. 47). Similarly, Greenberg, Watson, Elliot, and Bohart (2001), drawing on Carl Rogers's work, note that "the empathic therapist's primary task is to understand experiences rather than words. Truly empathic therapists do not parrot clients' words back or reflect only the content of those words; instead, they understand ... the nuances and implications of what people say, and reflecting this back to them for their consideration" (p. 383).

Empathy is often misunderstood as feeling what another feels. Empathy is a more profound process than simply mirroring back. Entering another's world and taking another's perspective conveys a willingness to suspend one's own assumptions in order to *know, to experience, to live for a moment* another person's way of experiencing, perceiving, taking in, and making sense of what occurs around her. Empathy also involves the capacity to put words to another person's experiences and ways of knowing and being, words that might not seem to be available to the other person. Empathy depends on the therapist's capacity to step back, reflect on, and give meaning to the other's experiences.

Case Example: Sarah

Sarah, a 22-year-old graduate student (see chapter 6 for a full discussion of this case) yearned for her professors to acknowledge her hard work, but believed she was not important enough.

P25:   I mean I ... even though I haven't felt as motivated umm...in the last 2 months, I still feel like I try to do what I can to put in as much effort as, as I can, you know, considering it's hard for me being depressed and being sad and even though I do that it still doesn't make them want to help me anymore or get back to me any quicker even though I just feel like I'm working as hard as I can.

T26:   So it sounds like, and again correct me if this is not accurate, but it sounds like in school, it's like you feel like you're struggling against the current so you're swimming upstream that you feel burdened by this sense of depression (Yeah) and sadness and so it's very hard for you to work and you're trying as hard as you can and your professors don't appreciate how hard you try. (Yeah.) They act like you aren't trying hard enough.

Here, the therapist uses the metaphors of "struggling against the current" and "swimming upstream" to capture the patient's sense of having to work so hard. The therapist offers a reflection that is emotionally evocative and echoes the patient's frustration and despair in feeling unappreciated and unrecognized for her efforts.

One reason empathy can be so difficult to achieve is that it can be difficult to suspend one's assumptions because it can be quite threatening to the therapist's sensibilities of the world and sense of self to do so. In illustration, patients who expect aggression and abandonment and who brace themselves with hostility and contempt of others may challenge the therapist's willingness to resonate empathically and understand what drives this way of relating. In addition, being that close to another's expectations (and experiences) of maltreatment threatens one's own optimism and security. On the other side, the meek, withdrawn, passive patient who may provide very little by way of a narrative about his experience and sense of self challenges the therapist to listen carefully to the quiet nuances and create some understanding of what is unspoken and deeply felt by the patient. The meek and passive challenge the therapist's desire to know and to accomplish something in the treatment, which can interfere with a therapist's openness to meeting the patient where he is.

Curiosity

Curiosity is at the heart of therapeutic exploration. If the therapist is to truly learn about the patient's life and subjective experiences, one of her most important tasks involves conveying an interest in knowing more. Curiosity conveys a willingness to know the patient in a nonjudgmental way. This attitude is captured in the simple, but profound statement: "Help me understand." Throughout the treatment, the therapist must model an attitude of curiosity and encourage the patient to think about his experiences. When the therapist asks the patient to *describe* what he feels, thinks, and perceives in interactions with others, she is inviting the patient to *think about* his heretofore unquestioned assumptions and reactions, perhaps for the first time. In doing so, the therapist's curiosity facilitates the kind of collaborative dialogue that helps her and the patient identify rigid, maladaptive modes of seeing the world and relating to it.

Reciprocity

Reciprocity, in this context, involves responding to what the patient has shared. Providing the patient with some feedback regarding the therapist's reactions to what the patient has said conveys interest and respect. Such feedback may come in the form of questions, comments, suggestions for further reflection, helping the patient see alternative explanations or possibilities, or identifying treatment goals. Reciprocity also involves discussing with the patient expectations for, procedures of, or approaches to treatment, as well as explaining reasons for pursuing a particular line of questioning or course of treatment. Orienting the patient to therapy is likely to foster expectations that the therapy will help, increase confidence in the therapist, and help the patient feel like a partner in the process. Reciprocity is how the therapist gives back to the patient in a way that fosters mutual commitment to the patient's progress and facilitates a collaborative relationship.

FOSTERING THE ALLIANCE: ADDRESSING PATIENT CHARACTERISTICS THAT INFLUENCE THE ALLIANCE

The prototypic therapeutic alliance would be characterized by mutual trust, respect, and caring in a way that fosters collaboration. Certain patients are more likely to be capable of such a positive alliance, while others will struggle because their key interpersonal difficulties are bound to get in the way of relating to the therapist (Constantino et al., 2002; Daly & Mallinckrodt, 2009; Gaston, Marmar, Thompson, & Gallagher, 1988; Kivlighan, Patton, & Foote, 1998; Mallinckrodt, Porter, & Kivlighan, 2005; Marmar, Weiss, & Gaston, 1989; Muran, Segal, Samstag, & Crawford, 1994; Satterfield & Lyddon, 1995; Zuroff et al., 2000). The capacity to trust and tolerate intimate connections with others is positively related to the readiness to enter into a therapeutic collaboration. In contrast, an alliance is less likely to develop with patients with significant personality pathology, such as those who anticipate abandonment, remain defensive, or interact in hostile ways (Crits-Cristoph et al., 2006). Significant transference/countertransference enactments affecting the therapeutic relationship are more likely to occur and require the therapist's active attention.

Another factor affecting the likelihood of a positive alliance forming is the patient's expectation for improvement (Meyer et al., 2005), which is bound to be influenced by the patient's interpersonal schemas. It is, after all, another person (not a pill or a procedure) who "administers" the treatment and who will either help or harm the patient. Thus, the patient's capacity to form attachments and to engage in positive interpersonal interactions can determine the degree of difficulty patient and therapist will have in establishing a working relationship. In this regard, competent practice is marked by skill in accommodating a patient's relational needs and making it possible for the patient to engage in the treatment. Adapting in ways that are responsive to the patient's needs and concerns is critical in working with all patients, especially those who carry negative expectations of their interpersonal encounters into the treatment. Such responsivity to a patient's relational needs involves (a) attending to the patient's immediate experience in session, (b) flexibility in one's approach, and (c) addressing relationship problems in the treatment in ways that show compassion, understanding, and openness to the patient's experiences. Addressing problems in the therapeutic relationship will be discussed in chapter 4.

Attending to Immediate Experience

Attending to the patient's immediate experience in the session has been linked to positive alliance early in treatment. It is important to pay attention to how the patient is feeling in session and experiencing the therapist, so that interventions can be tailored to the patient's immediate needs (Lazarus, 1993; Watson, 2010). Much of the patient's feedback is likely to be nonverbal and requires that the therapist tune into potentially subtle cues of the patient's inner experience. Tone of voice, fidgeting, averting eye contact, changing posture, or a grimace all may hint that the patient is troubled by something happening in the moment. Generally speaking, it is advised to follow up on these interpersonal cues, checking in with the patient in order to discover if something is troubling him. However, such attention to the patient's moment to moment experience can be overwhelming or intrusive for some patients. Recognizing this will be important in negotiating the alliance.

From a relational standpoint, patient and therapist are constantly finding ways to negotiate closeness and distance in their interactions. Some patients have a very strong need for connection while others hold back, afraid of closeness despite their yearning for it. As Greenberg, Watson, Elliot, and Bohart (2001) commented on apprehensive patients:

> Certain fragile clients may find expressions of empathy too intrusive, while highly resistant clients may find empathy too directive; still other clients may find an empathic focus on feelings too foreign. Therapists therefore need to know when—and when not—to respond empathetically. Therapists need to continually engage in process diagnoses to determine when and how to communicate empathic understanding and at what level to focus their empathic responses from one moment to the next. (p. 383)

This point can be made for all therapeutic interventions and ways of responding to patients, such as questions, linking statements, reassurances, or silences. Some patients will perceive a therapist's expressions of warmth and concern as offensive or reject them as mere pity. A patient may bristle at a question that the therapist thought was benign but touched too closely to an emotional sore spot. The reflection of an emotion may get spit back: "No, I didn't feel sad. Maybe a bit disappointed." At such times, the therapist could find herself bristling, feeling pushed away, perhaps annoyed, and wondering what happened. These reactions of the therapist offer clues about the patient's relational needs and concerns.

Flexibility

Flexibility involves altering one's therapeutic approach in the face of the patient's immediate needs in session and mode of relating with the therapist. One size won't fit all. Patients modulate intimacy in many ways: for example, missing sessions, arriving late, obsessively ruminating, avoiding emotions, disclosing little, or, paradoxically, disclosing too much, more than a therapist could process at once. We regard these as self-protective efforts. Interacting in ways that facilitate a patient's trust and willingness to collaborate requires flexibility and patience as the therapist searches for effective ways of connecting and speaking with a patient.

Therapists who are skilled in developing and preserving alliances respect a patient's way of being in relationships and adapt accordingly. For patients who struggle with closeness (i.e., avoidant or dismissive attachment styles), therapists look for windows of opportunity to engage the patient in progressively different and increasingly intimate ways of relating. For those patients who desperately seek an immediate connection with the therapist (i.e., the anxious/preoccupied attachment styles), pacing is more likely to involve, for example, tolerating the patient's emotional stickiness and demands for closeness, while also establishing clear boundaries or slowing down the patient's disclosures to help the patient avoid being overwhelmed. Skilled therapists innovate and draw on their creativity, humor, patience, respect, and intuition in their efforts to engage a patient in what will be a therapeutic connection.

DEEPENING THE ALLIANCE: HOLDING ONTO HOPE AND EXPANDING POSSIBILITIES

A strong, positive alliance is marked by a sense of working together in which the patient shares of herself in a way that helps the therapist understand and, in turn, the therapist compassionately brings meaning to the patient's experiences and offers something new. Ideally, both have an eye toward change and possibilities for something better in the patient's life. But, many times, these possibilities are hidden for the patient who has needed to hold on so tenaciously to rigid, maladaptive expectations of self and others. Introducing the idea that things could be different for the patient requires the therapist's compassion, sensitivity, patience, tact, and flexibility. It also requires the patient's trust in the therapist's wish to understand and offer support. These ingredients of a positive alliance make it possible for the patient to consider a different way of viewing herself and of dealing with relationships and life in general, even when she anticipates big risks. In turn, the alliance grows stronger and deeper as patient and therapist cope with difficulties and successes together.

4

Maintaining an Effective Therapeutic Alliance

There is consensus among most clinicians that the therapeutic alliance is an essential ingredient for successful therapeutic outcomes. It doesn't account for much outcome variance, but it always accounts for some and its qualitative importance is substantial (Horvath, Del Re, Flückiger, & Symonds, 2011; Norcross & Wampold, 2011). In order to maximize the likelihood of a positive treatment outcome, the ideal patient–therapist relationship would reflect a linear increase in the strength of the therapeutic alliance over the course of therapy (Stiles & Goldsmith, 2010). No therapeutic relationship is ideal, however, and fluctuations in the alliance will inevitably occur. No matter how solid, any human relationship will have periods of disagreement, misunderstanding, tension, conflict, and emotional distance. The test of a relationship is how well it endures such rough patches. Estimates of the percentage of psychotherapy sessions that evidence noticeable therapeutic alliance ruptures (i.e., significant interferences in a productive working relationship) range from 19% in the judgment of patients to 100% in the judgment of independent observers. The judgments of therapists lie in the middle (Safran, Muran, & Eubanks-Carter, 2011). It may be that patients, tend to underestimate the prevalence of alliance ruptures or, perhaps, independent observers, usually graduate students who may not be blind to the purpose of the studies, overestimate them. In any event, patient observations about the therapy relationship best predict treatment outcome, so their judgments should be seriously considered (Norcross & Wampold, 2011).

The remainder of this chapter will demonstrate the two essential competences, responsiveness and managing negative processes, that are instrumental in maintaining a positive therapeutic alliance in BDP. Responsiveness refers to the therapist remaining attuned to the state of the patient–therapist relationship and the nature of the patient's engagement in collaborative work. Regardless of the degree to which a therapist desires to adhere to the prescriptions of a particular treatment model, he must be willing to flexibly respond to the circumstances that arise as the therapy progresses, with the aim of preserving the patient's trust and cooperation.

Therapeutic alliance ruptures, as well as hostile interchanges in general, do not occur in every therapy session, but when they do occur the damage to a working relationship and to the ultimate outcome can be devastating. Consequently, it is an essential competency on the part of the therapist that he or she cultivates the ability to identify even subtle signs of negative process and to manage personal reactions to hostile communications by the patient without reciprocating.

In order to maintain a therapeutic alliance, the therapist's highest priority should be to manage the working relationship so as to minimize the occurrence of alliance ruptures. The first step in achieving this goal is to incorporate into the initial diagnostic assessment an identification of the patient's personality characteristics that may be relevant to the type of therapeutic work the therapist anticipates doing together with the patient. There is a body of process/outcome research that has identified specific personality characteristics that fit well with specific technical strategies (e.g., patients who internalize issues tend to respond favorably to insight-oriented approaches; Beutler & Harwood, 2000).

No matter what treatment model you implement with a patient, whether it's empirically supported or evidence-based, it is impossible to anticipate how any particular therapy is going to unfold and what specific challenges and difficulties will be encountered. Therefore, it is essential that the therapist remain responsive to the evolving contextual circumstances of the therapy relationship and to the changing needs of the patient (Binder, 2004; Norcross & Wampold, 2011; Stiles, Honos-Webb, & Surko, 1998). The hallmark of an expert in any domain of complex performance, such as the conduct of psychotherapy, is the willingness and ability to improvise when the circumstances require it (Binder, 2004). As noted in chapter 1, in a seminal study of master therapists who were conducting manualized treatments, Goldfried and his colleagues observed that these expert therapists did not go "by the book" to the same extent as did nonexpert therapists, even though the master therapists in many cases had written the manuals (Goldfried, Raue, & Castonguay, 1998). Therapist expertise involves knowing when to deviate from routinely prescribed techniques, which is usually when faced with an especially difficult or novel situation.

Regardless of how conscientiously a therapist works to maintain a positive therapeutic alliance, ruptures may still occur. Even in the absence of noticeable alliance ruptures, for innumerable reasons therapy may not be progressing or, sometimes, the patient may actually be deteriorating. For example, the therapist may be pursuing the wrong issue or approaching a problem with an ineffective technical strategy. If a lack of progress or deterioration goes unnoticed and is allowed to continue, eventually an alliance rupture will occur. There is a growing body of research unequivocally indicating that systematically collecting data about the status of the treatment every session and providing this feedback in some form to the therapist improves therapist performance and effectiveness (Lambert & Shimokawa, 2011; Norcross & Wampold, 2011). A system of patient feedback should be incorporated into every BDP.

Adhering to these recommendations will minimize but not prevent therapeutic alliance ruptures. Therefore, the competent BDP therapist should remain attuned to any sign of the occurrence of an alliance rupture. In a broad sense, alliance ruptures are of two types:

A confrontation rupture is evident when the patient explicitly conveys her dissatisfaction and hostility (Eubanks-Carter, Muran, & Safran, 2010; Safran & Muran, 2000). An example of this type of alliance rupture occurred midway through brief therapy with a single woman in her late 20s who had sought treatment to address her inability to establish a lasting, satisfactory romantic relationship with a man. Notable in her history was the traumatic death of her mother when the woman was a teenager and the equally traumatic emotional loss of her father a year later, when he remarried and focused his attention on his new wife and stepchildren.

Ann: So what are you thinking about this case now?
T: About this case? This feels like a review time for you about this?
Ann: No.
T: What led to your having this question?
Ann: Because I just, I just don't think anything can be done. I don't have, I just really don't.

T: Hhm. How are you feeling, how are you finding yourself feeling about that? That thought.

Ann: This is just really difficult at times. It, it really is. But, uh …

T: That it's difficult. Can you say something about that? In what way is it difficult for you?

Ann: Just everything. But I just don't think that there's anything that can be done except for me just to somehow just keep finding strength just to keep going on, and just hoping that some day things are gonna be different for me and that I'm going to reach a point where things will fall into place and I will be happy. But it's just, uh like all these people have been telling me, "You just have to hope things are gonna get better and you just have to wait."

T: Mm-hm. And so the difficult part in terms of this work is connected with that, is what? What is it about this that is real difficult?

Ann: It's just, it seems so pointless. And, I don't mean that maybe in the way that you might take that if I say that, like I said to you last time, that I don't mean to say that I don't think there's no value for this, but for me, I just don't think that there's any guidelines here that can help me. I really don't. It's just, it's just the way things are. And I just have to some way or another just be able to keep coping with it like I've been doing the past few years.

T: Mm-hm. I would think that would be leaving you with some feelings about the work here. It's disappointment or frustration?

Ann: It's frustrating.

T: Frustration. Uh-huh.

Ann: It is! Because I don't know (pause) from talking with you, uh, what can be done. Because basically I just see that there's nothing. I think my biggest problem is that I don't have any hope.

T: Then would you think then that would (pause) that's one of the things that (pause) that influences what (pause) what can happen in here with you and I? It's like that hopelessness …

Ann: I think it does, because I think I'm somebody who came in here without any hope of anything getting better anyway, and then I don't, I'm not really able to see that there is anything here that can give me …

T: Mm-hm. So your thought was in coming, sort of that maybe I could give you hope or some …

Ann: I, I don't know, I don't know! All I …

T: Whether this process could, you're saying …

Ann: … know is that (pause) when I came here, it was because, I don't know, I …

T: Well, I think that's important to look at. It's like you're, what you're saying is …

Ann: But see, it's like my girlfriend, we talked about it last week. And we just decided that really we haven't done anything wrong in our lives. Decisions that we've made or choices that we made, really have not been that much of an effect on how our lives have turned out for either one of us. And I don't think that when I came to you, maybe when you said this to me, it was the right thing, but yet at the same time, I don't know, you said, "just bad luck."

T: I said "bad luck"?

Ann: When you said that I had a right to feel the way that I felt, because I had had a lot of bad things happen to me, and it's just bad luck.

T: No. I didn't say it was bad luck.

Ann: And, uh…

T: I don't, I hope I didn't say "bad luck." I do …

Ann: But that's the way I see it now, and there's nothing that I could do to change that, and there's nothing that I just don't feel that there's anything that, I mean, I don't, I just [sigh], I'm tired of thinking about any of this. I just, I just really …

T: You're real …

Ann: Frustrated!

It appears that this woman's disappointment and frustration with her male therapist had been building up to this crescendo. Given her childhood experiences of the loss of her mother and the lack of emotional support from her father, it is understandable that she might have an expectation that a male to whom she looks for help would disappoint her. Nevertheless, her male therapist seemed surprised and stunned by her intense dissatisfaction. Although usually a very empathic therapist, who valued the importance of empathy in therapy, he was slow and tentative in acknowledging his patient's feelings of disappointment, frustration, and hopelessness. To make matters worse, he reacted defensively to her complaint that early in therapy he had explained her circumstances as "bad luck." This therapy continued to a mutually agreed upon termination but with no change in the patient's life difficulties. Although it can be very uncomfortable for a therapist to face this kind of challenge to his competency and humanity, it is crucial that he remain attuned to the patient's emotional state and committed to understanding what he has contributed to an alliance rupture.

A withdrawal rupture occurs when the patient or therapist, or both, emotionally disengage from the relationship. While they may appear to be working together, therapeutic progress ceases. Such a situation in a therapy relationship is like a marriage in which the spouses have emotionally drifted apart but go through the motions of maintaining the outward appearance of being a functioning family. For the therapist, this type of alliance rupture may not be as overtly uncomfortable as a confrontation rupture, but it is more insidious and more likely to go undetected until the patient prematurely terminates or the therapy has an unsuccessful conclusion. A withdrawal rupture probably contributes to many of the outcomes of the 5 to 10% of patients who get worse as a result of psychotherapy (Hill, 2010).

At the same time the therapist is alert to signs of an alliance rupture, there is no reason to assume that one must occur. There will be times when the therapist probes for the presence of a problem in the therapeutic relationship but finds no evidence of one. An example of this situation occurred early in the therapy with Sarah, the young woman briefly mentioned in chapter 3.

As a result of therapeutic work on the issues of Sarah assuming the role of caretaker for people important to her, and then feeling unappreciated, she reported some progress in the relationship with her boyfriend. She asked him to take on more responsibility in the house, reporting that he responded well to this request and agreed that he "should clean up after himself." However, she complained that after a few days he forgot and it went back to Sarah "doing it all again." She noted in a discouraged way that she had not "even asked him to do half the things in the house.... I haven't gone that far yet." Upon inquiry, Sarah indicated that she assumed from his inaction around their home that her boyfriend expected her to be the caretaker. The therapist validated how Sarah might come to that conclusion, but also remained curious about alternative explanations. He tentatively posed a question about the possibility that her boyfriend (and sister) might assume that Sarah wanted to take care of everyone because she invested so much energy in doing so. As a result, Sarah considered the idea that it had become a given that she does everything.

Sarah: Yeah. That's true. And that, I guess, brings up the feeling of, it makes me angry that they that that's a given.

T: Angry at whom?

Sarah: [deep breath, pause] Just angry. I guess angry at them. Why do they think it's a given? You know or, I guess I mean I understand my role in that but it's just I am very angry and not just at them. I don't think, just angry that it's a given. Why should that be a given that I'm going to take care of everyone else? And not have anyone take care of me?

Noting Sarah's reference to an ambiguous "them," the therapist immediately inquired about any of her anger being directed at him.

T10: Now do you feel any upset toward me for suggesting that you might contribute to the situation, unwittingly?

Sarah: Mmm. I don't feel that way. I mean, I guess I wonder if you think, you know, it's a given that I'm just supposed to be like this, take care of everyone else? But I'm not angry at you, I don't think.

T11: Is there any anything that I've said or that has transpired between us that would lead you to wonder that or feel that?

While denying any anger at the therapist, Sarah did imply that she may have viewed him as judgmental toward her. Viewing a therapist as judgmental would create risk for a patient and, thereby, undermine the therapeutic alliance. For this reason, the therapist explored this implication.

Sarah: That you think it's a given? [Yeah.] I don't think so. I think I mean before when I first started coming I really wondered whether you could understand me, you know, because I'm sure you haven't been through experiences like mine, and I'm sure you have a happy life and I didn't think you would necessarily understand what it's like to be me.

T12: Mmm. How do you feel now?

Sarah: I feel better. As the sessions have continued, I feel understood by you.

T13:   How do you think that happened?

Sarah: Mmm. I think we just, I mean, you just seemed to be very understanding and empathic about what I was feeling, and I didn't, I haven't really felt judged by you and, you know, I don't really have any reason to be angry at you or anything, so I think that it's been good.

T14:   Mmm. Would you be interested in um knowing from my perspective how I came to understand you more than I did when you first came in?

Sarah: Yeah, ok.

T15:   You talked to me. You told me about yourself.

Taking advantage of Sarah's expression of feeling understood by the therapist, in an impromptu comment her therapist reinforced the importance of Sarah talking openly about herself.

While it is important for the therapist to remain alert for "disguised allusions" to the therapy relationship, trying to conjure a rupture when none exists could become a self-fulfilling prophecy by producing confusion in the patient and a strain in the relationship. An example of this appeared in a published case study in which the therapist's repeated efforts to relate issues under discussion between patient and therapist to the therapy relationship was awkward and distracting for the patient (Kaspar, Hill, & Kivlighan, 2008). The patient appeared to have a relatively high level of interpersonal functioning and sought therapy for specific problems in her romantic relationships with men. While the language used was not psychodynamic, the therapist's approach could be characterized as heavily transference-focused; he repeatedly attempted to draw parallels between the patient's reports of her outside relationships and what transpired in the therapy relationship. In a posttreatment interview with a member of the research team, the patient expressed her confusion and discomfort with this technical strategy: "I don't really know if that's relevant or if that fits the situation I'm going through but I'm sure there's a purpose to it ... sometimes I could see how the two [situations] were connected, but sometimes I didn't. So it felt that maybe that, it just came across as a little bit artificial" (Kaspar et al., 2008, p. 25). While the treatment ended with mixed results, the clinical material presented depicted a generally empathic and skilled therapist.

The therapeutic alliance is an interpersonal phenomenon; that is to say, it is the joint product of the personal characteristics and interpersonal styles that both patient and therapist bring to the therapy relationship. As such, an alliance rupture can originate in an action by either patient or therapist. The original action can evoke a reaction from the other that initiates a negative transactional spiral culminating in an alliance rupture.

It is a fundamental working assumption in BDP that anyone motivated to begin psychotherapy has some difficulty, no matter how subtle, with finding a sense of safety, security, and emotional support in their important relationships. This situation is assumed to be true no matter what the initial complaints (e.g., symptoms of anxiety or depression, difficulties doing one's work effectively). A corollary assumption is that regardless of the strength of a patient's motivation to engage in treatment, there always will be a part of her that unconsciously seeks to obscure the therapist's view of her inner world and that avoids being entirely touched by the therapist's words. The ways in which a patient unconsciously seeks to protect herself from the imagined dangers of emotional intimacy are collectively referred to as resistances. Any attitude, belief, or behavior can function as a resistance if it impedes a genuinely collaborative therapeutic inquiry in the service of protecting the patient from some anticipated hurt. Since any degree of mistrust, no matter how subtly or indirectly manifested, represents a hostile sentiment and corresponding hostile behavior, it will be the therapist's natural inclination to have a hostile response—hostility breeds hostility (Kiesler, 1996). Once patient and therapist begin engaging in reciprocally hostile interchanges, an alliance rupture has occurred. However, hostility does not have to be conveyed directly; it can be expressed through emotional disengagement, an unconscious giving up on the possibility of a collaborative relationship. Another very subtle form of hostility is implied in mistrust in the "fundamental rule" of any psychodynamic therapy: open, candid expression of whatever cognitions and emotions come to mind. In the next clinical example, the patient attempted to simultaneously ingratiate herself with the therapist and control what she revealed. Apparently at some level of awareness she felt that in order to avoid negative interpersonal consequences, she had to maintain a rigidly positive attitude.

A middle-aged divorced woman, Nancy, began psychotherapy to resolve increasing anxiety and panic episodes that occurred every few weeks. Nancy attributed the latest episode to a recent visit from her mother, who lived in another city. She felt repeatedly pulled into giving her mother advice about how to deal with Nancy's emotionally neglectful and unfaithful father. It appeared that her mother played the role of helpless victim but dismissed any advice that the patient would offer. While Nancy was clearly disillusioned with and angry at her father, and while her history indicated a pattern of unhappy relationships with men, she stated that her current involvements with men were not a problem. Nancy was an educator and was familiar with how psychotherapy worked. She appeared to be self-reflective and to express herself openly. However, early in the therapy, the therapist became aware of being pulled by Nancy's repeated compliments into the role of an idealized figure—a wise and superbly empathic therapist. Below are a series of comments made in one early session by Nancy that capture her unconscious, defensive stance.

Nancy: … the therapy has been good to me … I can feel the effects of the therapy already …
T: In what way?
Nancy: Um, more control, personal control. It feels comforting to know I'm not crazy (referring to her panic attacks), and when I sat with the first person who interviewed me, I told him I thought I was going crazy. And then we were able to laugh at it together, because he didn't think I was crazy. And, you know, just going through the evaluation has made me feel better. I know I'm not having a heart attack. I'm just handling stress. So it makes it better.

A few minutes later:

Nancy: I can feel the benefit and that's good. I feel good about that. I feel in control, and that's important to me.

A few minutes later, Nancy again indicated the importance to her of self-control and control over her life:

Nancy: When I think of the control, I think of, um, me being in charge of me and me being in charge of my life and my decision-making, and, um, coming to this is part of my control. Or my physical body said, "You'd better do it, you know." But it's still me rationally in charge. Um, you've been very insightful, I feel like you've been insightful, you know. I've reviewed our conversations on the way home and whatever. I don't feel controlled …

50

A short time later, the patient voiced her sense of vulnerability but, at the same time, trust in the therapist:

T: I'm still not clear how talking with me makes you feel vulnerable.
Nancy: Because I'm verbalizing my feelings. You know, I'm letting you inside. I am being brutally honest, I think.
T: Okay.
Nancy: And I'm letting you inside.
T: All right, how does it make you vulnerable to let me inside?
Nancy: Because they're my insides, they're not your insides. I'm talking family business, so I'm vulnerable.
T: Mm-hm. Do you have some fantasies or ideas about how or in what ways that makes you vulnerable? I guess in terms of …
Nancy: In terms of telling you about me?
T: Yeah, and how I might respond to that?
Nancy: You could choose to be, to be judgmental. I mean, that's not your position, but you could. I trust you, so I wouldn't think that you would be malicious or, um, or gossipy or try to hurt me, knowingly try to hurt me. I'm not talking about that kind of vulnerability. I think that the kind I'm talking about is just sharing what's inside of me. You know. Opening my inside out and letting you look inside.

From the patient's repeated expressions of trust in the therapist, it appeared that the therapeutic alliance is strong. In fact, her phrasing quite graphically portrayed someone who is willing to open up completely and let the therapist look "inside." Her expressions of confidence in the therapist continued a short while later:

T: I'm not, I'm hearing that you're not …
Nancy: I'm not disappointed so far. I think I could be disappointed if I don't give all of me, or if I don't find … I liked you right away. No, so I can't imagine being disappointed at this point. You know, you haven't made any ridiculous statements. I don't know what you're thinking, but your body language and what you've said back to me has been helpful to me. So I don't think I'm going to be disappointed. If I am, it will be because I didn't share enough. And I came into this, you know, deciding that I was gonna put it all on the table for my own survival …

The patient continued to sound strongly engaged in a positive therapeutic alliance, but she voices her trust and commitment repeatedly and, in the process, at times sounded a bit ingratiating and flirtatious. Toward the end of the session the therapist appeared to be feeling hemmed in by the patient's extravagant and repeated compliments and expressions of trust:

Nancy: I don't find you, um, opinionated. I find you very insightful, by just the things you ask me.

T: You know, I feel like I would have a hard time disagreeing with you.

Nancy: Yes.

T: You know, like whatever, I mean even if I said something, I mean, even if I tried to disagree with you ...

Nancy: Hmm.

T: ... I almost feel like you might work it out so it wasn't a disagreement, quite.

Nancy: Hmm.

T: I mean this is kind of off the top of my head. Does this make sense to you?

Nancy: I don't know, unless.... Do you have a hidden agenda for me?

T: Well, you said a couple of times that you find me insightful or not dogmatic or....

Nancy: Yes.

T: Something like that. I guess I feel that you are, in this relationship, very, uh, flexible, very understanding, very...

Nancy: Yeah. I'm willing to be led, you know, this way and that way. It's interesting to me that we started with Daddy and we talked about relationships, because they do impact on me certainly, and he does. No, I appreciate going back and forth, that's okay. And it's amazing that, well, it's a compliment to you that you bring me in those directions ... I appreciate moving back and forth. And I think I'm pretty flexible, generally, anyway, you know, you are insightful. You are insightful, or at least you're asking me the right questions and saying the right things.

T: I'm just thinking you're the one having the insights.

The patient talked briefly about her mixed feelings about her father. Then:

Nancy: You're helping me, look at me, you know. And my gift to you would be that you always have someone that'll help you look at things …

In what appeared to be a somewhat uncomfortable and awkward way, the therapist attempted to comment on the patient's attempt to avoid any hint of a disagreement between them. Ironically, the patient saw his comments as more insightfulness on his part. After the session, the therapist's reactions to it reflected how restricted he felt by the patient's rigid attempts to maintain the appearance of an unequivocally positive relationship: "… it all feels very syrupy. It's difficult to tap into the problems. Everything quickly flips over to optimism and things are going well and things are getting better, and I'm insightful and I'm good at what I do and all of that. And I feel a little paralyzed by that. I thought the part where she was talking about feeling some sadness … that rang fairly true to me. But the predominant feeling was one of always hearing the right answer … I feel like she's trying very hard to please me."

THE ORIGINS OF THERAPEUTIC ALLIANCE RUPTURES

The terms *confrontation rupture* and *withdrawal rupture* refer to the consequences of some untoward situation that has developed in the patient-therapist relationship. The origins of these situations can take a variety of forms. There are misunderstandings in which the therapist has misinterpreted important information that the patient is trying to convey or has lost touch with the client's needs and expectations. For example, a patient wants the therapist to understand how deeply she has been hurt by the breakup with her boyfriend, and the therapist focuses on how the boyfriend had serious character flaws. There are impasses that typically are disagreements about the goals of therapy or about how therapeutic goals should be achieved. These disagreements can deteriorate into a power struggle, creating a stalemate in the treatment. For example, the patient wants to reduce the frequency of sessions from weekly to every two weeks, but the therapist adamantly maintains the position that they should meet at least weekly (Hill, 2010).

In psychodynamic psychotherapies alliance ruptures were originally conceived as the expression of transference/countertransference enactments (Safran & Muran, 2000; Strupp & Binder, 1984). The patient enacts a

prepotent maladaptive interpersonal mode of relating in the therapy relationship and unwittingly (unconsciously) draws the therapist into acting
a role that is part of the patient's internal drama (Strupp & Binder, 1984).
Historically, a basic assumption of psychodynamic therapies, regardless
of length, was that whatever problem brought the patient to treatment
would inevitably be enacted in interpersonal terms in the therapy relationship. Consequently, technical papers from Freud until the last decade
have depicted transference and countertransference as simultaneously
the largest impediment to therapeutic progress and the most propitious
opportunity to work on the major problem. Process/outcome research
over the past 20 years has challenged this fundamental assumption about
transference/countertransference with regard to short-term psychodynamic therapies (Høglend et al., 2011). This issue will be discussed in
more detail in chapter 7.

The last form of therapeutic alliance rupture to be discussed is the
angry patient. This situation usually occurs in response to something the
therapist has done or not done (Hill, 2010); for example, a therapist who
arrives late to a scheduled appointment or fails to congratulate the patient
for a job promotion. Sometimes, a patient is characterologically angry,
which may be the most difficult form of open hostility to deal with.

A red thread running through all of these forms of therapeutic alliance rupture is patient hostility, whether expressed directly or indirectly.
This hostility can be in reaction to an occurrence in the therapy relationship or an expression of problems that the patient brings in to therapy. In
either case, whether it's identifying it or managing it, therapists appear to
have more difficulty with patient hostility than any other situation they
face (Binder & Strupp, 1997; Norcross & Wampold, 2011). Furthermore, it
has been demonstrated that "a little bit of negative process goes a long
way" toward undermining a therapy (Henry, Schacht, & Strupp, 1986;
Henry, Strupp, & Schacht, 1990). A fundamental principle of interpersonal
theory is that a hostile action will always evoke a hostile reaction (Kiesler,
1996). Consequently, it behooves therapists to learn how to manage a hostile situation. How this is done will be discussed below. First, here is an
example of a patient whose hostility is first expressed passive-aggressively,
behavior that provokes an impatient reaction from the therapist. At that
point the patient reacts for a moment with more open hostility, and then
proceeds to demonstrate that her attitude toward her male therapist was
a transference reflection of her attitude toward important men in her life.

Patient and therapist were meeting for the first time since a holiday break:

Ann: Did you have a nice Christmas?
T: Yes, I did. Very nice. Thanks.
Ann: Good.
T: And you?
Ann: Hmm. Enjoyed it. Both my husband and I took the week between Christmas and New Year off, so it made it a little easier to catch up on a few projects. We didn't go anywhere or anything. You said you were going away for the holidays, right?
T: Well, we went away for a day and were in town the rest of the time.
Ann: Do you have family out of town?
T: Yeah, hmm. Yeah. I have some family I was able to visit for a day or so and then came back.
Ann: Hmm. They can't be too far, if you can do it in a day.
T: Oh, it's about a couple of hundred miles. Last time we met, we talked, you mentioned that you had called when you were feeling down, but you were feeling up these days.

This brief opening interchange appeared pleasant enough. However, there appeared to be an underlying tension: the patient appeared to be trying to control the topic of conversation and appeared somewhat annoyed that the therapist was reluctant to disclose many personal details; the therapist, in turn, did not want the dialogue to move in the direction of disclosing much about his personal life and shifted the focus back on to the patient.

Ann: Hmm.
T: Right?
Ann: Yeah, I was doing rather well.
T: Are you still feeling up?

There was a very brief interchange about the patient's gastrointestinal problems, followed by a long pause. Then, the therapist continued his attempt to explore the patient's subjective experiences.

T: And so how've you been feeling during the holidays?
Ann: Fine.

T: Entirely pleasant? Things at home are entirely pleasant?

Ann: (Sarcastically) When you live with three teenagers, are things ever entirely pleasant? Noo (chuckle) however, it's been rather, my son had some dental work done over the holidays. He's doing fine. Some minor upsets, like we didn't know whether our older son was gonna go back to school or not. We had told him if he did not maintain Cs or better, we wouldn't pay for his college, because he has a tendency not to, uh, has a tendency not to really work up to potential. And, so I was mildly upset when my husband really stuck to it because he got like three Bs, a C, and a D. And the D was in math, which he does have difficulty with, but he stuck with it, and I kept my mouth shut and, I guess it's gonna work out all right in the end. The only thing that did upset me was he did decide to go back to school. He's paying for it. And, the way, I mean the way he decided …

T: Your son decided to go back to school?

Ann: Uh-huh. The way he decided to do that was, I don't, I can't believe this, I really can't believe this. He said he didn't decide until the day of registration which, you know, is typically, he puts things off until he can't put them off anymore … and so he said he decided by the flip of a coin whether he was going to go back to school or not. And I said, "My God, you know, this is a very important decision and this is the way we decide it?!" He bothers me somewhat. He's a real charmer but it really, I guess it's maturity that he lacks. I'm hoping that will come with time.

A short time later, the patient compared her son with her daughter, who she felt "… does more with what she has … she's a planner." It appeared that the patient's initial attempt to control the conversation followed by her refusal to say much without the therapist's urging, evoked some expression of impatience (through a somewhat sarcastic question: "Entirely pleasant?"). The patient reacted to the therapist's behavior with sarcasm of her own—the tone of it conveying that what the therapist had said was simple minded. She then proceeded to talk about her husband and older son in a disapproving tone. She was not even able to acknowledge her son's willingness to pay his own way back to college but, instead, focused on the way he made the decision. In sum, the patient acted as though she was irritated with the men around her, and drew the therapist into enacting her picture of how men act.

Therapist Contributions to the Maintenance of an Alliance and What to Avoid

The personal attributes of a therapist that have been associated with maintaining a positive therapeutic alliance are: experience, flexibility, honesty, respect for the patient, trustworthiness, confidence in the benefits of BPD, interest and warmth, friendliness, openness, and active engagement with the patient (Ackerman & Hilsenroth, 2001; Messer & Wolitsky, 2010). Therapist activities associated with maintaining a positive alliance are: exploration of interpersonal themes, being reflective and supportive, facilitating collaboration in the setting of goals and means to achieving them, interventions that consistently address the focal themes of the treatment, facilitating expression of affect, being active, being understanding and affirming, attending to the patient's experience, and being generally active in the therapy (Ackerman & Hilsenroth, 2003; Messer & Wolitsky, 2010).

Attitudes, sentiments, and behaviors to avoid are: showing disregard, being distracted, self-focused, or disengaged from the process; lack of confidence in the ability to help; acting tense, tired, bored, distant, or aloof; being critical, and acting defensive or blaming; and generally being unable to provide a supportive environment (Ackerman & Hilsenroth, 2001; Messer & Wolitsky, 2010). Therapist techniques to avoid are: over-structuring or failing to provide enough structure; superficial interventions, belittling the patient, inappropriate use of self-disclosure or silence, and overuse of transference interpretations (Ackerman & Hilsenroth, 2001; Messer & Wolitsky, 2010).

When a therapeutic alliance rupture occurs, the BDP therapist can be guided in resolving the rupture by an evidence-based protocol (Safran & Muran, 2000). In general, this protocol first involves the therapist identifying a disruption in his working relationship with the patient, then disengaging from participating in whatever dysfunctional interaction is occurring, and inviting the patient to examine together what has being transpiring between them. The protocol also involves steps to take if the patient defensively avoids collaborative reflection on the patient–therapist relationship (Safran & Muran, 2000; Eubanks-Carter, Muran, & Safran, 2010).

Tolerance of Negative Affect

How a therapist can become effective in dealing with the maintenance of a therapeutic alliance will be discussed as part of the general topic of therapist training in chapter 11. A therapist competence that is a necessary foundation for effective management of the therapeutic relationship is the capacity to identify and to tolerate negative affect. Negative affects (e.g., anger, impatience, depression, anxiety, hopelessness) can emanate from either patient or therapist, or be the product of an interpersonal dynamic between them. A natural human tendency is to shy away from painful emotions, a reflex akin to automatically drawing your hand away from a flame. But, the effective therapist must learn to overcome the reflex to pull away from negative affect (for example, by downplaying its significance, immediately attempting to do something to "fix" the situation, changing the subject, or simply not seeing signs of the affect). He must learn to face the patient's uncomfortable emotions, help the patient accept them, and examine and understand them, in order to ultimately gain perspective and constructively manage them. In a similar vein, the therapist must learn to accept whatever personal reactions he experiences in working with a patient, and engage in self-reflection, in order to understand their meaning and role in his work with this patient. Negative affects are a fact of life and an inherent part of therapeutic alliance ruptures.

5

Performing an Integrative BDP Assessment

Our initial understanding of a patient's difficulties, needs, fears, and ways of relating ultimately guides treatment planning, interventions, and how we develop a therapeutic alliance. Assessment, however, is not a one-time endeavor, but rather an ongoing, iterative process in which we elaborate our early understanding into an increasingly coherent story of the patient's core subjective struggles in the context of her relationships. Competent assessment draws on skills in therapeutic inquiry, meaningful organization of clinical data, communicating our understanding to the patient, and relationship management.

THE ESSENTIAL CLINICAL COMPETENCIES ASSOCIATED WITH ASSESSMENT

Perform a Comprehensive Assessment

This essential clinical competency involves conducting a broad psychodynamic assessment to understand the patient's core struggles that will inform diagnostic understanding and case conceptualization. A comprehensive BDP assesses the patient's (a) emotional experiences, (b) self-experience and self-perception, and (c) patterns of interpersonal relating.

Therapeutic Inquiry

This essential clinical competency involves obtaining specific, detailed descriptions of interpersonal interactions and the patient's reactions during these interactions through the use of direct questions and elaborations. This inquiry leads to a coherent picture of the patient's core interpersonal difficulties that sustain maladaptive modes of relating.

Knowing When to Structure and Contain

This essential clinical competency involves judging when to guide the storytelling more actively based on the patient's level of functioning and quality of object relations.

KEY DOMAINS OF ASSESSMENT

We conduct the assessment with three major goals in mind: (a) evaluate the quality and severity of the patient's psychopathology; (b) generate initial hypotheses about the nature of the patient's psychological and interpersonal struggles that will guide treatment interventions; and (c) establish an alliance with the patient. While the initial assessment generally can be conducted in two or three sessions, the process of clarifying and elaborating a narrative understanding of the patient's difficulties continues throughout treatment.

Assessment involves gathering information about a patient in order to develop some understanding of what troubles the patient as well as how the patient copes with his suffering while getting along in the world. A shallow version of this understanding is represented by a descriptive diagnosis, most often codified according to the *Diagnostic and Statistical Manual of Mental Disorders* (American Psychiatric Association, 2000). A DSM diagnosis describes a cluster of observable behaviors and symptoms, which can be useful in identifying major areas of concern for a patient. However, a DSM diagnosis is impersonal. It does not help us know how a patient subjectively experiences his difficulties, the nature or the roots of a patient's suffering, or how the patient experiences himself and his interpersonal world. Moving beyond mere symptom presentation, we will discuss how to best assess and understand presenting concerns within the framework of a comprehensive psychodynamic/interpersonal understanding of the patient's core struggles.

As noted in chapter 2, in BDP relationships are at the core of understanding psychological development and functioning, with a particular emphasis on how early relationships come to have a lasting influence on an individual's sense of self, ways of approaching life's challenges and possibilities, and functioning in current relationships. For a comprehensive understanding, we attend to a person's (a) emotional experience, (b) self-experience and self-perception, and (c) patterns of interpersonal relating. For each of these key domains of assessment, we will detail the kind of information necessary for developing a narrative understanding of the patient's core pain; that is, what most troubles a patient, including hypotheses about the interpersonal roots of this pain. We have organized this chapter around key assessment questions that we are more likely to silently ask ourselves than to ask the patient directly. Their purpose is to guide therapeutic inquiry, including a therapist's clinical observations and efforts to organize the clinical data. In addition to gathering information, observing how the patient communicates (or does not communicate) and behaves with the therapist is an important source of information.

ASSESSING THE PATIENT'S CORE PAIN AND EMOTIONAL EXPERIENCE

Emotions and desires influence and motivate a person and are at the root of the struggles that bring people to treatment. Certainly, we pay attention to emotional experiences that a patient is aware of and can describe. Of equal interest is understanding the core emotional pain that may be more difficult for the patient to directly articulate but that emerges as a subtext in the patient's narratives about life experiences. This core pain, associated with unmet interpersonal needs or desires and subsequent negative feelings about one's self, is at the root of a patient's fundamental struggle to feel and live well—this is similar to Mann's (1973) concept of the "chronically endured pain," although we place greater emphasize on the interpersonal context in describing the pain.

We assume that this core pain has its origins in early interpersonal experiences and concerns and, in turn, shapes the maladaptive relational patterns that serve to protect self-integrity, but can perpetuate significant difficulties in life. In generally unconscious ways, people attempt to avoid this pain and may do so through restricting or distorting feelings, thoughts, or behaviors, or alternatively, through acting and reacting impetuously as a way of escaping distressing feelings. However, as discussed in chapter 2, these efforts to protect against the awareness of psychological pain often contribute to one's struggles, particularly because of subsequent difficulties managing the feelings and thoughts that do emerge into awareness. Assessing a patient's emotional experiences and capacities can provide a clearer sense of what troubles the patient most.

What Is the Patient's Range of Emotional Experience and Capacities for Pleasure?

In addition to understanding what the patient feels, it is important to consider the patient's range of emotional experience. This includes capacities to experience pleasure, joy, excitement, love, and concern. No one is immune to psychological pain; however, chronic distress that crowds out much of human emotional experience is a sign of significant constriction and rigidity associated with maladaptive interpersonal patterns. For example, patients prone to unrelenting feelings of shame, powerlessness, vulnerability, or doom and despair may be preoccupied with a core pain in a way that stifles possibilities for other more positive emotional experiences, self-growth, and interpersonal connections. This includes both patients who experience emotions intensely and have limited capacities to regulate emotional expression, as well as those who consistently dampen their emotional life. Both groups are likely to display a limited range of emotional experiences.

What Is the Patient's Capacity for Emotional Regulation and How Does the Patient Typically Express Emotions?

It is important to understand the degree of intensity of dominant emotions and emotional states, as well as a patient's capacities to manage emotional experience. Extreme emotional constraint and extreme reactivity in expressing emotions are equally disruptive. A person who habitually overregulates his emotional expression probably is no less vulnerable to intense, overpowering feelings and is as incapable of processing emotional experiences in adaptive ways as the person who underregulates emotional experience.

Emotional regulation involves conscious awareness of emotional reactions and the ability to reflect on and manage one's feelings in a way that is appropriate for the context. *Self-reflection* involves stepping back and thinking about what one's feelings and reactions may communicate about one's internal states of mind and motivations, as well as the immediate environment, especially the interpersonal environment. For example, an individual with the capacity for self-reflection is more likely to be able to tolerate an offense or disappointment, as well as to determine an appropriate response specific to the situation, than someone without this capacity. In contrast, patients with difficulties in regulating distressing emotional experiences may evidence intense reactions that may be exaggerated relative to the circumstance at hand. They may have difficulty controlling emotional reactions or be prone to urges to self-harm or other maladaptive means of coping (such as substance abuse, self-injurious behaviors, or promiscuity) that exacerbate distress in the long run.

ASSESSING SELF-EXPERIENCE
AND SELF-PERCEPTION

The concepts of self or sense of self, in some respects, have eluded clear definition in the clinical and empirical literatures. Nonetheless, how a person experiences, thinks about, and treats himself is important for therapeutic understanding. A coherent sense of self—experiencing oneself in a relatively consistent way despite different contexts—is the foundation for self-esteem and the capacity to fulfill one's potentials, desires, and ambitions, as well as key to intimate and mature relating with others (Clarkin, Lenzenweger, Yeomans, Levy, & Kernberg, 2007). Diagnostically, it is important to understand not only how a person describes and thinks about himself, but also the stability of the person's sense of self over time and context.

What Is the Nature of the Patient's Sense of Self?

Some patients speak directly about how they view themselves, for example, "I am stupid," "I am shy," "I am someone who laughs a lot when I get nervous," or "I get anxious about everything." With others, we can get an impression indirectly through narratives about other people that give some indication of how the patient perceives himself. When other people are seen as the only ones who are strong, successful, deserving, or needy, this may reflect a veiled comparison to the patient's perception of self as weak, incompetent, unworthy, or self-sufficient. With other patients, we may comprehend how a patient regards himself through how he interacts in therapy, perhaps ingratiating, demure, entitled, or domineering. Our observations provide clues, then, as to how a patient tends to see himself in relation to others.

It is also important to determine whether a patient's conceptions of her or his self (conscious and unconscious) are realistic. For example, a patient who feels incompetent may indeed lack competence. On the other hand, a patient who feels incompetent and describes herself in this way, may, in fact, quite competently deal with the challenges she faces in the world. She may, for example, report positive feedback she receives from others, but this does not temper her profound vulnerability to self-contempt, shame, and feelings of emptiness.

What Are the Patient's Self-Expectations and How Does the Patient Treat Herself?

A basic principle of interpersonal theory is that we develop a sense of self in relationships. As children, we not only identify with characteristics of our caregivers, we also internalize our experience of how they treated us. As a result, we tend to treat ourselves as we perceive primary caregivers have treated us. When a child must struggle with overwhelming or threatening experiences with caregivers, in the service of self-protection, she may come to have very little tolerance for her needs and feelings. Rigid expectations of oneself and rejection of one's subjective experience may reflect those efforts to preserve early attachments and avoid further pain. These efforts often come at the cost of self-regard and authenticity. For example, Sam, a 25-year-old man, who grew up witnessing recurrent violence between his parents and feeling chronically frightened and neglected, learned to minimize his feelings and to focus on taking care of his mother's needs, instead. As a result, at the first signs of anxiety or sadness, Sam became acutely self-critical, calling himself weak and selfish. Consequently, he had great difficulty in relationships because getting close to others evoked his longing for comfort and nurturance, Sam treated himself as if he were a needy, demanding child who would take too much. He retreated from relationships to avoid the shame associated with his beliefs that he would burden others.

Is the Patient Able to Sustain a Coherent and Stable Sense of Self Over Time?

A continuous sense of self over time and context is important to adaptive functioning as it enables one to carry a sense of personal history that informs present living and helps anticipate the future. Severe disturbances in self are marked by discontinuity in self-experience (often associated with lapses in memory, such as not remembering how one felt from one therapy session to another) and identity diffusion (subjective feelings of not having a clear sense of self or a tendency to shift identities in response to the influence of others). Those with a shifting, fragmented sense of self are more vulnerable to feeling confused about personal qualities (Who am I?), experiencing blurred boundaries between self and other, and feeling empty and untethered in the world. One also may experience extreme fluctuations in self-esteem, marked by highs and lows that are dependent on external feedback and context (indicating disruptions in self-esteem regulation). Such incoherence and discontinuity in sense of self (and therefore others) also can have significant impact on the quality of interpersonal relating, as well as the patient's capacity to explore patterns in relating. It may be more difficult for the patient to provide a historical account of her relational experiences because she experiences her life story unfolding without a coherent theme. Therefore, the therapist may need to piece together a narrative more from his direct experiences with the patient or from the fragments of stories the patient can tell.

ASSESSING PATTERNS OF INTERPERSONAL RELATING

A person's interpersonal experiences and dominant mode of relating to others are at the heart of understanding a patient's struggles in BDP. A primary goal of BDP assessment is the construction of a story that captures key difficulties in a patient's expectations of, reactions to, and modes of interacting with others. As such, BDP assessment focuses on dominant themes in a patient's narratives of early and current relational experiences.

Describe Family and Other Significant Relationships at Various Points Throughout Life

A primary aim of BDP assessment is to obtain information with which to begin constructing a rich and detailed picture of a patient's family, peer, and romantic relationships throughout life. This task involves obtaining specific, detailed accounts of important relationships at key developmental phases, as well as interpersonal experiences associated with critical life events. It is important to get clear impressions of a patient's relationships in adulthood, particularly romantic and sexual relationships and work-related interactions. Knowledge of early childhood experiences provides a context for making sense of the desires and expectations a patient brings to current relationships. Positive change in enduring patterns of relating, however, must happen in current interpersonal interactions. Thus, it is important to have a clear understanding of chronic distortions in perceptions of self and others, as well as rigid modes of relating that have developed since childhood and that have been reinforced in adulthood.

What Are the Dominant Interpersonal Themes? What Is the Nature of the Patient's Dominant View and Expectations of Others?

We listen for the wishes, needs, emotional experiences, and fears that recur in the patient's descriptions of her relational encounters. Interpersonal patterns or themes that emerge repeatedly across different relationships and developmental phases are likely to have an enduring influence on the characteristic manner in which an individual negotiates emotionally significant relationships. When listening to the patient's interpersonal narratives, it is helpful to attend to questions such as those listed in Table 5.1. These questions help identify the primary theme(s) in a patient's personal story. Drawing on these questions will also help pinpoint when to inquire for more concrete examples of interpersonal interactions and exchanges.

What Is the Patient's Capacity for Attachment and Ability to Care for Another?

The BDP therapist pays attention to how a patient may feel she has been treated by others. Equally important is how one cares for others and plays the role of an attachment figure. Being in relationships, expressing love, and sustaining intimacy with others are hallmarks of psychological

Table 5.1 Guide for Assessing Dominant Interpersonal Themes and Expectations

---

How does the patient tend to describe relationships?

Are relationships caring and intimate, frightening and harmful, volatile and destructive, tumultuous, chaotic, competitive, collaborative, or reciprocal?

How does the patient tend to feel in relationships?

This is apt to be linked to the patient's core pain and desires in relationships.

How are other people characterized?

Others may be perceived, for example, as friends, confidants, enemies, abusers, victims, caretakers, someone to be taken care of, possessions, "trophies," burdens, partners, subordinates, superiors, or authorities.

What issues or conflicts does the patient most struggle with in relationships?

We generate clues about the specific nature of a patient's longstanding struggles to find a balance between simultaneous strivings for attachment and autonomy, dominance and submission, and need to be nurtured and nurturing others. Perhaps, for example, a patient may struggle with self-assertion, being controlling, feeling controlled, lack of trust, being too trusting, trouble cooperating, fearing exposure, avoiding closeness/ intimacy, avoiding commitment, falling in (or out of) love too quickly, detachment, fear of harming others, or sensitivity to rejection.

What is the patient looking for from others?

For example, is she looking for accessibility, availability, nurturance and caretaking, attention or recognition, safety, dependability, acceptance being wanted, or independence and freedom?

What are the patient's typical modes of behaving and interacting with others?

Does the patient tend to be passive, assertive, aggressive, hostile, kind, nurturing, giving, controlling, blunt, rude, offensive, uncompromising, obsequious, rejecting, or withdrawn?

---

health. Of course, the capacity for attachment is not simply either present or absent, since human functioning naturally fluctuates. We can feel ambivalent and become frightened in relationships, and our capacities for empathizing with others can falter. It is also the case that one can become overly involved in caring for another, suggesting possible difficulties with self and other boundaries. In assessing a person's ability to love and care for others, we consider dimensions of balance and degree.

Quality of Representations

The stories a patient tells about relationships and people in her life typically will provide clues for understanding the nature of her recurrent interpersonal struggles. The therapist listens "in between the lines" partly to assess the degree to which a patient has an appreciation for, and tolerance of, the multiple motivations, intentions, desires, and needs that drive others' behavior. Integrating disparate personal qualities into an increasingly complex, nuanced conception of another allows for greater possibilities in relating (Kernberg, 1975, 1984; Livesley, 2003). By contrast, there are individuals who tend to think in simplistic, narrow, rigid ways about their own and others' qualities, motivations, and intentions. Highly confusing, inconsistent experiences with parental figures or significant others can overwhelm the child's ability to integrate positive and negative experiences of self and other into coherent representations (Livesley, 2003). For example, a parent may in one moment lovingly dote on a child and at another moment behave in a cruel, contemptuous way, rejecting the child's overtures for closeness. Extreme fluctuations in how others behave in front of and toward the child can lead to discontinuous experiences of self and others. The consequent representations become split between global impressions of good and bad that are disconnected from each other. Such discontinuity in representations of self and other can result in unstable, erratic ways of relating to others because of rapid shifts in how one anticipates and experiences relationships.

What Is the Potential For Establishing an Alliance with the Patient in Treatment? What Will the Patient Need in Order to Make Use of Therapy?

It is important to attend to clues about how the patient perceives and reacts to the therapist during the early sessions, and to note the difficulty or ease with which the patient interacts with and reveals personal information to the therapist. How the patient interacts with the therapist and the initial rapport established between them can reveal much about the patient's core interpersonal struggles. This evidence may be an important source of information in understanding the patient, particularly with those persons who are less able to provide a coherent narrative of their experiences. In addition, information about the patient's key relational experiences, interpersonal concerns, and ways of relating can tell us something about how a patient may engage in the treatment. Having some indication of the patient's capacity to use relationships and form attachments helps the therapist determine what it may take to establish a productive working alliance with the patient. This was discussed in chapter 3 on forming an effective therapeutic alliance and in chapter 4 on maintaining the therapeutic alliance.

GETTING THE STORY: THERAPEUTIC INQUIRY

An initial purpose of therapeutic inquiry in BDP is the development of a coherent picture of the patient's core interpersonal difficulties that sustain maladaptive modes of relating. The therapist works to construct a narrative that captures a *dominant interpersonal theme* associated with the patient's core psychological pain. This theme is relatively generic, such as a search for acceptance, feeling unworthy of love, anger, or jealousy. The consequent elaborated narrative provides a *"personal story line"* that is unique to the patient (Schafer, 2004, 2005b). This story line is more specific and traces a person's particular desires and concerns, expectations, experiences, and reactions in relationships. In establishing a person's recurrent concerns and pattern of relating, it is important to understand as clearly as possible what happens in actual interactions. These "scenes" of the person's life are specific, concrete examples of interpersonal encounters that provide us with a vivid picture of how the person experiences and relates to others (Binder, 2004).

BDP emphasizes a narrative based approach to inquiry that focuses on obtaining specific, detailed descriptions of interpersonal interactions through the use of direct questions and elaborations. This approach effectively facilitates identifying a focal interpersonal theme and constructing a more elaborated, coherent story of the patient's struggles. To get a flavor of the patient's relationships, the therapist needs specifics of context, tone, emotions, dialogue, outcome, and subsequent feelings and conclusions that the patient has carried from relational encounters. Thus, it is important to use focused questions and reflections in order to obtain specific details of the patient's interpersonal encounters. This approach focuses on content, but not to the exclusion of empathically connecting with the patient's story. Indeed, it is important to get enough detail so that the therapist can enter into the patient's relational world and thereby resonate emotionally with the patient's subjective experiences.

Questions and comments serve to encourage the patient to elaborate her story. The therapist's inquiry is an invitation for the patient to become more aware of herself by way of communicating with another person (Schafer, 1992). The patient has an opportunity to discover herself with the "support of the benevolent but tough-minded curiosity of the therapist" (Schafer, p. 300). There are several inquiry strategies that can facilitate a clear understanding of how the patient relates to others and approaches interpersonal situations.

Pursue Details

Details make stories human, and the more human a story can be, the better. (V. S. Pritchett, quoted in Moore, 1989)

Obtaining details of several specific, concrete examples of what happens in interpersonal interactions is the most effective strategy for getting a clear picture of what the patient struggles with in relationships. The BDP therapist should look for opportunities to follow up on general statements made by the patient and seek "scenes" in a person's life through questions or prompts such as: "Imagine for a moment that your father is a character in a movie. How would you describe him?" "Can you tell me about a specific interaction you had with your ex-wife in which you felt put down?" "Is there an example of when you experienced that with your sister?" "Can you walk me through that interaction, step by step? What you said, what he said, how you felt, what you were thinking." Encourage the patient to give these concrete examples in the form of interchanges that step-by-step construct the dialogue with another person.

Get Clarification and Elaboration

The therapist should ask for clarification if he does not understand or is having difficulty connecting with a patient's experience. Ask for elaboration of key words or expressions that stand out as distinctive to the patient's experience or narrative, or that may seem odd, contradictory, or out of place in some way. In no instance should the therapist assume that he knows precisely what a patient means.

Case Example: Sarah

In the following excerpt, Sarah, who was discussed above, is speaking about the death of her mother when Sarah was 13 years old. The therapist reacts when Sarah unwittingly uses the present tense (highlighted in bold).

C55:   Yeah. And then, you know, those last few years when she was sick, I wanted to take care of her and I was really happy to do that, honestly, **because she's really taken care of me a lot and I feel like she's tried to protect me** from my dad in terms of how his behavior impacts me and how I feel about it, and I guess it was my turn to do that for her and to kind of take care of her.

T56:   You know when you're, just now as you're talking about how she took care of you, you put it in the present tense, like she was still doing it.

C56:   What do you mean?

T57:   You said she "tries" to take care of you.

C57:   Oh, I didn't realize I, I had said that.

T58:   I think maybe it's hard even after all these years to acknowledge that she's gone.

C58:   Maybe. I didn't, I didn't even know that I had said that. I'd like to believe that she's always with me.

T59:   Yeah. You still feel that way that she's with you in some way?

C59:   In some way. In some way. Not the way I'd like her to be.

Even though one might rationalize the use of the present tense as a simple error, calling attention to it allowed the therapist to empathically highlight how strongly the patient felt connected to her mother, how difficult it was for her to accept her mother's death, and the power of her wish that mother was still living. This captures the patient's core psychological pain, because, since her mother's death, the patient has felt lonely, unnurtured, and unprotected, surrounded by people she perceives as not having enough time or concern for her needs.

Be Curious and Raise Questions

Wonder aloud about what the patient is communicating in order to convey curiosity and encourage a dialogue with the patient. The goal is a dialogue, an exploration *with* the patient, a "give and take" that clarifies, elaborates, and deepens awareness and understanding about the patient's experiences. We may tentatively note links, themes, or parallels between different aspects of what the patient is saying. Reflecting back the core of the patient's narrative in such a tentative and exploratory way fosters collaborative story telling with the patient.

Suggest Alternatives

Point out the implications of what the patient is saying. Also suggest alternatives to the patient's interpretations of, or reactions to, others, and elicit the patient's reactions. Again, the objective is to facilitate the patient's curiosity about her assumptions and reactions and to begin questioning previously unquestioned assumptions. And always, the ultimate objective is to encourage and facilitate a dialogue. Through such a dialogue, the therapist can get a clearer idea of the patient's expectations and the extent of rigidity of the patient's conceptions of self and others (Binder, 2004).

Attend to Process as Well as Content

In addition to listening to *what* the patient says, also attend to *how* she says what she says. For example, note occurrences such as when a patient changes topic suddenly; the sequence of what the patient tells; incongruence between what the patient is saying (content) and overt emotional experience (for example, laughing when telling of mother's terminal illness and death); tone of voice, intonations, and clarity of speech, especially changes from typical presentation (for example, stuttering or faltering in speech when otherwise usually articulate). Observe, too, the patient's reactions in response to a suggestion; for example, did the patient feel criticized, bristle as though being contradicted, or agree too readily? These kinds of shifts in emotional expression and nonverbal reactions (such as fidgeting, averting eye contact, smiling or laughing, or changing postures) are cues to potentially important inner experiences.

KNOWING WHEN TO STRUCTURE AND CONTAIN

During the early sessions when assessment is paramount, balancing listening versus asking guiding questions in the process of story construction depends on the circumstances. Sometimes the therapist can wait for the story to unfold and ask for more information slowly over several sessions. Other times, you may feel the need to fill in more details of the picture as quickly as possible. One factor in judging when to guide the storytelling more actively involves the patient's level of functioning and quality of object relations (QOR); that is, the capacity for relating to others in a generally positive, realistic, flexible, and consistent manner (Piper, Joyce, McCallum, Azim, & Ogrodniczuk, 2002). Those patients with a high QOR are more likely to engage productively with the therapist. They spontaneously tell coherent stories about experiences and relationships outside of the therapy, and the focal theme of their narratives will be more apparent. Translating the salient theme into the beginning of a coherent individualized story occurs relatively quickly and smoothly because these patients are able to reflect on and narrate their experiences. In this case, the therapist allows the story to unfold and listens for dominant themes in what the patient has to tell. This therapist may ask questions or make comments for the purposes of conveying empathy, fostering alliance and collaboration, or minor clarifications.

In contrast, with relatively low functioning patients (low QOR), the narratives are more likely to be less coherent and, instead, fragmented, superficial, sketchy, or excessively detailed. Interpersonal stories may be more idiosyncratic and fragmented so that a salient theme may be harder to identify. In this case, a coherent story will take relatively longer to construct. Therefore, the therapist may need to piece together a narrative more from his direct experiences with the patient or from the fragments of stories the patient can tell. It is likely that the salient theme will become more clearly identified in an evolving transference/countertransference enactment. Articulating the theme being enacted requires first disembedding from the enactment and then articulating what has occurred between therapist and patient. The technical strategy of the treatment is more likely to be transference-oriented (Høglend et al., 2011; Safran & Muran, 2000; Strupp & Binder, 1984). These types of patients characteristically have significant personality pathology. Typically, they receive a DSM diagnosis of a Cluster A or Cluster B personality disorder. They also may receive a severe version of a Cluster C personality disorder.

Low QOR patients may have great difficulty telling a coherent narrative without direction from the therapist. The stories may become tangential, the patient may be so anxious that she cannot think clearly enough to speak coherently about her experiences, the patient may not appreciate the relevance of speaking about interpersonal experiences without clear guidance from the therapist, or the patient may become so emotionally distraught in telling her experiences that the therapist needs to help her soothe and contain her emotional reactions. In such cases, it may be helpful to first observe the patient's difficulty and invite her to share what may be contributing to her difficulty in telling her story. In addition, the therapist may need to structure the interview by actively selecting the content of what is discussed, directing a line of questioning toward concrete examples, redirecting the patient toward relevant information, and actively reflecting back what she is telling in order to give it more coherence and structure.

Keep in mind that "incisive questions" are more probing and confrontative (Binder, 2004). It is important to judge how well a patient can tolerate probing questions. Patients with more concerns around trusting others may experience such questions as intrusive or threatening. Patients with difficulty tolerating uncomfortable psychological experiences may be overwhelmed by such probing questions. It is important to monitor patient's reactions closely for such elements as increased anxiety or agitation, decreased disclosure, or marked shift away from the topic at hand—and gently retreat from a probing inquiry as needed. In addition, containing the patient's emotional reactions may involve stepping in to help the patient slow down, calm down, and find ways to quiet intense emotional reactions. This is not necessary for every patient, but certainly for those patients who may raise concern regarding potential for self-harm or impulsive activities in the face of emotional distress.

It should be noted, on the other hand, that novice therapists tend to underestimate their patients' psychological resilience and needlessly shy away from emotion-laden issues. The novice fears that his patient will decompensate if asked an uncomfortable question. Often, this fear is a projection of the therapist's own discomfort with certain feelings and issues; at other times, it simply reflects the novice therapist's nervousness and uncertainty in the face of an unfamiliar task.

Structuring or containing may also be necessary with hostile or highly guarded patients as well. Managing such challenging assessments involves keen attention to establishing rapport and being very clear and direct about the goals of the assessment and the intentions of the therapist. In this regard, with hostile patients, a therapist is less likely to leave the inquiry open-ended and, instead, more likely to be explicit about the kind of information needed for the assessment. When a patient's disturbance appears to be so severe that it completely interferes with conducting the interview, then the therapist's attention shifts to reviewing the patient's mental status and determining the need for immediate medical evaluation or hospitalization. In this case, the therapist will become very active in structuring the assessment and directing the content.

A FINAL COMMENT: ON ITERATIONS OF ASSESSMENT

Assessment is an ongoing, iterative process in which fragments of the patient's story are progressively elaborated and connected with greater detail to form a more comprehensive picture that deepens our understanding of the patient's experience. Each time a patient speaks about his experiences offers the potential to reconstruct the story in a way that opens up new ways of seeing and thinking about what may have occurred. When a patient is able to think differently about his experiences, this is a hint of change in the patient's characteristic mode of perceiving and relating to self and others. The therapist, too, will hear the stories differently, having more context and understanding of the patient's life and more experience of how the patient relates. This process of furthering understanding and self-understanding is an essential part of therapeutic change, making assessment and intervention inextricably intertwined. To paraphrase the social scientist Donald Schön (1983), who studied expert performance across knowledge domains: the patient is changed in the process of understanding her and understood in the process of change.

6

Developing a BDP Case Conceptualization and Intervention Plan

The essence of empathy is seeing the world through the patient's eyes and conveying an understanding that is emotionally salient and makes meaning of the patient's experiences. Connecting with a patient's core emotional pain requires a rich understanding of what troubles the patient and how the patient perceives and responds to her experiences. This chapter will describe how to develop a case conceptualization by organizing a welter of information around a predominant theme. The organizing principle is a narrative structure that is used to create a meaningful personal story around the identified theme. This initial understanding of the patient guides subsequent clinical observation and inquiry, therapeutic engagement, clinical decision making, and multicultural and ethical sensitivity. In BDP, a therapist cannot effectively help a patient without a conceptual "blueprint" of the patient's struggles (Binder, 2004). When coupled with relational skills, including a keen understanding of how people struggle to be in relationships, case conceptualization may in fact be the linchpin of therapeutic competence (Betan & Binder, 2010; many recognize case conceptualization as a core competency in psychotherapy, e.g., Binder, 2004; Eells, Lombart, Kendjelic, Turner, & Lucas, 2005; Ivey, 2006; Kendjelic & Eells, 2007; National Council of Schools and Programs in Professional Psychology [NCSPP], 2007; Persons, 2006; Scheiber, Kramer, & Adamowski,

2003; Sperry, 2010; American Psychological Association Presidential Task Force on EBPP, 2006).

ESSENTIAL ELEMENTS
OF A CASE CONCEPTUATLIZATION

The identification of themes and patterns across seemingly unrelated information begins a process of explaining why this patient experiences these particular problems at this particular time (Ivey, 2006). Case conceptualization involves moving between describing how the patient struggles and making clinical inferences about the meaning and origin of these problems (Eells, 2010). Clinical inferences include not only theory-guided hypotheses about the origins of the patient's problems, but also the factors that contribute to their persistence. In order to capture a working understanding of the patient, a comprehensive case conceptualization will answer the following questions:

What Are the Patient's Struggles?

This includes the patient's symptoms, as well as psychological, behavioral, and interpersonal problems. Here, the concern is with describing what the patient reports about her subjective feelings and relational problems, as well as what we observe in the patient's behaviors and attitudes. Being descriptive means staying "close to the data"—what the patient reports directly and what we can observe in the patient's behaviors, nonverbal cues, and emotional reactions or lack thereof.

What Contributes to the Patient's Vulnerability to Struggle in this Particular Way (Origins and Predisposing Vulnerabilities)?

What makes the patient more or less susceptible to experiencing such difficulties and distress? BDP case conceptualization identifies a patient's dominant relational schemas and focuses on early interactions with significant caretakers that contribute to the patient's maladaptive perceptions of self and others. In addition, it is important to understand how negative expectations of others' intentions and reactions can leave the patient vulnerable to experiencing distress in current relationships.

77

What Helps Perpetuate the Patient's Struggles and Maladaptive Modes of Functioning (Maintaining Influences)?

A basic assumption in BDP concerns the enduring impact of internalized relational schemas that continually affect the way one interprets interpersonal interactions, as well as shape the modes of relating that contribute to confirming one's expectations about relationships. The case conceptualization offers a story of what repeatedly happens in the patient's relationships that leaves her distressed or symptomatic. Rather than merely describing the patient's relationships, we consolidate what we have learned into a narrative that highlights a key pattern in her way of relating, as well as its consequences. In drawing these links, we are making clinical inferences regarding the patient's inner experiences, motivations, and efforts to protect against emotional pain.

What Are the Directions and Avenues for Treatment?

The case conceptualization ought to inform specific treatment goals and interventions, as well as identify specific psychological or interpersonal needs that could influence or disrupt treatment.

THE ESSENTIAL CLINICAL COMPETENCIES ASSOCIATED WITH CASE CONCEPTUALIZATION

Specify the Presenting Problem(s)

This clinical competency involves the ability to clearly specify the patient's difficulties that will be the focus of treatment.

Establish an Interpersonal Theme

This clinical competency involves the ability to identify and track a primary interpersonal theme in the patient's descriptions of her relationships.

Develop an Effective Case Conceptualization

This clinical competency involves the ability to develop a coherent, individualized narrative about a patient's core assumptions about relationships, as well as typical ways of interacting interpersonally that perpetuate the patient's difficulties in life.

Develop an Effective Intervention Plan

This clinical competency involves the ability to select interventions that are based on the patient's unique relational concerns and increase the patient's awareness of the problematic ways of interacting with others that perpetuate emotional and interpersonal difficulties.

BDP CASE CONCEPTUALIZATION

The Cyclical Maladaptive Pattern (CMP)

The BDP model of case conceptualization provides a framework for capturing a patient's assumptions about relationships, as well as typical ways of interacting interpersonally that perpetuate the patient's difficulties in life. As we discuss in chapter 2, we place relationships at the core of understanding psychological functioning, emphasizing in particular how early relationships have a lasting influence on an individual's sense of self, expectations of others, and ways of moving through the world and approaching life's possibilities. Applying an integrative psychodynamic/ interpersonal theory as a broad conceptual foundation, the BDP therapist seeks to articulate a patient's unique personality and interpersonal style, current difficulties, life history, and cultural context. Accordingly, we emphasize a narrative approach that allows description of the essential themes underlying a patient's relational stories using the patient's own words and the therapist's empathic constructions to give meaning to the patient's current struggles.

We organize the case conceptualization around the patient's cyclical maladaptive pattern (CMP), an enduring, repetitive pattern of engaging in relationships that perpetuates a patient's difficulties (Binder, 2004; Levenson, 2010; Strupp & Binder, 1984). The CMP captures, in a narrative format, the person's expectations of others, problematic modes of relating with others, experience of others' responses, and consequent negative experiences of self. In the following, we offer guidelines for generating a BDP case conceptualization, including descriptions of each component of the CMP and an extended case example.

GUIDELINES FOR GENERATING
THE CMP CASE CONCEPTUALIZATION

In psychotherapy, we listen to stories and also tell stories. These stories grow more meaningful as we come to understand the complexity and specific nuances of what our patient has experienced, felt, and suffered. In telling a therapeutic story, the goal is to pull together fragments of experience into a coherent whole, a narrative that draws links among basic motivations, feelings and behaviors, expectations of and reactions to others, and beliefs about one's self. The story we tell opens up possibilities for change as it highlights unconscious choices the patient repeatedly makes and, therefore, choices that can be unmade.

In narrating a patient's experience, the therapist must strive to tell how the patient feels in words that are emotionally meaningful and immediately evocative. In contrast to dry, rather shallow descriptions of a patient such as depressed or anxious, consider the evocative and telling nature of language such as the patient "experiences profound loneliness," "feels hollow and empty inside," "at the core, feels unloved and unworthy," "feels useless," "hates himself," "wishes he never existed," "feels as if he doesn't really exist," "wishes to disappear," "wishes simply to be seen by others," "carries long-held, unremitting guilt," "believes no one understands and will never care to understand," or "feels desperate for…" or desperate to be…." The main idea here is that the therapist needs a rich vocabulary and language for describing the patient's subjective experiences and internal world in experience-near, meaningful expressions that convey our empathic connection and understanding.

Step 1: Describe the Presenting Problem(s)

The first task is to clearly specify the patient's difficulties that will be the focus of treatment. Patients vary in how specifically they view their problems, as well as in the extent to which they view their difficulties in an interpersonal context. Some patients are more likely to focus on symptomatic difficulties such as depression, anxiety, or substance abuse, while others may cast their difficulties in terms of relationship problems, such as conflict in a primary romantic relationship, with family members, or with work colleagues. Still others may feel distressed about their sense of identity as represented by confusion about career goals, a lack of ambition, a sense of failing to achieve their ideals, or loss of faith in something previously valued. It is often the case, too, that what therapists identify as the core problems differs from what the patient initially presents. In the following case example, although the patient initially reports feeling depressed and unmotivated in her school work, it is important to note predominant interpersonal concerns that emerge as problems to be addressed in treatment. The following vignette is taken from a first interview that was made for training purposes.

Case Example: Sarah

Sarah, a 22-year-old, European American woman sought therapy feeling increasingly unhappy and inadequate as a result of difficulties performing at school and strain in her relationship with her boyfriend. She describes feeling "really depressed.... I just don't feel like doing anything. I'm in school right now but its hard to go to my classes and I'm having trouble with, with school and getting things done and [sigh] I'm really just sad all the time. I really don't feel like there's much of a point to everything that I'm doing." Sarah feels under pressure at school because, despite trying, she is unable to complete her work to her own or her professors' satisfaction. She questions whether she belongs in her academic program and believes that her professors and peers also see her as incapable. Sarah complains of feeling unmotivated and finding it difficult to focus on her work. Sarah also describes feeling dissatisfied in her current romantic relationship because she feels obligated to take care of her boyfriend and wishes to feel more appreciated and nurtured by him. Sarah describes a longstanding history of feeling sad and unhappy since her mother died of cancer when Sarah was 13 years old. She reported that her father quickly remarried and noted feeling she and her sister were "pushed aside" as if they were no longer as important to him as his new family. As a result of feeling that her father wasn't emotionally available, Sarah took care of her younger sister. Her concern for her sister's loneliness and need for support overshadowed her own sadness in losing her mother.

Step 2: Establishing an Interpersonal Theme

Understanding symptoms and presenting problems in an interpersonal context focuses attention on the stories patients tell about their relationships. In order to identify a primary interpersonal theme, the therapist listens for the wishes, needs, and expectations that recur in the patient's descriptions of her relationships. He or she seeks to identify a recurring theme (a red thread running through the patient's discourse) across the patient's concerns, complaints, beliefs, emotional reactions (or lack thereof), and ways of interacting interpersonally. This theme is likely to reflect the patient's core pain—the unmet interpersonal needs or desires and subsequent negative feelings about one's self—that helps sustain maladaptive modes of relating. The interpersonal theme emerges as the therapist listens across the stories a patient tells. What is the patient trying to communicate about what she has always felt, wanted, or needed in life? Whether or not the patient is aware of it, she is giving her current, preferred version of the events, experiences, actions, and interactions that have led to this point in time. She is consciously and unconsciously giving meaning to her current circumstances, the point where she is in her life history.

In order to identify a broad interpersonal theme, it sometimes helps to have previously articulated thematic categories from which to choose. A patient's interpersonal needs or desires may center on one or more of the following distinct, but related, themes: (a) receiving nurturance and caretaking, (b) getting attention or recognition, (c) being accepted by others, (d) needing others' dependability/availability, (e) experiencing safety with others, (f) being wanted by others, (g) being independent, (h) self-definition. Keep in mind that patients often have multiple needs or expectations of self and others that conflict with each other and that simultaneously contribute to maladaptive modes of relating.

Case Example: Sarah

The following transcript material presents Sarah's descriptions of key interpersonal relationships. This section focuses primarily on illustrating how we might extract a dominant interpersonal theme by attending to concerns and feelings that recur across Sarah's stories. Key interpersonal information is highlighted in bold. Later, we will refer to the case material to identify her interpersonal patterns. Asked how she experiences her depression and views herself, others, and the world, Sarah responds:

C4: I guess in terms of myself I don't really feel good about myself. I don't feel like I, you know, I'm getting my master's right now, and I just don't feel like I'm smart enough to be able to finish the program and like I really deserve to be doing what I'm doing and **I think other people probably feel the same way** about me, and I don't know I just don't think that, **it seems like I do a lot for other people and no one really wants to do anything for me**.

Although speaking of her view of her self, in fact, Sarah begins by telling an interpersonal story. In addition to her self-doubt, she believes that her professors and peers also see her as incapable. She thinks perhaps that others are as disappointed in her as she is in herself. She then moves to another experience of others, suggesting that no one really wants to do anything for her even though she does a lot for others.

First, pursuing Sarah's idea of not being smart enough, the therapist asks about the nature of her academic program and her performance. In this vignette, an interpersonal concern **revolves around a sense of inadequacy, not being good enough for herself or for others**. The therapist asks about the instructors' feedback in an effort to begin to flesh out the interpersonal interactions. What we learn is that the patient assumes the instructors are frustrated, but she has not received any direct confirmation from them.

C12:   Mmm. I mean I think that **maybe my instructors are probably frustrated with me** about not having as much motivation as I probably should to make it in doing this and it's just, it's frustrating too because professors are pretty busy. **I don't think they have enough time for me** to help me do what I need to do so …

T13:   Now have they told you that, or are you inferring that from what they've said? [Here, the therapist hopes to distinguish between the patient's assumptions about others' intentions and others' actual behavior]

C13:   Well, it just doesn't, well, they never told me that, but it just seems like they're pretty busy. They don't have enough time to help me out.

T14:   Hm. Do you ask and they tell you they're too busy or … [The therapist is seeking specific information about the interactions Sarah has with her professors.]

C14:   No. I guess they don't ever tell me they're too busy, but I know sometimes I've emailed them and it's taken like three or four days to get back to me. So, I assume that if **it was important**

enough they'd probably get back to me right away. But it doesn't seem like that ...

Sarah is frustrated because she perceives her professors as "too busy" and not having enough time to help her out. She assumes, without evidence, that other students are not experiencing delays in hearing back from professors. She concludes that her needs, and by implication that she, are not important enough. This interpersonal concern about not being important enough extends to other relationships, as well. When the therapist suggests that she may be taking their delay in responding personally, perhaps misinterpreting their actions, Sarah responds,

C19:   I don't know, it just seems like that's kind of always how it's been for me. Even my boyfriend kind of does the same thing. **It doesn't seem like what I need is as important as what I need to do for him**, and it's a lot about him and how he's feeling and that's what he uses to relate with me. So, I mean it's not just my professors....

C22:   Yeah, similar in the sense that, you know, I feel like maybe my professors are more, I don't know, more subtle with how they feel about me, but my boyfriend makes it pretty clear that, I don't know, he makes me feel like I'm not good enough.

T23:   How does he do that? [Here, the therapist is seeking a more specific description of the interpersonal interaction.]

C23:   It's just little things like even, I'll go out of my way to make a nice dinner and something won't be, you know, won't taste right. It won't have enough salt or it won't be, it will be too spicy or something like that. **I just feel like I went out of my way to do something nice and it wasn't good enough,** and I think more often when I do things like that, even when its little things, **I don't feel like he appreciates them**.

In her relationship with her boyfriend, Sarah feels that her needs take a backseat to what she does for him. She describes her sense of going out of her way to meet his needs and often feels criticized or unappreciated in return. Similarly, with her professors, Sarah elaborates:

C25:   I still feel like I try to do what I can to put in as much effort as I can, you know, considering it's hard for me being depressed and being sad, and even though I do that it still doesn't make them want to help me any more or get back to me any quicker, even though I just feel like I'm working as hard as I can.

In these vignettes, the predominant theme that emerges is **Sarah's recurring feeling of being unappreciated despite trying so hard**. In a similar vein, Sarah has assumed a great deal of responsibility for taking care of her younger sister. Sarah's sense of obligation to care for her sister began when their mother fell ill and subsequently died of cancer when Sarah was 13 years old. She links her longstanding feelings of being sad and unhappy to this time in her life. Describing her father as emotionally unavailable, she noted that he quickly remarried and focused more on his new wife and stepchildren.

C32:   Yeah, she, umm, died from cancer and it was, it was just a very difficult time for me. I had my little sister who's 4 years younger than me, and it just changed my world. **Like my father really wasn't there for me in terms of support**, and I really feel like I had to take care of my sister. **I was more worried about her and I couldn't really, I felt like I wasn't allowed to feel sad or feel depressed**. I kind of had to keep it all in because I had my sister to take care of, and, like I said, my dad wasn't really there for her so it was really pretty much my job to do that.

T33:   When you say your dad wasn't there for you or your sister, can you explain what you mean? [Here, the therapist does not assume he understands, but asks for elaboration of what appears to be a key interpersonal experience around loss and disappointment, perhaps even abandonment.]

C33:   Well he got into another relationship pretty quickly. Umm, and I don't know if that was going on even before my mom passed away, but he got married within a year of her dying and he really put a lot of focus on the family. The person who he married already had two kids, and he put a lot of effort into that family, and I **feel like we were kind of pushed aside and just weren't important enough**. So that's how we felt. He was there to financially, of course, help us and do what he needed to do, but emotionally I felt like he wasn't there and it was basically me giving all the emotional support to my sister.

Here, again, in Sarah's concern about not being important enough, she despairs over always disappointing her father. In fact, she moved in with an aunt for one year because "it just didn't seem like my dad wanted me around." She returned to his home only because she believed her sister needed her since their father was not giving much attention to her sister. Since then, Sarah has served this caretaking role for the sister, always, it seems, at the expense of her own needs.

T36:   And then you moved back after about a year. What made you decide to move back?

C36:   Because I missed my sister and I thought that she needed me, especially when she would call me and tell me how dad just wasn't really there for her and was doing a lot of things with the other kids and, you know, I felt like she was pretty lonely, and so I, **I didn't really want to move back, but I felt like I had to do that for her.**...

Sarah is still taking care of her sister, currently helping her apply to colleges.

C65:   Well I guess it's, it just feels like it's my job to be that for her. Be the person who can help her and maybe, if my mom didn't get sick, then maybe it would have been her to do that. But, you know, she's not here now I have to do it for her. I don't want her to ... go through it....

C69:   ... I think she would be disappointed. I think she'd be angry. I guess if I told her one day that she needs to do it on her own, all this college stuff, I think she would be pretty upset with me.

T70:   Uh huh. Now if you're doing all this stuff for her how much does that take away from the time you need to do your own work in your program?

C70:   It takes a good bit of time away, but I guess I feel pretty overwhelmed too, and that kind of pushes me to the other end of feeling like I can't do anything at all. You know, it's hard to get the motivation to do that much with my own work when I spend so much time trying to make sure she's doing what she needs to do. So it definitely takes away from my own work.

We learn that Sarah feels unappreciated for all she does for her sister, as she feels with her boyfriend and professors. Sarah has not communicated her limits or needs because she believes that asking her sister to be more independent would disappoint and anger her sister. This prospect causes Sarah to have guilty feelings. It appears that Sarah's guilt is associated with the idea that expecting more self-sufficient behavior from her sister would be tantamount to abandoning her as she believes her father and her mother have done to her. Discussing her reluctance to let her sister know that she is struggling, Sarah says:

C73:   Well, there's no one else to help her, you know, so I feel like I'm the only one that could do it. And I don't think, I mean you know, you just asked me about feeling appreciated, **and I don't think that, like she's never really shown me her appreciation. I think it's just what she expects**. So, I guess that's the difference, so that it makes it harder in the relationship too, because there's another relationship where I don't feel appreciated. But it's different because, you know, I guess maybe in my relationship with my boyfriend I don't have to be there but with my sister, she's my sister. I have to.

T74:   So she expects you to be doing all these things and, well, how do you feel about that?

C74:   (Sighs) It just goes back to that feeling of, just things are unfair. Its not, I just see people around me that don't have to deal with this and I don't understand why I have to do it. I don't understand why I had to become a mother when I was 13, **and I just I don't think other people have to go through this**, and it makes me mad that I have to, and that this is what I was dealt, you know, and I'm angry about that, and, you know, I sometimes, what annoys me the most is like when I see like couples out that are happy or I hear about, you know, a friend who just went on a vacation with their parents and things like that. **I don't want to hear that. I just it makes me more angry**, and no one I know has to change their plans or has this whole other obligation, that they can't do what they need to do with their lives because they have somebody else to take care of.

When Sarah hears that a friend went on vacation with her parents, she is angry. She conveys her anger and resentment toward others for having what she does not. Sarah believes that others haven't suffered as she has. In adolescence, as today, she believes her peers would not understand, thinking:

C48:   Well I just don't think anyone would understand what I'm going through. It just seems like all the other kids just had that life of, they're born with everything that was perfect and just you know if they had their mom and dad and they had their really good life and here I was with … I don't know, it can't really get much worse than what I had and everyone else is living their perfect lives, **and I just don't think that there's anybody there that could have understood me.**

Sarah conveys how lonely and disconnected from others she feels. No one understands the sadness and anger that have followed her like dark clouds since her early adolescence. No one understands how difficult her life has been and how hard she works despite her burden. Sarah is dismissive and angry.

The dominant theme that emerges from these interpersonal vignettes is loneliness and lack of appreciation. An individual story can be developed from it. Sarah wish desperately for attention and caring, wanting others to recognize how hard she works to give them what they want and to acknowledge how painful and burdensome her life has been. Instead, she feels underappreciated, inadequate, and not important enough for anyone in her life. Recognizing this broad interpersonal theme and accompanying *personal story line* sets the stage for articulating the specific interpersonal patterns that Sarah unwittingly enacts and that perpetuate her primary concerns.

Step 3: CMP Case Conceptualization

Identifying a broad interpersonal theme is the foundation of the BDP case conceptualization that is progressively elaborated into a specific, individualized story following the narrative structure of the CMP. Developing a narrative that pulls together fragments into a coherent understanding involves identifying those elements in the patient's communications that are most relevant to the theme. For the therapist, this story construction process involves the generic skills of interpersonal pattern recognition. This skill depends on a process of selectively attending to and selectively dismissing chunks of clinical material in terms of whether or not they appear to be relevant to the theme. Not every story or experience will fit. In general, the more emotionally evocative a story, the more likely it is to be relevant to the patient's dominant core pain.

As the therapist identifies critical scenes, recurring "characters," emotional sequences, and central concerns in a patient's stories, he begins to organize these chunks (like pieces of a puzzle) into a progressively elaborated and coherent maladaptive personal story line (Schafer, 2005). By conceptualizing a case in this way, the therapist is in the role of a coauthor. When listening to the patient's narrative depictions, the therapist should picture specific scenes in his mind's eye, in as much detail as possible. Visualizing the story depends on pursuing the kind of specificity gleaned from concrete examples of interchanges between characters in a story. A therapist who is able to visualize the story as it crystallizes will be more likely to judge what aspects of the story are especially meaningful for the patient. The standardized story structure of the CMP components can help key aspects of relational experiences stand out and guide the therapeutic inquiry.

The CMP provides a narrative structure for the maladaptive personal story line that will be the focus of therapy. It is in the form of a wish or intention that is thwarted by an anticipated negative reaction from significant others. In the form of a self-fulfilling prophecy, the patient is prone to unconsciously act in ways that evoke reactions from others that reinforce her negative expectations. Negative expectations are further reinforced by her interpretations of the motives of others' reactions, which are usually in line with her expectations. The patient then reacts negatively to herself and automatically initiates defensive strategies to protect herself from the anticipated negative reactions of others. This recurrent maladaptive interpersonal pattern is subjectively experienced as the core pain that is at the root of patient's fundamental struggle to feel and live well.

An essential aspect of this cyclical pattern of interpersonal relating is the way one's expectations of and appraisals of interactions produce behavior that, paradoxically, invites exactly the response from others that one anticipates. However, the original structure of the CMP (Strupp & Binder, 1984) leaves implicit this motive for self-defeating behavior. An additional component can be introduced into to the CMP framework— Acts of Self-Protection—in order to capture how a person attempts to protect himself from (but unwittingly elicits) negative expectations and painful emotions in relationships. In doing so, we attend more explicitly to how a person becomes caught in a vicious cycle by behaving in ways that often elicit responses from others that match or confirm generally negative expectations. In this revised CMP framework, the elements of one's style of relating include: (a) needs and desires in relationships (acts of self), (b) expectations of others, (c) acts of self-protection, (d) acts of others, and (e) consequences for self-regard and self-treatment (acts of self toward the self).

Needs and Desires in Relationships (Acts of Self)

The first component of the primary interpersonal theme represented in the CMP is the patient's particular needs and desires in relationships that impact her sense of self and well-being. Every person brings needs and desires to relationships with others. Wanting to be loved and nurtured, recognized and appreciated are at the core of being human. Connections with others who are dependable, attentive, caring, and loving build a sense of security and self-worth that enable an individual to pursue talents and interests and explore the world (reflecting autonomy and initiative). The need for a secure base (Bowlby, 1988) from which to launch and explore, knowing we can return for comfort and connection, never ends. When someone seeks our help, it is safe to begin with an assumption that this crucial security in attachment is missing, limited, or significantly distorted. In attempting to understand what one needs and is looking for in interpersonal relationships, consider first what the person did not seem to experience in his early relationships and, therefore, what he is left longing for and desperately seeking. Patients are likely to cast their needs and wishes in terms of what is missing in relationships and in themselves: for example, "I'm lonely" (wish for connection), "No one wants to be around me" (wish for acceptance), "No one cares" (wish for caretaking/nurturance), "I can't make my own decisions" (wish for autonomy), "I am stuck" (wish for self-determination), "I don't know who I am" (wish for self-definition).

To fully articulate the patient's core pain, there must be a hypothesis addressing why one believes he cannot have what he most needs or desires. This is a statement about one's self that ultimately sustains maladaptive modes of relating by setting up one's expectations of others and efforts to protect oneself against distressing interpersonal and/or emotional experiences. For example,

The patient is longing to be loved but feels undeserving of love.
The patient is longing for acceptance but feeling worthless.
The patient needs to be nurtured and taken care of but feels disgusting.
The patient wishes to be recognized for her effort but feels inadequate.
The patient needs to be taken care of but feels he is unimportant.

The CMP story begins with a statement of conflicting voices inside the patient's mind: one that calls out for what the patient desires or needs followed by the patient's objection, so to speak.

Expectations of Others

The CMP calls explicit attention to one's expectations of others, highlighting enduring schemas that influence how one anticipates and interprets interactions with others. Although there is a link between these schemas and actual interpersonal experiences, one's experiences of others can be distorted in the process of internalization, and earlier schemas influence how we perceive subsequent experiences. When developing an understanding of a patient's expectations of others, it is helpful to keep in mind how narrow or rigid his expectations of others can become.

Early messages from caregivers echo throughout life. A caregiver's disinterest, impatience, contempt, rejection, hostility, anxiety, clinginess, or disappointment may leave a child with an enduring sense that others cannot tolerate her needs, self-expressions, or strivings. As a result, the child may come to expect similar reactions in all interpersonal interactions and relationships—regardless of how others respond in actuality. This is the power of schemas to shape what we expect and experience and to create a continuous feedback loop across time. Expectations of others will emerge prominently in a patient's relational narratives when the therapist begins to listen for them.

Acts of Self-Protection

As discussed in chapter 2, children cope with painful relational experiences by finding ways to accommodate caregivers or cope with overwhelming feelings, often involving suppressing their own needs and desires. Such efforts to cope, however, can result in maladaptive relational patterns that may have served to protect early attachments, but that come to contribute to and perpetuate significant difficulties later in life. The Acts of Self-Protection component captures a person's ways of protecting against the anticipated hurtful behavior of others or negative emotional states that have developed as a result of painful relational experiences. It is important to keep in mind that one's behaviors are often contradictory to one's wishes and needs in relationships. For example, a person may wish for affection from others, but in feeling unworthy and expecting to be rebuffed, she may treat others dismissively, acting as though she does not need anyone. As a result, the patient's expectations of being rejected are likely to come true as others withdraw in the face of her apparent disinterest. Although trying to protect oneself in reaction to one's negative expectations of others can take as many different forms as there are relationships in the world, acts of self-protection may fall into the broad categories of either (a) inhibiting oneself in some way (e.g., passivity/dependency, disavowing one's needs and feelings, or restricting self-expression) or (b) rejecting others (e.g., hostility or withdrawal) in order to ward off anticipated negative interpersonal experiences.

Perceived Acts of Others

This refers to others' actual responses, but more frequently the behavior is perceived idiosyncratically by the patient. The therapist should attend to how and to what extent a patient may misperceive the responses of others, especially their intentions. These misperceptions and distortions reflect the patient's dominant expectations of relationships. However, it may very well be that the patient's perceptions of others' reactions are not distorted; instead, others may indeed be reacting in quite negative, unempathic, angry, controlling, demeaning, condescending, ingratiating, and paternalistic ways that are complementary to the patient's mode of relating. This is at the heart of understanding the cyclical maladaptive pattern: others respond or are perceived as responding in exactly the way the patient expects, thereby perpetuating the patient's core pain and protective mechanisms.

Consequences for Self-Regard and Self-Treatment (Acts of Self toward the Self)

As discussed in chapter 2, one's interpersonal experiences have a profound impact on one's sense of self. Maladaptive relational experiences generally leave a person vulnerable to disparaging beliefs about oneself and painful feelings that perpetuate one's difficulties. In addition, the internalization of interpersonal experiences also leaves the person prone to treat himself as a perceived other had treated him. Therefore, attending to the meanings one carries about self-worth and self-efficacy, as well as attending to characteristic self-treatment, is a vital component in understanding how a patient unwittingly contributes to perpetuating her maladaptive relational patterns. Attacks on one's own sense of self-worth generally trigger one's keen awareness of interpersonal needs and wishes, bringing us back to the first component.

Case Example: Sarah's Cyclical Maladaptive Pattern

As seen in the case of Sarah, she wants to be appreciated for being "a good girl," one who stifles her needs and instead takes care of others despite her pain. She wishes for recognition and acknowledgment of her efforts, but feels she is not good enough or important enough in the eyes of others. Sarah struggles with an enduring sense of sadness and resentment at being burdened with taking care of others. Underlying her caretaking and efforts to please others, Sarah longs to be nurtured and cared for. However, she expects others to neglect her, to be unable to understand her struggles, or to regard her as undeserving of their attention. Expecting to be disregarded or overlooked, Sarah does not want to suffer greater loss and rejection. She protects herself by keeping her feelings to herself, as well as alienating herself from others. Sarah rejects or diminishes her peers, infantilizes her sister, and avoids asserting her needs with her boyfriend and her professors. A proneness to self-neglect, reflecting her perceptions of neglect of others, reinforces her defensive posture. As a result, others have no understanding of how neglected and unappreciated she feels. They do in fact misunderstand her experiences. Sarah then perceives others as not making time for her, being self-absorbed, and simply expecting her to take care of them. She is left feeling angry, resentful, and lonely. Turning on herself, she feels guilty and inadequate, undermines her performance at school with a lack of motivation, and withdraws from others, thereby perpetuating her sense of loneliness. Table 6.1 summarizes Sarah's CMP.

INTERVENTION PLANNING

Coalescing the patient's interpersonal stories into a narrative of the dominant maladaptive pattern of relating provides the therapist with a blueprint that can help keep the treatment focused on the patient's most critical and enduring core pain. In this regard, the case conceptualization provides a focus for further therapeutic discourse with the patient.

Table 6.1 Components of the Cyclical Maladaptive Pattern

Wishes: What the patient wishes for and feels in relationships. "The patient wishes for...."

Example: Sarah longs to be nurtured, as well as recognized for her efforts.

Expectations of Others: The patient's expectations of others' responses, intentions, and feelings. "The patient expects others to...."

Example: Sarah expects others to neglect, disregard, or misunderstand her.

Acts of Self-Protection: The patient behaves in these ways to ward off what is expected and feared in relationships (often contradicts wishes). "In order to fend off [negative expectations of others], the patient tends to...."

Example: In order to avoid feeling rejected and alone, Sarah avoids expressing her feelings and needs to others, who, in turn, do not know how much she is struggling.

Perceived Acts of Others: Others respond in these ways or the patient sees it that way.

Example: Sarah perceives others as not responding to her needs and expecting her to take care of herself.

Self-Regard and Self-Treatment: As a result of experiences with significant others, the patient feels and acts toward oneself in certain ways.

Example: Sarah feels resentful and angry; her guilt, however, leads her to withdraw from others, perpetuating her sense of loneliness and deprivation. Her tendency for self-neglect reinforces her sense of deprivation.

The therapist presents an emotionally evocative version of the case conceptualization that captures the dramatic tone of the patient's story and demonstrates empathic attunement. This is a starting point for collaborating in an ongoing dialogue that fleshes out the patient's most currently influential interpersonal schemas and the painful emotions associated with them. The patient has the opportunity to modify his maladaptive personal story line as a result of such a collaborative dialogue—that give-and-take in which patient and therapist together pursue a meaningful understanding of the patient's struggles and identify alternatives for how the patient makes sense of his experiences.

The objective of developing a case conceptualization is to raise the patient's awareness of a dominant, repetitive pattern of dysfunctional thinking and corresponding maladaptive pattern of relating that contributes to disruptions in the patient's sense of self, mood, and coping. BDP is specifically geared toward increasing the patient's insight into how his typical expectations and reactions foreclose possibilities for positive interactions with others; with greater awareness comes the chance to identify and try out new ways of relating with others. As the patient attempts new ways of thinking about and relating to others, concomitant changes in a patient's sense of self and expectations become possible (Binder, 2004).

An inherent characteristic of a maladaptive interpersonal pattern is that the patient perceives herself to be a character that has no choice but to play out the established plot of her personal story. Over the course of therapy, the ultimate objective is to convince the patient that she is not a character but rather an actor who has more freedom than she imagines to improvise her role and influence the plot. In this regard, treatment goals should represent desired changes in the outcome of the story; that is, expanding possibilities for the patient to have a different ending. More general targets for treatment, such as decreased depressive affect, increased self-esteem, increased frustration tolerance, diminished anger, and improved interpersonal relatedness are indicators that desired changes are being made in the unique maladaptive personal story line and in the patient's ability to influence the unfolding plot.

Broad objectives that are relevant to every treatment include helping the patient engage in the therapeutic discourse, increase his insight into relational patterns, generate more flexible and realistically positive beliefs about himself and others, and expand his emotional and behavioral repertoire of interpersonal interactions (see Table 6.2). The strategy for implementing these objectives must be highly individualized for the specific patient and cast in terms unique to the patient's relational struggles and core pain. For example, building a positive alliance with a patient who is generally mistrustful will require interventions distinct from those suitable for a patient who is passive and readily agreeable. Both patients will have difficulties collaborating, but for different reasons that must be addressed appropriately. Similarly, interventions to expand a patient's behavioral repertoire should address the unique interpersonal deficits. For example, a timid and demure patient who repeatedly gets taken advantage of by others may benefit from increasing assertiveness skills; in contrast, an overbearing patient probably would not need assertiveness skills, but rather skills that help her learn to slow down and listen to others before making a decision. The purpose of treatment objectives

Table 6.2   BDP Treatment Objectives

1.	Alleviate suffering and improve functioning.
2.	Construct an interpersonal story in order to articulate and structure the patient's primary interpersonal concerns into a guiding framework for a treatment focus.
3.	Develop patient's awareness of the problematic ways of interacting with others that perpetuate emotional and interpersonal difficulties.
4.	Promote self-reflection. Increase the patient's capacity to step back from immediate experiencing and observe the story being enacted. This includes learning to observe one's own thinking, feeling, and behaving, as well as the other person's reactions.
5.	Through the therapeutic dialogue, disrupt maladaptive interpersonal patterns and expand possibilities for ways of perceiving relationships and self.
6.	Develop new ways of relating and behaving.
7.	Facilitate internalization of therapeutic inquiry skills—facilitate actively thinking about one's own reactions and behaviors and generating new ways of thinking and responding.

is to achieve treatment goals, which should be based on the content of the problem formulation.

There is an array of psychodynamic, interpersonal, cognitive, and behavioral interventions that can be effectively integrated into BDP. The way a therapist uses these interventions must be rooted in a clear identification and understanding of how the patient's dysfunctional cognitive and emotional processes and corresponding maladaptive interpersonal patterns contribute to the patient's primary problems. Furthermore, these interventions are bolstered by the BDP approach to therapeutic discourse, which invites the patient to reflect on and regard her troubles in increasingly nuanced ways.

7

Interventions
Inquiry and Dialogue

In human communication, stories are all we have. (Schafer, 2005b, p. 278)

We are in the era of neuroscience. Clinicians are increasingly fascinated with the neural activity that underlies subjective experiences and overt behavior. Brain imaging methods such as positron emission tomography (PET) allow scientists to map the areas of the brain that "light up" simultaneously to a particular subjective experience, including events and experiences that occur in psychotherapy. But human beings have evolved with sense organs that are directed primarily outward; sight, smell, hearing, and touch are sensory functions all more sensitive to stimuli external to the body than within it. Humans are "wired" to respond to their external environment subjectively and behaviorally (Bowlby, 1988a). Neural activity is represented in subjective experience as self-awareness. This self-awareness inhabits a representational world composed of self-representations and object-representations that are ineluctably linked together by interaction scenarios with each having a characteristic affective tone (Beebe, Lachmann, & Jaffe, 1997; Mitchell, 1988; Sandler & Sandler, 1978). This internal representational world begins to be populated in infancy through internalizations of perceived interactions with the outside world. Although this representational world is laid down as personality structure, it must be replenished continually from interactions with the world, especially people.

The life-sustaining importance of contact with other human beings was noticed in the 1930s by pediatricians who observed infants waste away while in hospitals if they were not provided with some minimal amount of personal attention and contact by the personnel responsible for them. This fatal condition was called hospitalism. In the 1940s, the condition was observed in foundling home infants by Rene Spitz, a psychoanalytically informed physician who pioneered the child development research strategy of systematic, theory-guided infant observation. Spitz observed hospitalism in those foundling homes with staff organizations that inadvertently discouraged frequent, stable contact with the infants in their care. Hospitalism is associated with profound psychological and physical damage, including retarded physical development, disruption in perceptual-motor skills, and disruption in the development of language. The important point to be made is that, at least in infancy, significant deficiencies in interpersonal contact produce physical damage to the brain and sufficiently traumatic interpersonal experiences at any stage of life can produce damage (van der Kolk, 2000).

The need for human contact does not disappear at the end of childhood. Contact, especially in the form of intimate and stable relationships, remains a basic motivational striving throughout life (Wallin, 2007). Even persons who find themselves physically cut off from other people attempt to maintain their internal representational worlds, to be emotionally sustained by them, and to avoid the experience of complete aloneness. The desperate measures that a person forced into a solitary existence will take to maintain a sense of human contact was dramatically depicted in the movie *Castaway*. A Federal Express executive was stranded on a desert island after a plane crash. To avoid the experience of being completely alone for years, he formed an imaginary relationship with a volley ball that he named "Wilson." The executive had regular conversations with "Wilson," and when the volley ball was accidently washed out to sea, the executive almost drowned trying to rescue his sole "friend."

There are reciprocal influences between human subjective experience/overt behavior and neural activity. All human subjective experience and overt behavior is produced by neural activity; on the other hand, brain functioning can be profoundly impacted by reactions to external events. This reciprocal influence has implications for mental health interventions. Through their influence on neurochemistry, psychotropic medications can directly impact delimited areas of cognitive/affective and behavioral functioning, but more comprehensive and complex changes in human behavior can be produced only by interpersonal encounters. Drugs can stabilize moods, but they cannot inspire selfless or creative actions; they can manage painful emotional states and control disruptive behavior, but they cannot produce creative and productive ways of avoiding or resolving those emotional states or of replacing disruptive with constructive behavior. The collaborative efforts associated with a psychotherapy relationship are likely to have more comprehensive, complex, and profound impacts on neural activity than any pharmacological intervention aimed at brain functioning.

This chapter will look more closely at the processes and procedures associated with discourse in BDP. Therapeutic "discourse" is composed of two overlapping phases: (1) inquiry and (2) dialogue. The two essential competencies associated with competent therapeutic discourse are construction of a personal narrative and deconstruction of a personal narrative.

Construction of a Personal Narrative

Once the initial case formulation has been used to identify a content focus for BDP, this content focus must be progressively elaborated into a detailed narrative that provides a context for the patient's difficulties that is meaningful to him or her. The construction of this narrative requires the therapist's interpersonal skills to establish and maintain an interpersonal environment that feels sufficiently safe and secure for the patient to openly share subjective experiences and the intimate details of past and current relationships. In concert with her interpersonal skills, the therapist must use skill at facilitating the patient's introspection through evocative questions and observations.

Deconstruction of a Personal Narrative

A point is reached in the construction of the patient's personal narrative when there are sufficient details to begin looking for intrapersonal and interpersonal processes that maintain the patient's dysfunctional modes of relating to himself and his environment. This aim is achieved with the aid of the therapist's skill at identifying in the patient's verbal reports maladaptive patterns of relating that run like red threads through the patient's history and current life. It also is achieved through the therapist's ability to self-monitor her interactions with the patient, in order to identify immediate manifestations of these maladaptive interpersonal patterns. Another skill used in the service of narrative deconstruction is the therapist's capacity to detect logical inconsistencies and contradictions in the patient's stories, and other disruptions in his syntax, which signal the presence of dysfunctional cognitive/affective and interpersonal processes. Motivating all of these therapist skills is her attitude of curiosity about what makes people tick.

INQUIRY

An "inquiry" involves seeking information by asking questions. It is a search for truth, information, or knowledge (Abate, 2002). As mentioned in chapter 1, psychotherapy begins with the therapist initiating an inquiry into the nature and origin of the patient's presenting complaints. A person seeks out a psychotherapist because he feels his unhappiness or dissatisfaction can no longer be tolerated and he has no hope of improving conditions by himself or with the help of family or friends. At the same time, the patient typically is uncertain about what therapy entails and may be apprehensive about what he may experience. Grappling with these concerns, the patient should meet a therapist whose attitude is consistently interested, respectful, nonjudgmental, noncritical (even when provoked), and genuinely committed to help. From the beginning of the relationship, the therapist's stance should be reasonable, mature, and trustworthy. She should project a professional but friendly attitude, appreciating the seriousness of the patient's concerns but, at the same time, not be averse to using humor at appropriate times to lighten the mood. Therapy is a serious business but does not have to be a grim business. Always, the therapist should seek to foster a symmetrical relationship between equals. The therapist has the knowledge and skills sought by the patient, but both are human beings, equally deserving of respect. The therapist has an objective, which is to understand the psychopathology behind the patient's presenting problems. But she should never neglect to acknowledge the patient's strengths. In all of these aspects, the therapist should be consistent, for the consistency of the therapist's stance, as it is communicated over a period of time, is in itself a powerful therapeutic factor.

The suffering person may overtly or covertly appeal to the therapist to prove his worth quickly by doing something to relieve the person's suffering or resolve his problems. Novice therapists typically are in a hurry to begin using the technical interventions they have learned. Cognitive scientists have observed, however, that experts in any complex performance domain (psychotherapy being one) spend a relatively great deal of time seeking to understand and analyze a problem situation before they plan what to do (Chi, 2006).[1] Also, the degree to which the therapist's presence and empathic listening constitute a powerful antidote to demoralization and a reassurance that this person can be of help is often underestimated.

After inviting the patient to talk about himself and what brought him to therapy, the therapist should be receptive and attuned to what the patient is communicating directly and indirectly, verbally and nonverbally. Every verbal communication has the potential for a tacit, nonverbal communication, which may reveal more about the content of the explicit words and which may also reveal how the patient is experiencing the patient-therapist relationship; that is, "disguised allusions" to the therapeutic relationship (Strupp & Binder, 1984; Watzlawick, Beavin, & Jackson, 1967). In the same vein, the therapist must remain sensitive to the fact that any of his interventions may carry a tacit interpersonal message conveying a conscious or unconscious view of the patient. First and foremost, he should minimize "mixed messages" that overtly convey a therapeutic message but, at the same time, may implicitly convey a hostile or blaming message (Henry, Schacht, & Strupp, 1986): "A little bit of bad process goes a long way" toward undermining a therapy (Hans H. Strupp, personal communication). Even with the best of intentions and the most skillful of interventions, the meaning to the patient of a therapist's words is not objectively given in the words themselves. The patient will interpret the content and intention through a filter of expectations based on selective past experiences that may be consistent with core interpersonal themes (Strupp & Binder, 1984; Wachtel, 1993).[2]

The therapist listens empathically: he immerses himself in the internal world of the patient, he feels himself into the subjective experiences of another person (Schafer, 2004). From this vantage point the therapist sees the world through the patient's eyes. The therapeutic inquiry begins with a cluster of problems or symptoms. These complaints are held together by some narrative theme yet to be identified. The therapist furthers the inquiry with empathically guided observations, comments and, above all, incisive questions (Binder, 2004). As Confucius said, "true virtue lies in the asking of questions" (E. A. Levenson, 1988, p. 549).

As the patient describes his current life and history, the therapist seeks to identify recurrent interpersonal patterns that reflect a unifying narrative theme, which can be elaborated into a maladaptive personal story line (i.e., a plot consisting of characters with motives, yearning, fears, plans, etc.). The story can be maladaptive for several reasons that are not mutually exclusive: (a) it is based on the internalization of childhood experiences that were misperceived or misunderstood at the time, because the situations were emotionally disturbing or the significant adults involved conveyed confusing or incoherent messages about relationships; (b) it is based on the internalization of childhood experiences that were psychologically traumatic; (c) whatever the origins of the story line, it has exerted a distorting influence on the individual's personality development and now impedes the individual's flexible adaptation to the circumstances of the moment. Whatever psychological potentials the individual possess, he is often constrained by a relatively limited repertoire of modes of relating that are rigidly enacted when activated by external or internal cues. The patient cannot see this story line because he is surrounded by circumstances and characters that, to some extent, are unwittingly recruited and directed by the patient to play specific parts in what appears to be a fateful drama. Strupp and Binder's (1984) "cyclical maladaptive pattern" and Wachtel's (2011) "cyclical psychodynamics" capture the ineluctably intertwined actions and reactions between a person and his interpersonal environment that perpetuate the dysfunctional and distressing story line. He cannot see it because it is all around him. This story line is maintained by unquestioned assumptions and beliefs. The basis of these beliefs and assumptions may be hard to examine because it is associated with painful emotions and distressing and unacceptable fantasies and wishes. To make matters worse, the patient unwittingly acts in ways that evoke reactions from other people that serve to confirm the most distressing of the patient's beliefs and assumptions.

If the therapist successfully conveys the interpersonal stance that has been described as well as demonstrates through his interventions that he is attentively and empathically listening, then the patient will begin to develop trust in his ability to help and a therapeutic alliance will begin forming. In the classic psychoanalytic therapies of the 20th century, a popular therapist stance was the detached observer who listened in the shadows to the patients' associations, searching for hidden clues like Sherlock Holmes dispassionately searching for clues at a crime scene. This stance required the careful selection of patients who were highly motivated for a therapy that required the patient to actively produce clinical material while passively accepting the ostensibly objective therapist's opinions about the meanings of the material. The psychodynamic therapist of today most likely views his role as that of a participant observer, who must balance attention to nurturing a therapeutic alliance, sensitivity to his reactions to and impact on the patient, and facilitation of progressively expanded understanding of dysfunctional modes of construing events and interacting with others.

Understanding and being understood are at the heart of therapy. Everything else evolves from them. The initial rapport established between patient and therapist is the result of the initiation of what the patient perceives as a potentially helpful intervention: "In large measure the inquiry is the intervention: the therapy is viewed as a process of inquiring more and more deeply into the individual's experience in order to further his self-understanding" (Wachtel, 2011, p. 144). Be careful not to jump to conclusions about understanding what the patient is saying. A mindset of "disciplined naivety" helps avoid misunderstandings. Interventions that are reflections of what the patient has just conveyed can be rapport building, unless the therapist has misunderstood the patient. In that case, reflections merely reflect misunderstanding.

The therapeutic inquiry begins with the therapist encouraging the patient to discuss the problems and distressing experiences that brought him to treatment. Regardless of the initial language the patient uses to describe his difficulties, the therapist tries to couch them in interpersonal terms or within an interpersonal context. Comparable to any social encounter in which two people become familiar with each other, the therapist questions the patient, who is encouraged to talk about himself. The therapist listens, becomes curious about certain details and spontaneously asks further questions, which generate further information from the patient. As the therapist listens to the patient talk about his life, the former searches for a theme in the welter of information coming at him. This theme captures in a word or two the kernel of a possible narrative to be constructed.[3] For the more experienced therapist, this searching appears to involve a tacit interpersonal pattern recognition process; something akin to searching for and discovering a familiar face in a crowd. Once a theme is identified, the purpose of the inquiry shifts to constructing a maladaptive personal story line based on the identified theme. A case formulation is an individualized superstructure built upon a conceptual foundation composed of theories of personality development and functioning and of developmental psychopathology. Accordingly, a competent dynamic/interpersonal therapist must have developed a concise, personal theory composed of an integration of object relations, attachment, and interpersonal theories (Binder, 2004).

The therapist begins to consciously search for a recurrent interpersonal pattern in the clinical material; he begins to "connect the dots." To be more specific, a novice therapist is more likely to engage in the analytic thinking process of constructing an interpersonal pattern a few dots at a time. The more experienced therapist is more likely to engage in analogic thinking, in which an interpersonal pattern is discovered more or less whole because it reminds the therapist of previous patterns he has seen— the dots are largely already connected. Constructing a salient, individualized story line based on an identified interpersonal pattern requires a competency in identifying narrative connections that may seem obscure or contradictory. It should be noted that conceiving of a patient's difficulties in terms of a personal story line "implicitly recognizes that it is always possible to develop and communicate meaning in more than one way" (Schafer, 2005b, p. 273). From any recurrent interpersonal pattern there are many potential stories that could be developed, and the therapist must ensure that the story he constructs is plausible, coherent, clear, comprehensive, and, above all, meaningfully explains for the patient the reasons for his suffering. Donald Spence (1982) observed that, "There seems no doubt but that a well-constructed story possesses a kind of narrative truth that is real and immediate and carries an important significance for the process of therapeutic change ..." (p. 21).

Case Example: Louise

For illustrative purposes, here is a relatively straightforward example of the rapid emergence of a theme, followed by the accompanying narrative. Louise was a 56-year-old woman who had been married to her second husband for 19 years. She had several grown children from both marriages. We will return to Louise in chapter 8 on "Monitoring and Evaluating Clinical Outcomes." The first interview began like this:

T: What was it that you felt you needed some help with?
Louise: Well actually I think I have several things, but one thing is the stage in my life. Of course I'm where I've never been before.
T: Mhm. It's true of everybody.
Louise: Yeah, my support system in the way of relatives (becomes tearful).... Up to this time I've had my mother, aunts, neighbors that

I've had some relationship with, some friends that I worked with, and all of a sudden my relatives are gone (her mother had died 6 years previously), my neighbors have moved away, my friends that I work with … one in particular, has taken other work (her youngest child has graduated from college) … and I really feel deserted. I do feel, given time, that I can handle, regroup so to speak. I can't replace these people, but perhaps by changing some things I can find some other satisfactions.

The theme of loss was immediately evident. The idiosyncratic implications for Louise of these losses began to emerge a few minutes later.

Louise: Well this is, you know, it may be a fact that I have depended on many people, I say I am a dependent person, I'll say that for one, if you're gonna say, of my problems, I'm dependent. And I've depended on a lot of different people: my mother, my aunt, my neighbor, my friend, and my husband. And I guess it's a little frightening for me now to feel that I depend upon him exclusively. And then if he is, should be out of the picture, then that leaves me alone, right? And that is scary. And it's not, I don't mean to minimize that, I guess is that I feel I need to protect him in a way, not be too dependent upon him, not put too heavy a load of my existence upon him … and in the past I've had other people that have kinda filled in the spaces for me.

T: You feel you don't want to depend on him too much, is that it?

Louise: That is right, yes.

T: What would that be like for you, to be too dependent on him? In what way would you be making too many demands on him?

Louise: Well, he, I would expect for him, and this is the person that I'm depending upon, this person is going to keep me furnished with conversations to begin with, but all sorts of things, entertainment for another thing, emotional support for another thing, bring their inside world to me too. His world …

Over the past few years, and especially the past 2 years, Louise had experienced recurrent losses of people important to her. She felt, in part, "deserted" by these people. Using her husband—the remaining important person who is physically close to her—as an example, Louise described how she took from the "inside world" of others in order to fill up her own inner world. She described a subjective experience of emotional depletion:

daily tasks are "'sapping" her, and she had a feeling of emptiness when she was alone, like there are "holes" in her life without people around with whom she had steady relationships. Louise was afraid that putting the entire burden on her husband of filling her emptiness might be too much for him, and left her too dependent on one person. Louise said that she lacked self-confidence, which was why she depended on other people so much. Gradually her resentment at those who had "deserted" her emerged: "It's like I need these people, and these people don't need anybody."

Louise: I'm talking about the people that I have ongoing relationships with, attempting to have satisfactory relationships with, it's like that they need people, surely … but maybe they don't need me. And that hurts. Because if I selected them for me to want to have a relationship, then I want it to be a reciprocal kind of thing … I don't really feel that I get rejected, so much as I'm just sort of passed over.

For Louise, the theme of loss was part of a story about her need for emotional sustenance from people upon whom she relied, and how they did not appear to realize how important their presence was for her, or they didn't care. She was acutely aware of feeling needy, empty, and afraid, but, strikingly, she had not been aware of her feelings about the losses that precipitated her concern over being too dependent.

T: And you're in a sense grieving these losses.
Louise: (Cries). I never thought about it just that way (continues to cry). I should grieve shouldn't I? Because I lost, I lost a lot. I have spoken of the fact that they're not longer around, I've been aware of it, I've missed them. But it's kinda like a head thing, you know. You can know things at different levels. I know they're gone. I know they're not here. I know I haven't replaced them. And maybe I've just kept peddling so hard, I haven't really stopped to realize that maybe I've been hurt about that.

DIALOGUE

In order for psychotherapy to be beneficial, it must progress from the inquiry phase to the dialogue phase. This transition occurs when the patient indicates that the prepotent theme that has been chosen as the focus of therapy has been elaborated into the beginnings of a maladaptive personal story line. This story line shows promise of meaningfully capturing a portion of the patient's life associated with his troubles. One definition of a "dialogue" is an interaction in which two people clarify understanding for one or both of them as a way of working toward the solution of a problem. A related definition refers to an open and frank discussion of ideas in the process of seeking mutual understanding. This discussion includes error-correcting feedback and the coconstruction of a shared understanding (e.g., personal story line) (Abate, 2002). These definitions of "dialogue" exquisitely capture the essence of the therapeutic interaction during the heart of therapy. Two people bound together by the aim of achieving shared therapeutic goals in a relationship of growing trust and mutual respect, and sometimes even fondness. This therapeutic alliance includes an agreement on the nature of the work that they will do together and their reciprocal responsibilities. But to reach this point and beyond, the therapist must track the development of the maladaptive personal story line within and across sessions.

Tracking the Therapeutic Focus

Tracking a focal story line across a therapy is a competency that is not discussed much in the psychotherapy literature (Binder, 2004). The mental processes involved in tracking are not often studied and are not well understood. Certainly, interpersonal pattern recognition is a skill that is an essential part of tracking a focal story line. The ability to follow a story line across a therapy is likely the same ability we use to follow the plot of a novel, or movie, or a television show across episodes. Tracking begins with a mind-set: the maladaptive personal story line embodies an organizing theme in the patient's personality that is timeless. Consequently, regardless of the time interval between sessions, whether a day or a month, whatever the patient says or does at the beginning of a session is a seamless continuation of the story line where it left off at the end of the last session.

In a dynamically oriented therapy, the standard method of beginning a session is to invite the patient to talk about anything that comes to mind, based on the principle of "psychic determinism"; that is, the unconscious mind is organized such that a prepotent theme will inevitably be expressed in one way or another. Accordingly, it is assumed that if the patient begins spontaneously, indications of the maladaptive personal story line will inevitably emerge. The therapist, however, must be flexible about this strategy. Especially when meeting weekly or less often, the patient may ask the therapist what they had been talking about in the previous session. Often it moves things along for the therapist to answer this question with a brief summary of where they had left off in their exploration of the story line. At other times, the therapist will spontaneously provide this reminder, because he thinks it is likely to efficiently refocus on the most important issues.

Once the discussion begins, the therapist may not be able to find evidence of the focal theme and may begin to feel lost. There can be several reasons for this to occur:

1. Content indicating the presence of the maladaptive personal story line is present but the therapist has missed it. That familiar face is in the crowd, but the therapist has not noticed it. If the therapist feels lost, his first act is to concentrate more and look harder for evidence of the focal theme in the patient's communications.

2. The focal theme is not identifiable in the patient's verbal communications, because it is being expressed paralinguistically through a transference/countertransference enactment. In this case, evidence for the content focus is in front of the therapist's nose; that is, the evidence is all around him, he is living it with the patient. In this case, the most relevant therapist skill is "reflection-in-action"—the ability to stand back and see the interaction pattern that is being enacted, freeze the action, and "metacommunicate" with the patient about what is transpiring (Safran & Muran, 2000; Schön, 1983). In other words, the therapist as a participant-observer temporarily stops participating and focuses on observing.

3. The therapist cannot find evidence of the focal theme because the patient unconsciously is defensively avoiding any topic relevant to the therapeutic focus. In this case, when the therapist sees no other alternative, he points out that they have moved away from what has been their primary topic of examination.

4. The therapist feels lost because the patient's communications reveal no coherent story line. Often this situation is associated with the patient going into excessive detail, and the therapist cannot construct a clear picture from all the verbiage. In this situation, the therapist should consider the possibility that the patient is so anxious that his

cognitive processes have been disrupted and he is suffering from a subtle thought disorder. It may require psychotropic medication to improve the clarity of the patient's thought processes to the point where a productive therapeutic dialogue can ensue.

5. The maladaptive personal story line that is being pursued turns out not to be the one to which the patient most strongly resonates. In this case, the therapist must reinitiate an inquiry to identify a more resonant story line.

Constructing the Primary Maladaptive Personal Story Line

The therapeutic content focus or core issue agreed upon by therapist and patient during the course of the inquiry phase is in the form of a rough sketch of the primary maladaptive personal story line. During the dialogue phase of therapy this story line is progressively elaborated. Together therapist and patient examine the latter's current and past experiences, particularly "relationship episodes"—reported interactions that may have meanings and emotional loadings relevant to the central focus (Book, 1998; Luborsky & Crits-Christoph, 1997). The therapist uses his interpersonal pattern recognition skills to selectively attend to or ignore discrete episodes in the process of tracking a recurrent pattern. The aim is to construct from the initial rough sketch of a maladaptive personal story line parallel mental pictures in the minds of therapist and patient which are vivid and precisely detailed. These mental pictures reveal the theme (i.e., the underlying meanings in the story) and the plot (i.e., the unfolding actions and motivations of the characters) that have been unwittingly authored by the patient and contributed to by others who have been unknowingly recruited into various roles. The maladaptive personal story line is embodied in the patient's dysfunctional mental working models of interpersonal relationships and corresponding characteristic maladaptive patterns of interpersonal relating (Binder, 2004).

A therapeutic dialogue is furthered by stimulating the patient to reflect on his experiences and his reactions to them. The therapist facilitates this self-examination in a number of ways, the primary methods being (a) incisive questions and (b) empathic reflections, clarifications, and elaborations. Depending on the context and the way it is worded, an incisive question can serve clarifying, confrontative, and interpretive functions. The patient may not have a ready answer to a question, but questions, at least, can stimulate thinking about aspects of his life that heretofore he has taken as givens.[4] Questions that have a clarifying function are exemplified by the therapist's interventions at T4, T10, and T11 in the segment from the middle of Sarah's therapy, presented at the end of the chapter. Questions that have a confrontative function are exemplified by interventions at T20, T23, and T36.

Empathic communications articulate the patient's immediate experience, as well as how this "story arc" fits into the crystallizing primary maladaptive personal story line. These communications facilitate self-reflection, which enables the patient to get in touch with experiences just outside of awareness. Self-reflection makes it possible for the patient to gain perspective on the story in which he has been absorbed without realizing it and has been living without being aware of alternative possibilities. The therapist's empathic communications draw from her capacity for empathy, as well as from memories of similar experiences shared by other patients and memories of her own personal experiences. Perhaps above all the therapist draws from the common sense acquired from a life lived. She knows that she is on the right track when she and her patient feel like they are on the same "wavelength."

Empathic communications are most effective when conveyed as though they were the patient's own experiences viewed through his eyes and reported in his own words. The therapist describes the subjective experiences of which the patient is aware, as well as feelings, beliefs, expectations, attitudes, and fears of which he is unaware. There are some beautiful examples of this type of empathic intervention in a six-session brief therapy conducted by Hannah Levenson and produced for the latest American Psychological Association series of video recordings of master therapists (H. Levenson, 2010).[5] The patient, Laura, was a single woman in her 20s, who was in a master's program in business administration. Laura reported that there were two issues causing her increasing stress: (a) the time involved in pursuing the graduate degree and (b) maintaining a romantic relationship with a man who lived a long distance from her home. In the first interview, it became clear that Laura's romantic relationship was the chief source of distress; she felt that while she devoted herself to pleasing her boyfriend without complaint, he was unappreciative and did not reciprocate.

In the first session, Laura expressed frustration with her boyfriend never offering to come to her home, while she drove an hour in order to visit him weekly.

Laura: ... I will go every time to his house. We have more things to do at his house, but I wish that he once in a while would come and see me when it is not convenient (her voice starts to tremble). He will see me on the days he goes to visit his sister who lives near my apartment.

Levenson: So, Laura, what is going on inside with you right now. I see something is going on.

Laura: (Tearing) It is upsetting.

Levenson: I can see that on your face.

Laura: I'm just frustrated (crying). Sorry.

Levenson: No, this hurts I can see that. It's like "why isn't he going out of his way for me? I go out of my way for him. Why isn't he giving when it is not convenient?" It is of concern to you.

A short time later Laura related an especially hurtful incident with her boyfriend, Brian. They were at the house of a friend of Brian's, who she did not particularly like. He left her there to go to a bar with his friend. He returned very inebriated, and Laura cried all night.

Laura: He has blatantly said to me, "I don't need a clingy girlfriend" ... the way he said it hurt so bad (voice trembling). "Why am I here if you don't want me here" (crying). I want to be here, but if you don't want me to be here, I won't be here."

Levenson: "... so here I have allowed myself to really get close, I have allowed myself to become attached to you, to give to you, and now this is particularly frightening, because now that I am out on a limb, what will happen if you cut that limb down?

In the second interview, Laura reveals that when she was a child, her father had a severe drinking problem. When Laura was a little girl, there were times when father had passed out after a bout of heavy drinking. Levenson captured the inchoate fear of that little girl. As is typical in families where a member has a substance abuse problem, in Laura's family distressing issues and events were not discussed.

Levenson: So I can see a lot got pushed down in your family ... so don't say to your father, "This really hurts me when you are drinking (Laura nods). This is not good for me. I am a child in this family. I don't feel safe."

Development of skill in the use of empathic communications is crucial to maintaining a positive therapeutic alliance and furthering therapeutic dialogue. Therefore, another concrete example will be presented. In chapter 4, we encountered Nancy, a middle-aged, divorced woman suffering from anxiety and panic attacks. She was stuck in a chronic scenario with her mother, who was bipolar and in an unhappy marriage. This scenario involved mother repeatedly conveying to Nancy that she wanted to be rescued from her unhappy state but dismissing Nancy's advice, including the advice that she leave Nancy's father, who was gone most of the time and unfaithful. Nancy, however, persisted in responding each time mother made her implicit pleas for help. More generally, in Nancy's family she had the role of caretaker. An impending event that increased Nancy's stress was her daughter leaving for college, which would leave Nancy living alone. In chapter 4, we saw how from the beginning of therapy, Nancy showered her male therapist with compliments, which left the therapist feeling "paralyzed." Toward the middle of the 25 session therapy, the topic was Nancy's role as a caretaker for people important to her. Early in the session it had been established that it was much easier for her to give emotional nurturance than to receive it (the transference dimension of Nancy taking care of the therapist by continuously complimenting his skills was not addressed after the first few sessions). The context of the therapy segment to be presented was a discussion of the possibility of Nancy taking a vacation as one way of nurturing herself. But she would have to go by herself and was nervous about facing social situations alone:

T:	… It's not as if you get nothing. Because I think you're a giving person and giving feels good.
Nancy:	Yeah.
T:	There's a certain amount of return …
Nancy:	Yeah.
T:	… for that.
Nancy:	Sure.
T:	Uhm, and probably much of the time that's enough to get by on.
Nancy:	Yeah.
T:	Some of the time it's not.
Nancy:	What I'm finding is the beginning part is enough to get by on, but it's a vicious cycle, and the giving part is wearing me out. Because I don't take any time for me.
T:	I think you take care of a lot of people. Who takes care of you?

Nancy: I don't know. I don't know. The good Lord, I guess (tearful). I don't know (long pause). Who takes care of me? It makes me mad (pause while softly crying). It makes me mad that I have to take care of myself, and I'm taking care of everybody else. And who takes care of me? When I talk to my parents, for example, not that they should, I'm not angry with them for this, but I'm angry with myself. I guess when I talk to my parents, I'm taking care of them. They don't hear my needs. They don't, I'm sure they care, but they don't really hear them.

T: You don't feel taken care of by them.

Nancy: No.

In this example, the therapist asks a simply worded but deeply empathic question at just the right moment. Nancy is emotionally touched perhaps for the first time in the therapy. Tears and strong feelings are evoked. In a one year posttreatment follow up interview, there was evidence that she had been able to noticeably reduce her role as caretaker for her family.

The patient's awareness is further expanded by highlighting assumptions, expectations, and construals of situations that have been unquestioned, perhaps for a very long time. All of these mental contents are incorporated into the maladaptive personal story line. The therapist uses her imagination to enrich the "textural quality" of the patient's personal narrative by articulating implications and consequences inferred in the threads of the story (E. A. Levenson, 1988). To be more specific, a prototypic interchange reflective of the dialogue phase of a therapeutic discourse would go like this: The patient reports a recollection of an interpersonal episode that occurs to him. With the patient's help, the therapist explores the memory of this episode until he is able to construct a richly detailed mental picture of it. Then, again with the patient's help, the therapist explores the possible implications and consequences of the pictured episode. In Sarah's therapy session starting on page 126, therapist intervention T19 (p. 130) is an example of spelling out the implications of her view of others: "Oh, so as long as you're paying me, I'll be willing to understand and listen?" (T24 and T26 are other examples, see p. 131). In therapist intervention T28 (p. 132), the hypothetical origin of a *maladaptive personal story line* begins to be created: "She died at a time, a very difficult time for mothers and daughters. I mean you're beginning, you're an adolescent and you're beginning to go out and start carving a life away from the family. And yet at the same time very much needing the family to be there for you as a place of security, safety. And then all of a sudden it's taken away from you [Yeah, yeah]. It's almost like you resolved never, you're never gonna put yourself in that position again where you need anybody to take care of you, to lean on. You're going to make everybody dependent on you" (T31 offers further elaboration). T28 and T34 also spell out the consequences of Sarah's maladaptive ways of construing events as well as her expectations about future events.

The therapist should always look for an opportunity to use emotionally evocative language. Such language stirs the patient to resonate with the intervention. In searching for where to pick up the immediate thread of the patient's story, the therapist should look first at patient communications that are emotionally loaded. Active emotions are usually associated with immediately relevant issues. Emotions convey important information but, in addition, have physiological and subjective elements not found in cognitions. Emotions convey important information about how a person is construing situations and events and about how he is viewing himself and others. They are particularly reactive to signs that invite the individual to participate in a pleasurable experience or that warn the individual to flee a potentially hurtful or dangerous situation. They always are part of an interpersonal context and are embedded within a personal narrative. In other words, from a dynamic/interpersonal perspective unraveling the interpersonal implications of an emotional reaction is an important part of constructing a primary maladaptive personal story line. A daunting challenge is to distinguish between an emotional reaction that signals the most plausible interpretation of a situation and one that reflects a faulty interpretation which has been overly influenced by prepotent assumptions and expectations associated with the patient's story line.

The therapist should always attend to "feelings in the moment," a situation that occurs when the patient's narrative is accompanied or interrupted by the emergence of noticeable affect. However, people vary considerably in their capacity to experience and express emotions, in terms of the variety and intensity of feelings. This can be largely a matter of temperament, which is unchangeable (McWilliams, 1999). People also vary considerably in their capacity to describe emotions, in terms of clarity, detail, and depth. The opportunity to explore an immediate emotional state can enhance the clarity and depth of meanings of elements in a personal narrative. Emotions can "shine a light" on important story elements. But the therapeutic contribution of emotions is only as great as the patient's capacity to experience, convey, and explore them. Some people need to ventilate their feelings, others need to learn to label and describe them, others need to explore what meanings they convey for their personal narratives, while still others may not be able to comprehend their feelings sufficiently to use them productively in therapeutic work. Emotions are one of several channels for conveying personal meanings, and when this channel is unavailable for use in the work of therapy, it still is possible to effectively use others channels to convey and explore personal meanings (e.g., cognitive productions such as fantasies, dreams, memories, expectations, attitudes, reports of interactions).[6]

A patient construes the world and interacts with it in ways that produce distress and dysfunction. The ways in which the patient's characteristic transactional patterns unwittingly recruit others into behavior that is consistent with the guiding maladaptive personal story line and, thus, reinforce the patient's worldview are most effectively revealed through a detailed collaborative investigation. Immersed in a repetitively maladaptive story line—an interpersonal rut—the patient cannot figure out why his problematic life offers so few choices. A psychodynamic therapist's question usually is "What does it all mean?" But before personal meanings and their impact can be thoroughly understood, we have to encourage the patient to ask: "What is going on around here?" (E. A. Levenson, 1988). That is to say, we have to flesh out the story line.

An attentive therapist will usually identify elements of a maladaptive personal story line, and, in collaboration with his patient, he usually will be able to construct a partial story. It is our experience, however, that therapists often fall short of constructing as complete, comprehensive, and detailed a story as is possible. The therapist may not use all the pieces of the puzzle that were revealed through the inquiry and dialogue. He may not sufficiently imagine the implications and consequences of various story threads, and he may not pursue his therapeutic investigation with sufficient thoroughness. We believe that with regard to therapist competence one of the major challenges facing the teachers of psychotherapy, as well as clinicians pursuing their own professional development, is the progressive enhancement of the skills involved with constructing a complete maladaptive personal story line.

Among the purposes of therapist interventions are: (a) to generate, clarify, and elaborate interpersonally relevant information; (b) to identify problematic thinking, affect management, and interpersonal patterns; and (c) to promote the practice of self-reflection and interpersonal pattern recognition. Above all, however, the purpose of a therapist intervention is to promote further dialogue that seeks the coconstruction of a complete maladaptive personal story line. In this effort, the therapist should always strive to find a productive balance between intervening and listening. He should do nothing to impede the patient's contributions to story construction. He should not be a "ghost writer" of the patient's personal story. The therapist should not assume anything about elements of the patient's story that are unclear. When there is narrative ambiguity, the curious therapist probes for precise details. He tries to maintain a mind-set of "disciplined naivety" (Binder, 2004).

Deconstructing the Primary Maladaptive Personal Story Line

The therapeutic discourse begins with the inquiry phase, which leads to the identification of evidence for what appears to be a story line that is emotionally evocative for the patient. This evidence most often is in the form of a recurrent pattern of maladaptive interpersonal relating. In the therapeutic dialogue that follows, therapist and patient systematically coconstruct a personal story line that gives context and meaning to the maladaptive interpersonal pattern and, ultimately, to the patient's troubles. To the extent that they have constructed a story that is true to the patient's subjective picture of his life, it feels like the only story he could have lived. As they look closely at the story they are constructing, however, it becomes evident that the story does not hold together.

A meticulous examination of a patient's stories about his life and subjective experiences ideally should result in a clear, coherent, and richly detailed picture. Psychological distress and interpersonal difficulties, however, are associated with a breakdown in the narrative coherence of a person's self-described story lines (Angus & Greenberg, 2011; Binder, 2004; Goncalves & Stiles, 2011). Therefore, during the process of coconstructing a primary maladaptive personal story line, the therapist should take care not to interfere with the patient's idiosyncratic narratives. These narratives will be characterized by restricted themes, inconsistencies, and contradictions in plot lines, ambiguities and gaps in recollections, superficial descriptions of intentions and motives, and evidence of conflict. This narrative incoherence provides an opportunity to challenge and disrupt even chronic patterns of dysfunctional thinking and corresponding maladaptive modes or relating. The patient's assumptions, expectations, and interpretations about details, situations, and events associated with his maladaptive personal story line can be called into question. "Deconstruction of a prepotent maladaptive interpersonal theme interrupts the spontaneous, automatic operation of the underlying dysfunctional internal working model and creates the possibility of perceived new meanings and implications for previously unquestioned [ways of construing the world and interacting with it]" (Binder, 2004, p. 149). Heretofore unquestioned features of the story can now be questioned. Sometimes therapist and patient simultaneously have the same realization about some aspect of the story. As mentioned before, they are on the same wavelength, and this can be exhilarating (even patients who are characteristically detached from their emotions can experience this). Humanistic clinicians call this sharing of an experience "meeting" the other person (Bohart, O'Hara, & Leitner, 1988). The beginning of the deconstruction of Sarah's maladaptive personal story line begins at T32 (p. 133): "As we talk about this it seems to me that you really are stuck in a horrible dilemma, because in order to, from the perspective that we're talking about, in order to protect yourself from what you feel would be just a horrible hurt, and to put yourself in a position where you rely on somebody emotionally and then expect to be abandoned, just fall and be hurt. That in order to avoid that at any cost, you maintain this extreme self-sufficient position in relation to important people in your life where you do things for them, you take care of them, and then they expect you to. So you don't have to rely on anybody. Everybody relies on you. [Yeah.] But, on the other hand, you're left feeling lonely, underappreciated, and overwhelmed." [Yeah.]

If upon scrutiny the personal story line that therapist and patient have authored does not hold its narrative coherence, then other more fulfilling story lines become possible. As William James (1881) phrased it: reality is a "theater of simultaneous possibilities" (p. 288). The prepotent maladaptive personal story line can be modified or replaced by one that is not as associated with negative emotions like loneliness, fear, guilt, shame, and anxiety (Wachtel, 2010). The specific direction taken by the patient–therapist dialogue is determined by the meanings given to the story elements and the unique way those elements are organized. The direction of the story also is determined by the idiosyncratic contribution of the therapist to the unfolding story line. The individualized version of the character played by the therapist in the patient's maladaptive story line will significantly influence this story line, like an actor renders his version of an iconic character in one of Shakespeare's plays. Relationships associated with a new, healthier story line can be more satisfying and fulfilling. The patient is less prone to being stuck in unhappy scenarios that get rigidly enacted with monotonous repetition. He can achieve the flexibility and creativity to write hitherto unimagined stories. The therapist's interventions with Sarah at T47 and T49 illustrate the beginning of a potentially new and healthier story line for her: "What do you imagine if you try to sit down with your sister and talk more openly than you have up to this point about your relationship with your mother, about the arrangement that you two have had for years? ... if she saw you, your worst fear realized, you're sitting there and ... all of a sudden it dawns on her, she has this realization that you're not as strong as, you can't do everything and be everything for her. And you don't want to. What would happen?"

The dynamic/interpersonal therapist uses any type of intervention that serves to expand the patient's awareness of how he perceives himself and his world. In other words, any intervention can be used if it serves a clarifying, confrontative, or interpretive function. As mentioned previously, incisive questions often are the most therapeutically evocative interventions. Curiosity and common sense are the most effective mindsets for producing incisive questions. "Common sense" in this context refers to the therapist's ability to access from memory stereotypes of culturally defined healthy and reasonable scenarios for innumerable situations which can be compared with the patient's report of the way he construed and acted in a similar situation. When the patient's report deviates from the therapist's stereotype, this deviation alerts the therapist to the possible presence of the patient's maladaptive personal story line (Binder, 2004). Finally, the therapist should not ask questions that encourage the patient to provide closed-ended or dead-ended answers, or a choice from a limited set of alternatives.

In Sarah's therapy session, once the deconstruction of her maladaptive personal story line had begun, the therapist looked for opportunities to show Sarah how it negatively influenced her construal of, and reactions to, current situations. His interventions at T39 and T41 (p. 135) illustrate questions that have an interpretive function. In these cases, the therapist wondered about the possible unnoticed impacts on their relationship of Sarah's maladaptive personal story line.

An interpretation of any type should not be a pronouncement. It should always be given in the spirit of collaboration, as a suggestion, observation, hypothesis, inference, or speculation to consider. A "good" interpretation fits into the primary story line; it "resonates with the patient's experience and evokes and amplifies that experience" (Wachtel, 1993, p. 4). It should be articulated as succinctly as possible and, as much as is comfortable for the therapist, using the patient's language. Above all, it should never connote blame or fault. The therapist's interpretation at T52 links a current conflictual relationship with Sarah's conceivable subjective experience of a traumatic childhood event: "It sounds like, without even necessarily articulating it explicitly, your fear was that if you were more honest with your sister, that it would either drive her away or kill her [Yeah]. Sort of like you felt, you described as a 13-year-old when your mother died." The insight this intervention produces can facilitate the creation by Sarah of a new, healthier narrative for herself.

THE ROLE OF TRANSFERENCE AND COUNTERTRANSFERENCE

The first generation of psychoanalytic clinicians who developed formal short-term therapy models adapted without much modification psychoanalytic treatment concepts to a brief format (Davanloo, 1978; Malan, 1976; Mann, 1973; Sifneos, 1972). Accordingly, they used the traditional conception of "transference," as the displacement of feelings and attitudes originally about childhood figures now projected onto the person of the therapist (Weiner & Bornstein, 2009). Whereas the classic view of transference was that it developed over weeks or months, these first generation brief dynamic therapists assumed that it was present from the first encounter. Furthermore, they assumed that the transference reflected a circumscribed conflict originating in childhood and now continuing to cause problems for the patient in the form of symptoms or interpersonal dysfunction. This circumscribed conflict was termed the *core conflict*, or *nuclear conflict*, or *chronically endured pain* and usually was the content focus for the treatment (e.g., Malan, 1976a; Mann, 1973).

The early brief dynamic therapy models were based on a set of assumptions about the technical strategies that facilitate therapeutic change:

1. The influence of transference is always present in the patient–therapist relationship, even in the face of increased activity characteristic of the brief therapist.
2. Explicit transference manifestations as well as allusions to the transference in the patient's communications and behavior should be interpreted as soon as they appear.

3. Interpretations typically were in the form of pointing out parallels between current transference manifestations and memories of dysfunctional childhood relationships, usually with parent figures.
4. These "genetic transference interpretations" or "transference/parent links" were assumed to be the most robust facilitators of symptom resolution and characterological changes, because they gave the patient "immediate affective resonance" with and insight into his salient problems.
5. Suitable patients were those whose "quality of object relations" were sufficiently mature (i.e., at most, mild personality disorders) to sustain a strong therapeutic alliance—they were self-reflective and could tolerate anxiety-producing observations and realizations, like a genetic transference interpretation.
6. Persons who had relatively immature "quality of object relations" (i.e., moderate to severe personality disorders) required more "supportive" therapy in which transference interpretations were not used.

The second generation of brief dynamic therapists introduced new treatment models beginning in the late 1970s and early 1980s. These treatments were characterized by new developments in psychoanalytic theory—particularly the increasing influence of object relations, attachment, and interpersonal theories—as well as a new trend toward theoretical integration and technical eclecticism (Horowitz, 1986; Luborsky, 1984; Strupp & Binder, 1984; Weiss, Sampson, & the Mount Zion Psychotherapy Research Group, 1986). They also had different conceptions of transference. Time-limited dynamic psychotherapy (Strupp & Binder, 1984) viewed the therapeutic relationship as a dyadic process and the therapist as a participant-observer. Accordingly, transference was conceived of as the product of the patient's preconceived expectations about how relationships will unfold and how he will be treated. Based on these preconceived expectations, the patient selectively attends to behavior of the therapist that could plausibly be interpreted as confirming these expectations; he also selectively construes the attitudes, sentiments, and intentions of the therapist to confirm the former's preconceived expectations. Another essential component of this conception of transference are behaviors of the patient that unwittingly elicit overt and covert responses from the therapist that are consistent with the patient's expectations.

Corresponding to this new conception of transference was a modern conception of "countertransference" also based on object relations and interpersonal theories. The first generation of brief dynamic therapists maintained the traditional conception of countertransference as manifestations of psychological vulnerabilities of the therapist evoked by the patient's transferential feelings and behaviors and which interfered with the therapist's objectivity and empathy (Gelso & Hayes, 2007). They appeared to believe that in brief therapy countertransference occurred intermittently and that competent therapists should be largely immune to it. The second generation of brief dynamic therapists tended to give a larger role to countertransference, along with their more modern conception. For example, time-limited dynamic psychotherapy (Strupp & Binder, 1984) viewed countertransference as a form of "interpersonal empathy" in which the therapist for a time and to a degree inevitably is drawn by the patient's transferential behavior into enacting a role that represents a character in the latter's salient maladaptive interpersonal pattern. Whereas the traditional conception of countertransference limited it to internal reactions of the therapist, Strupp and Binder broaden the concept to include overt reactions. They viewed transference and countertransference as the unwitting enactment of the patient's salient maladaptive interpersonal pattern and, therefore, ineluctably intertwined. The therapist's aim was not to avoid transference/countertransference reactions but to minimize the time and extent to which he or she participated in them.

With these newer conceptions of transference and countertransference came alterations in techniques for their therapeutic use. The default interpretive technique shifted from the transference/parent link to here-and-now interpretations: an exploration of how the patient's salient maladaptive interpersonal pattern was shaping the patient–therapist interaction. Strupp and Binder (1984) explicitly recommended that the therapist should look for every opportunity to identify and interpret explicit references to the therapy or therapist as well as disguised allusions to them. Transference/parent link interpretations should be used sparingly and only after, in the therapist's judgment, the patient has accepted the influence of patterns in his interpersonal behavior of which he heretofore was unaware.[7] With the exception of these important changes in the conceptions of the ingredients of therapeutic process and in technical strategies, the second generation of brief dynamic therapy models was based on the same set of assumptions as the first generation models.

Malan (1976b) published the first set of findings that purported to establish empirical support for key assumptions about the role of transference interpretations in brief dynamic therapy. He produced a significant positive correlation between frequency of transference/parent (T/P) linking interpretations and treatment outcome. Almost a decade after his study was published, Marziali (1984) published her attempt to replicate Malan's findings with more rigorous research methods (e.g., identifying instances of T/P linking interpretations using transcripts rather than therapist process notes, and different raters for identifying T/P linking interpretations and for judged outcomes). She was not able to demonstrate as strong an association as had Malan. Beginning in the 1990s, independent research teams interested in the role of transference interpretations in brief dynamic therapy mounted larger studies with more sophisticated research designs (e.g., Connolly et al., 1999; Ogrodniczuk, Piper, Joyce, & McCallum, 1999). Their findings did not support the traditional assumptions regarding the positive and essential role of transference-focused work in brief dynamic therapy. These researchers came to a conclusion voiced by Per Høglend (1996), a leading researcher on the role of transference interpretations in brief dynamic therapy:

> Interpretations of the here-and-now transference manifestations are potentially potent and accurate. But the relationship with the therapist may seem unimportant to the patient compared to the interpersonal difficulties outside of therapy. (Høglend, 1996, p. 129)

> A moderate use of transference interpretation may be more productive with subgroups of patients.... However, it may be sufficient *or even more important* to focus on interpersonal relationships outside therapy. (Høglend, 2003, p. 286, emphasis added)

A related set of findings concerns the nature of therapeutic alliance "ruptures," their role in therapy process/outcome, and methods for dealing with them. These findings have been produced by a research team led by Jeremy D. Safran and J. Chris Muran at Beth Israel Hospital in New York City (Safran & Muran, 2000). Safran and Muran have demonstrated that alliance ruptures occur in many if not most brief therapies and if not identified and resolved, can contribute to poor treatment outcome. Their empirically tested method for resolving alliance ruptures is constructed around what they term *metacommunication*: the therapist engages the patient in a discussion about what is transpiring in their relationship, to which they are both contributing, that is interfering with their working collaboratively.[8] Metacommunication is an extreme form of here-and-now transference analysis; metacommunication as a technical strategy is associated with the assumption that the problem between patient and therapist does not necessarily reflect the problem that bothers the patient outside of therapy, while here-and-now transference analysis assumes that the problem between patient and therapist is a reenactment of the problem brought into therapy by the patient.

Binder's (2004) manual for brief dynamic/interpersonal therapy was heavily influenced by published findings about the relationship between transference interpretations and treatment outcome. He also recognized the congruence of Safran and Muran's findings on alliance ruptures with the accumulating findings concerning the role of transference analysis. To quote Binder (2004):

> In sum, there is converging clinical and empirical evidence suggesting that a transference-focused technical strategy is no longer warranted in time-limited dynamic therapies. Instead, the most frequent area examined in detecting the influence of dysfunctional internal models of interpersonal relationships and corresponding maladaptive interpersonal patterns is that of relationships currently significant to the patient. Furthermore, the most frequent type of linking interpretation is one that draws parallels between maladaptive interpersonal patterns in the patient's current relationships and reconstructions of problematic childhood relationships with significant parental figures. (p. 173)

As a general rule, we would recommend that transference interventions be used when either of two conditions exist:

1. The therapist identifies evidence of transference-countertransference patterns reflecting the maladaptive interpersonal theme that is the focus of treatment, and the patient evidences receptivity to examining these patterns.
2. The therapeutic alliance is significantly strained, indicating that transference-countertransference enactments have reached a critical threshold of influence (2004, p. 174).

In place of a general transference-focused strategy for brief dynamic therapy, Binder (2004) recommended an emphasis on establishing and maintaining a therapeutic discourse that fostered what he considered to be the primary change processes in this form of therapy:

1. Cognitive insight
2. Practice in detecting maladaptive mental and interpersonal patterns if they occur in the patient–therapist relationship and in outside relationships.
3. Creating new and more satisfying interpersonal experiences in the patient–therapist relationship and in outside relationships.
4. Internalization of new and more satisfying interpersonal experiences and the consequent modification of interpersonal schemas and corresponding internal working models of interpersonal relations.

Competence in furthering a productive therapeutic discourse has a foundation of several generic interpersonal skills: (1) interpersonal pattern recognition; (2) self-monitoring and self-regulating; and (3) improvising to adapt to the immediate contextual demands of the interpersonal situation. (Binder, 2004)

Since the publication of Binder's 2004 brief dynamic treatment manual, a major study of the relationship between transference interpretations and outcome in this form of therapy has been published (Høglend et al., 2006). This was the first study of the long-term effects of transference interpretations that used a randomized experimental design. More specifically, the research design was a dismantling, randomized, clinical trial in which a transference-focused treatment of up to 40 sessions was compared to a nontransference treatment of the same length. The same therapists, all highly experienced, conducted both types of treatment, after up to 4 years of training in each type. The main effect of the treatment comparison appeared in the first publication of study findings: there was no difference in long-term (up to several years posttreatment) outcome between the two treatment conditions. In addition, a significant mediator variable was identified: "quality of object relations" (QOR)—reflective of the person's level of maturity of interpersonal functioning. In the most recent data analysis, the findings were contrary to key assumptions that historically have guided the conduct of transference-focused brief dynamic therapies. These findings were: (a) transference work had the strongest positive effect with patients with relatively low QOR within the context of a relatively weak therapeutic alliance; (b) for patients with a relatively high QOR and a relatively strong therapeutic alliance, use of transference interpretations was associated with a relatively poor outcome; and (c) patients with a relatively high QOR and a relatively strong therapeutic alliance had a better outcome in the nontransference treatment than the transference-focused treatment (Høglend et al., 2011). The research findings on the relationship between transference interpretations and treatment outcome that have been published in the last few years, as well as the continuing research on therapeutic alliance ruptures and resolution (Muran & Barber, 2010), support the technical recommendations made in Binder (2004): in brief dynamic therapies, a transference-focused technical strategy is warranted when difficulties arise in the patient–therapist relationship with patients evidencing significant personality disturbance. When working with a patient who functions at a relatively mature level of interpersonal relating and in circumstances in which the therapeutic alliance is strong, making transference interpretations may seem out of place to the patient and create strain in the therapeutic relationship (for a case illustration, see Kasper, Hill, & Kivlighan, 2008). In these circumstances a transference-focused strategy could prove useful but is more likely to be ineffective or actually contribute to poor treatment outcome. This recommendation is contrary to traditional clinical wisdom regarding psychodynamic therapies (Høglend et al., 2011) as well as to technical recommendations associated with most of the major contemporary models of brief dynamic therapy.

The technical recommendations proposed here have another surprising implication concerning how psychodynamic therapies are characterized. Traditionally, transference-focused therapies have been seen as "expressive"; that is, a probing, explorative approach in which the patient has sufficient psychological resilience and self-reflective capacities to face uncomfortable emotions and truths, particularly as they are manifested in the immediacy of the therapeutic relationship. While potentially anxiety-producing, this approach has been considered necessary for producing significant psychological change. As Freud (1958/1912) said: "For when all is said and done, it is impossible to destroy anyone in absentia or in effigy" (p. 108). Conversely, dynamic therapies in which the area of work is outside the therapeutic relationship have been seen as "supportive"; that is, an approach necessary with patients who are relatively fragile psychologically and who require cautious handling that does not challenge personality defenses. The goal is to restore or maintain the patient's precarious psychological balance rather than aim for significant psychological change.

What the research findings have indicated, however, is that in brief dynamic therapies a transference-focused approach is actually supportive, since it is most effective in dealing with therapeutic alliance ruptures when working with patients who have significant psychological vulnerabilities. The aim of the transference-focused strategy is to shore up a precarious working relationship by examining what is currently transpiring between patient and therapist. Conversely, a nontransference-focused approach is actually expressive, since it results in significant psychological change (as indicated by a variety of measures of symptoms, functioning and perceived quality of life) by an approach that closely examines the patient's reported experiences outside of therapy and in the past, in order to bring into focus troublesome issues, no matter how anxiety-producing this exploration becomes. It appears that Freud was wrong: you can at least mitigate "in absentia" the chronic impact of old psychologically damaging relationships.

Case Example: Sarah[9]

Sarah was introduced in chapter 6. She had been depressed about her work in graduate school and about the problems in her relationship with her boyfriend. The initial story line to which Sarah had resonated was feeling unappreciated no matter how hard she worked to please people who were in various contexts important to her. Sarah begins a session in the middle of her brief therapy by reporting progress in her relationship with the boyfriend.

T1: Why don't you, as you know, as I've talked about before, just start wherever you'd like, whatever's on your mind. Because the way the mind works, whatever is important to talk about, and we've established a focus in terms of the pattern that's associated with your sadness, so wherever you start it'll be relevant sooner or later.

S1: Ok. Well (sigh) things at school haven't really changed much. I still don't like what I'm doing, and I'm not sure if I should be doing it. But I know we've talked a lot about my relationship with my boyfriend, and I guess things there have changed a little bit. I've been able to tell him more that he needs to take some responsibility in the house and do things and it's, you know, sometimes he'll actually listen and do what I need him to do and then he'll kind of just forget again.

T2:   I like the way you put that, sometimes he'll "actually" listen! [Yeah.] That's an extraordinary event that he's actually listening?

S2:   (Laughs) Yeah. Exactly that's, well, I mean compared to the relationship we've had thus far, it is a pretty unique event for that to happen at all. But I also think, like you told me last time, that I hadn't really placed any expectations on him before. I hadn't really made it clear to him how I've been feeling and how it was important to me for him to do these things. So, I mean but that's pretty, a small change. That's the only thing that's kind of happened, me being able to say that to him. And there's still other stuff that, you know, when it comes to the criticism and things like that it just still seems to be a part of the relationship. And, I don't know, maybe I just have to deal with that.

T3:   Now, how did he respond to your pushing him more, listen to you?

S3:   Well, I think he was ok with it. He said that he agreed that he should probably put in even more effort in doing at least his part, as opposed to me cleaning up behind him. And I feel like still most of the responsibility is mine in terms of cleaning and things like that. But before it was cleaning up after him, too, so I think he realized that first part that maybe he should clean up after himself. And he says "ok" and he does it for maybe a few days, maybe a week, and then it almost goes back to, or it does go back to me doing it all over again. And I haven't' even asked him to do half the things in the house. Like maybe if I did the dishes and he could do the laundry. I don't think he'd be ok with that. So I haven't gone that far yet.

T4:   Well, do you think it's a matter of just being hard to break old habits, or he really believes in his heart that you should be doing everything for him?

Here is an example of a clarifying question. The therapist is attempting to clarify in his own mind whether the patient has unwittingly chosen a selfish boyfriend or by her behavior has unwittingly recruited him into this role.

S4:   Hmmm (pause) it seems like he really thinks I should be doing everything. That's just what he expects from me is to be the caretaker of all that needs to be done.

T5:   Now what gives you that impression?

S5:   I guess because he never does anything.

T6:   Well, I can see how you could come to that conclusion but [Yeah], if I've heard you right, you've begun to put some pressure on him and let him know that you feel he should do more [yeah]. And he's sort of at least grudgingly going along but [right] that really there's, again correct me if I'm wrong about this, but it sounds like you could be much more, you could be more explicit and more consistently encouraging him to do more.

S6:   Well, I just think that, I mean if someone cares about you shouldn't they understand what you need? And why would I, I guess I just don't understand why he just wouldn't do some of it. Just know that he's supposed to do it. I don't understand why he doesn't. I guess understand me or understand that I'm overwhelmed and that he needs to help me do some of this stuff. Why wouldn't he just do it? I mean, and because he doesn't I assume that he thinks that I'm supposed to do it all.

T7:   Well, I think it's understandable that you'd feel that he really doesn't want to do it and he doesn't appreciate how burdensome this is for you. But on the other hand, one of the things we've seen is that you feel this very strong obligation and feel compelled to take care of people. In other words, your boyfriend, your sister, it could be that whether they consciously think this, their reaction to how much energy you put into taking care of them, then their reaction is, "This is what Sarah wants to do, so I'll let her take care of me."

S7:   So, you're saying that basically just the role I've had in their lives of pretty much doing everything for them, they've kind of just expected that from me.

T8:   Yeah. I mean they've just gotten used to it and sort of taken as a given. Similar to, perhaps, how until we started talking about it you took it as a given that that was your role, to take care of people, that you had to do everything.

S8:   Yeah. That's true. And that, I guess, brings up the feeling of, it makes me angry that they that that's a given.

T9:   Angry at whom?

S9:   (deep breath, pause) Just angry. I guess angry at them. Why do they think it's a given? You know or, I guess I mean I understand my role in that but it's just I am very angry and not just at them.

I don't think, just angry that it's a given. Why should that be a given that I'm going to take care of everyone else? And not have anyone take care of me?

T10: Now do you feel any upset toward me for suggesting that you might contribute to the situation, unwittingly?

The therapist is probing to determine if there is a transference implication in the patient's anger at "them." He asks another clarifying question. Sarah's answer does reveal an uncertainty on her part about his attitude toward her inhabiting a caretaking role.

S10: Mmm. I don't feel that way. I mean, I guess I wonder if you think, you know, it's a given that I'm just supposed to be like this, take care of everyone else? But I'm not angry at you, I don't think.

T11: Is there any anything that I've said or that has transpired between us that would lead you to wonder that or feel that?

Here is another clarifying question. In this case, it is intended to help Sarah gain some perspective on her assumptions about other peoples' attitudes toward her. If this exploration of their interactions continued, it would represent a strategy of here-and-now transference analysis. However, Sarah's concerns about her therapist's attitudes do not appear to constitute a significant thread in their relationship.

S11: That you think it's a given? [Yeah.] I don't think so. I think I mean before when I first started coming I really wondered whether you could understand me, you know, because I'm sure you haven't been through experiences like mine, and I'm sure you have a happy life and I didn't think you would necessarily understand what it's like to be me.

T12: Mmm. How do you feel now?

S12: I feel better. As the sessions have continued I feel understood by you.

T13: How do you think that happened?

S13: Mmm. I think we just, I mean, you just seemed to be very understanding and empathic about what I was feeling, and I didn't, I haven't really felt judged by you and, you know, I don't really have any reason to be angry at you or anything, so I think that it's been good.

T14:   Mmm. Would you be interested in knowing from my perspective how I came to understand you more than I did when you first came in?

S14:   Yeah ok.

T15:   You talked to me. You told me about yourself

S15:   I haven't done that with other people?

T16:   Well, that's my impression.

S16:   Yeah. I don't., I always kept it in.

T17:   How come?

S17:   Because I was worried that they wouldn't understand. That they wouldn't be able to give me what I need.

T18:   Did you feel that I wouldn't understand?

S18:   Yeah. In the very beginning, I did and I think that, you know, the environment that we're in made it different in a sense that that's what we're here for me to talk to you about what I need and to talk to you about what I'm going through and that's what you're here for.

T19:   Oh, so as long as you're paying me, I'll be willing to understand and listen?

The therapist's question implies an assumption about their relationship of which Sarah was not necessarily aware. This is an example of a question with an interpretive function.

S19:   Well, you may not have. You could have been someone who I experienced that similar kind of feeling with of not feeling understood, but it didn't. It didn't work that way. I think just, you know, before I, my fear of you, that they won't understand took over in my other relationships but here this is the purpose: for me to talk and to talk about my stuff and for you to listen and tell me what you think

T20:   So, in our relationship right, if not right from the beginning pretty quickly you viewed the purpose of our relationship as such where you'd expect me to listen and, hopefully, to understand. [yeah] What is it about the relationship you have with two other important very important people in your life—your sister, your boyfriend—what is it about those relationships that holds you back, that makes you wary about whether they'll really listen and understand and be at least empathic?

The exploration of transference elements in the therapy relationship produced limited results, so the therapist turned their attention back to relationships with important people in her life. His question encouraged Sarah to confront wariness about relying emotionally on them.

S20: Yeah. I guess I've always thought that it's just not their job.

T21: Can you expand on that? I'm not sure what you mean.

S21: Um (pause), I guess I just don't expect them to be that for me, to be those people for me, to understand me, to take care of me, because, like we said, it's always been the other way around, or it's been more my role and my obligation to be there for them. I remember in the first session you'd said something about, "Do you, have you ever even given your sister the opportunity to see how much she could do on her own?" And I think that maybe one of the things I'm realizing is that I've never really given either of them much of an opportunity to see if they could be that for me and understand me.

T22: Why do you think you haven't?

S22: Because I've been scared. Scared of finding out that if I do put myself out there and they won't be able to do it, that I guess it will disappoint me and that's scary.

T23: Now is there anything that either of them have done that would cause you to feel so strongly that if you, as you say, put yourself out there for them to do something for you, to support you, that they would disappoint you?

This is another question with a confrontative function.

S23: Hmm (pause) not really. I don't think I've given them a chance. I really have not had any expectations.

T24: I wonder where that comes from, then? Because it sounds, correct me if I'm wrong, but it sounds like a very strong fear on your part, a very strong expectation. I sort of, you know, I get this image of those old trust building exercises. "If I turn around and just let myself fall and my sister or my boyfriend can catch me," you know what I'm talking about [right], they won't be there and I'll be hurt. [Yeah, yeah.] Why would you feel that way?

S24: I guess that's how I feel with what happened with my mom.

T25: What, what do you mean?

131

S25:   Well, I mean, you know, our relationship was good and like there were definitely things that I was able to talk to her about and she was able to talk to me about, and then she left. And sometimes I wonder if it was, if I was too much for her. Maybe when I was going through something and just talking to her about it, I mean she never really showed me but she also just left and so I guess maybe that has something to do with it.

T26:   Well you make it sound like she just packed her car and took off because you were just too much to deal with. You're just too much or that you killed her.

S26:   Hmm. I guess I'm just realizing now that I feel that way. I hadn't experienced it like that before. I guess there's a part of me that I just feel like, I mean I knew it wasn't in her control, you know, she couldn't do anything about it. But it still feels like she just left me on my own.

T27:   Now as you're expressing that sentiment, is it stirring up any feelings?

S27:   (Sigh) Just that loneliness again, feeling just abandoned and alone.

T28:   She died at a time, a very difficult time for mothers and daughters. I mean you're beginning, you're an adolescent and you're beginning to go out and start carving a life out away from the family. And yet at the same time you very much need the family to be there for you as a place of security, safety. And then all of a sudden it's taken away from you. [Yeah, yeah] It's almost like you resolved never, you're never gonna put yourself in that position again where you need anybody to take care of you, to lean on. You're going to make everybody dependent on you.

Using a combination of Sarah's memories and basic propositions from developmental theory, the therapist creates a partial story of the origin of Sarah's current rigid, dysfunctional expectations about how people upon whom she would rely for emotional support would disappoint her. The story also explains her corresponding maladaptive mode of relating as a caretaker who has minimal needs, herself. This is a partial story that contains the hypothetical consequences of Sarah's loss of her mother (followed by the emotional loss of her father). She resolves never again to depend on anyone. It is plausible and Sarah appears to resonate to it. She and her therapist were on the same "wavelength."

S28:   Yeah. At least that way I don't have to worry about how much it's going to affect me if they leave. I guess I get, I have more control over the situation that way.

T29:   How do you think that fits into this compelling feeling you have that you've got to do everything for your sister, your boyfriend.

S29:   I think it fits in just right where, how powerful, I guess, that fear is for me of not wanting to experience that again, and taking care of everyone else so that I don't become dependent on them for taking care of me, so I don't get hurt. So I don't have to experience that again.

T30:   So you don't have to experience it again, but you did ...

S30:   I did?

T31:   Well, you did right after, shortly after your mother died, because then I imagine you felt abandoned by your father.

S31:   Yeah. I still feel, I mean I still feel the same. I mean, in one place is the fear of not wanting to be abandoned again and hurt. But right now I'm hurting regardless, because I don't feel important enough, so it doesn't seem any better to act on that fear really or not let myself open up.

T32:   As we talk about this it seems to me that you really are stuck in a horrible dilemma, because in order to, from the perspective that we're talking about, in order to protect yourself from what you feel would be just a horrible hurt, and to put yourself in a position where you rely on somebody emotionally and then expect to be abandoned, just fall and be hurt. That in order to avoid that at any cost, you maintain this extreme self-sufficient position in relation to important people in your life, where you do things for them, you take care of them, and then they expect you to. So you don't have to rely on anybody. Everybody relies on you. [Yeah] But, on the other hand, you're left feeling lonely, unappreciated and overwhelmed. [Yeah.]

The story that began with origins is now elaborated into a description of Sarah's primary way of relating to important people in her life, as well as an explanation for this way of relating. The theme is abandonment and loss, and the plot concerns protecting oneself from ever being vulnerable again to experiencing an emotionally traumatic abandonment. Sarah's resonance to this story deepens. She and her therapist continue on the same wavelength.

S32:   Yeah. Yeah. That's what I mean. It does feel like a dilemma. One way I'm gonna feel a certain way that's just going to be just as bad as choosing the other way.

T33:   You think there's any way out of that?

S33:   I don't know. I hope so.

T34:   Well, it seems to me like it's all based on your conviction that if you do rely on anyone, the more important they are to you; the more you rely on them, the more, I don't know if you could say more inevitable—inevitable is inevitable—but it's inevitable that they're going to disappoint you and you're going to be hurt.

The therapist repeats that part of the story concerning the consequences of Sarah's hypothesized experience of emotionally traumatic abandonments as a teenager.

S34:   Yeah. Is that not true?

T35:   No, it's not.

Sometimes the therapist can be most helpful by simply offering a strongly held opinion. In this case, the therapist makes clear that he does not agree with Sarah's overgeneralization that her desire for emotional support will always be thwarted.

S35:   So it's not like it was …

T36:   When is the last time you gave it a chance, gave somebody a chance?

Here is another confrontative question.

S36:   My mom. (Pause. Sighs)

T37:   Well, if you set your expectations of what you can expect from the important people based on relations with your mother, then it's understandable that you feel that's inevitable. And you're gonna be disappointed.

S37:   Yeah. And it's not true?

T38:   And don't forget she didn't leave you. She died.

A bluntly stated reality.

S38:   Right. (Sigh). I hear you. It's just, it's hard to change.

T39:   Now we're seeing that the issue of important people in your life who you rely on, disappointing you, disappointing you by leaving, is a very important one. Given that, have you thought at all about our eventually stopping, our relationship ending? [Yeah.] Because I mean we're half way through the time that we agreed to meet.

The therapist suggests a possible link (connecting two dots) in Sarah's pattern of anticipating abandonment by anyone upon whom she became dependent. This is another example of a question with an interpretive function.

S39:   Yeah. I do think about it. I do think about it. Yeah. Maybe in some ways I hold back in here too. Because I don't, I guess I don't want to say anything or do anything that would make you leave any earlier than the time we decided on.

T40:   Can you describe how you hold back?

S40:   Mmm. I think it's more, maybe outside of here, or sometimes in here, where I just think more to myself, remind myself that this is temporary, and that this relationship is going to end, and that it is not going to be forever. And I guess in that way I hold back from maybe completely being in the relationship, always being aware that there's gonna be an end.

T41:   You know, I wonder if, and from my perspective, if it wasn't very important for you to hold back from allowing yourself to be completely in a relation with me. Like today for example, we're talking about very painful recollections and painful situations, and it seems like they resonate, talking about it makes sense to you, what we've talked about. It resonates for you. But, on the surface anyway, it seems to be touching you emotionally very little. You maintain a lot of control. And I wonder if that's one way you keep yourself out of the relationship with me, by holding, I mean not deliberately necessarily, but just automatic, you're at a distance from your feelings, disconnected from your feelings, of the strength of your feelings.

The therapist suggests a transference implication in Sarah's emotionally inhibited mode of relating to the therapist. This is another example of a question with an interpretive function.

S41:   I could see that. Maybe that's one way that I wouldn't want to overwhelm you with my feelings, or maybe burden you. It's a heavy weight because I have too much.

T42:   Now as, as we're talking about that, did it stir up anything?

S42:   (Sighs) I guess it's sadness and how entrenched this is for me and how out of control …

T43:   And perhaps sadness from what you miss in the relationships, because you need to keep that kind of distance? [Yeah.] Because I wonder if that contributes to the resistances there with your boyfriend?

S43:   Yeah. I think it definitely does, and I think with my sister too, that it's one sided and it's not an emotional relationship.

T44:   To enjoy and get as much satisfaction out of a relationship as you could, would put you at great risk in terms of what you feel is inevitable. If you put your, you know, if you put your heart out there.

S44:   Yeah. That's what it feels like.

T45:   Another dilemma.

S45:   Yeah. But, I guess slowly (sighs) I'm realizing that I have to do that, or that I need to be able to do that to have a real relationship. That it would make me happier. That just doesn't change the fact that it's really hard to do that, because I feel like it's been 13 years trying to be this person that keeps it inside and controls it and just don't want to burden anyone else. I mean I understand that. I mean I understand the part, I understand that you're telling me that is part of what I need to do. It's just hard to change.

T46:   So what, what can you do next?

S46:   (Sighs) I guess, small steps in expressing what I'm feeling and what I'm going through, with the important people in my life. I think I'd like to start with my sister. I don't know, maybe we can even talk about our mother. And just talk about each other's experiences and feelings and maybe build a stronger relationship.

T47:   What do you imagine if you try to sit down with your sister and talk more openly than you have up to this point, about your relationship with your mother, about the arrangement that you two have had for years? [Right.] What do you imagine you

136

would, what's the word I'm looking for, reluctance, sources of reluctance, risks, dangers, what would make it difficult for you?

Here is another function served by a question. The therapist invites Sarah to imagine a new story line and asks Sarah about the risks she anticipates by going in that narrative direction.

S47:   Yeah, to do that? Hmm. I guess I mean what I've always been scared of is, is will she be able to handle the fact that I'm not that strong sister that she's thought I've been or that she's seen me as for the past 13 years? Of really being self-sufficient and taking care of my own stuff and feelings, and that she might not see me as all that anymore.

T48:   What do you fear she would do?

S48:   What she would do?

T49:   Yeah. If she saw you, your worst fear was realized, you're sitting there and—I'm kind of exaggerating this—but all of a sudden it dawns on her, she has this realization that you're not as strong, as, you can't do everything and be everything for her. And you don't want to. What would happen?

The therapist continues to encourage Sarah to elaborate in her imagination of the new story line. What are the imagined consequences of this new story line?

S49:   (Long pause.) Hmm. I don't know. I don't know if I know exactly what she would do. But I feel like, or I just got this sense that, our relationship would feel just so much more real and that maybe there might be a part of her that's disappointed but maybe even relieved that I ...

T50:   That's bad?

S50:   No. actually I just kind of got that feeling that, the good feeling that could be a real step for us. And that (pause), yeah, in some ways I think that it could be a relief for her to see that I have these struggles too, and that she's not alone. And maybe we can connect.

T51:   And this, this is the consequence that has held you back from talking with her?

Sarah's imagined new story line leads to what immediately is, in retrospect, an obvious healthy alternative but which until that moment had eluded Sarah. It is amazing how fixed, maladaptive expectations can blind a person to the obvious.

S51:   This is a consequence of, actually I was so overwhelmed with the fear of being, her not being able to handle it and that I just didn't think about this as a possibility until we're sitting here right now.

T52:   It sounds like, without even necessarily articulating it explicitly, your fear was that if you were more honest with your sister, that it would either drive her away or kill her. [Yeah.] Sort of like you felt, you described as a 13-year-old when your mother died.

The therapist offers an interpretation of Sarah's unconscious expectation of the consequences of pursuing the new story line that depicts Sarah relating to her sister in a more emotionally open way.

S52:   Exactly and it just didn't come together for me until now. That's what I have been acting on in our relationship. And I hadn't realized that what I felt about my mother is what I carried through these relationships until now. So it's given me a different sense of what it would be like if I did talk to her. Hmm.

The therapist pursuing a discourse driven primarily by questions that in context served several functions, and leading to the articulation of an old, maladaptive personal story line and the beginning of a new, healthier story line, has led Sarah to important insights into the nature and origins of her chronic fear of traumatic loss of emotional support from those upon whom she would rely.

NOTES

1. At the same time, due to their ability to efficiently analyze problems in their knowledge domains, in absolute terms experts spend relatively less time in problem analysis.
2. A rigid predilection on the part of the patient to interpret the therapist's communications within the confines of expectations is consistent with a core interpersonal theme and is the essence of transference (Gill, 1982).

3. Generic thematic categories have been proposed. For example, Summers and Barber (2010) have identified six "core psychodynamic problems": depression, obsessionality, fear of abandonment, panic, anxiety, and trauma.

4. At the end of the chapter is an excerpt of a session transcription from the midpoint of Sarah's treatment (whom we met in earlier chapters). The transcript begins with the opening discourse and follows it almost to the end. Annotations elucidate the nature and purpose of those therapist interventions that illustrate ideas presented in this chapter. The respective speaking turns of therapist and patient are sequentially numbered, so the reader can refer to specific illustrations of the ideas that are discussed in this chapter.

5. Reproduced with permission of APA Video Media. For this book, several identifying aspects have been altered.

6. The role of emotions in the therapeutic dialogue also can, in part, define a treatment model. The brief dynamic therapies described respectively by Binder (2004) and H. Levenson (2010) both derive from time-limited dynamic psychotherapy (Strupp & Binder, 1984), which was an integration of object relations, attachment, and interpersonal theories. The two derivative treatment models have progressed in different directions with regard to the technical role of emotions. In his model, Binder has incorporated elements from cognitive theory and therapy, as well as concepts and principles from the cognitive sciences having to do with the nature and development of expertise. Accordingly, emotions are viewed as important background to the development of a meaningful narrative explanation of the patient's troubles. The relevant skills needed by the therapist are interpersonal pattern recognition and the ability to articulate another person's subjective experiences in narrative form. By contrast, Levenson has incorporated emotion-focused elements into her approach. Accordingly, the process of identifying "the feeling in the moment" is in the foreground of technique. The narrative context of the emotional moment is in the background. The relevant skills needed by the therapist are a focused resonance with another person's affective experience and the ability to translate that experience into words.

7. Lester Luborsky (1984) created a highly structured formulation model, the core conflict relationship theme (CCRT), that he argued was a representation of transference. The CCRT allows for the organization of clinical material into a therapeutic focus with minimal inferences, it facilitates the tracking of a focus, it is teachable, and it can be operationalized for research. The CCRT is a cornerstone of Luborsky's brief dynamic therapy model, supportive-expressive treatment. It is largely identical to Strupp and Binder's (1984) cyclical maladaptive pattern (CMP) but has much more extensive research support.

8. The more general usage for "metacommunication" is a discussion about the meanings of a verbal communication that are in addition to the literal meanings associated with the words used. These additional meanings are conveyed through paralinguistic messages and are, essentially, messages about messages. The nonverbal message can be congruent or incongruent with the verbal message.

9. The case of Sarah is based on an actual patient who was treated as part of the Vanderbilt II psychotherapy research project (Strupp, 1993). The excerpts presented here are a completely improvised simulation of how that treatment could have evolved to a good outcome. Unfortunately, the actual therapy had serious problems that led to a poor outcome.

8

Monitoring and Evaluating Clinical Outcomes

It is no longer sufficient to be conscientious in giving patients your maximum effort to be helpful; you must also produce empirical evidence of the products of your efforts. Third party payers and patients themselves increasingly want evidence of the benefits of psychotherapy and, when it comes to reimbursing you, of your outcomes in particular. Managed care companies have realized that the products they are selling are outcomes rather than specific healthcare services (Lambert, 2010). Consequently, these companies are going to want proof that you are providing their clients with useful services. It would not be surprising if in the near future professional organizations (e.g., the American Psychological Association, the American Psychiatric Association) mandate that obtaining treatment outcome data is an ethical requirement of psychotherapists. Yet, relatively few practitioners collect data on the progress and outcome of their treatments. It is likely that even fewer have received training in this competency area. For example, in a survey of 2,000 randomly selected clinical psychologists, only 37% of those who responded said that they used outcome measures in their practices (Hatfield & Ogles, 2004). This shortcoming is increasingly hazardous to the livelihood of individual practitioners. It also interferes with professional development, since without systematic feedback on his or her performance across many patients a therapist has no firm basis on where to focus his future knowledge acquisition and skill development activities. Research has demonstrated that it is a grave mistake to rely on self-evaluations to assess the quality of one's performance (Dunning, 2005).

THE THERAPIST AS A "LOCAL CLINICAL SCIENTIST"

The practitioner who constructs a systematic method for evaluating his treatment outcomes is being consistent with the broader professional goal of working with a scientific attitude and, more specifically, of engaging in "evidence-based" practice. The generation of evidence about one's practice is one part of being a "local clinical scientist" (Stricker & Trierweiler, 1995); a practitioner who informs his or her work with systematic observations and thought. The local clinical scientist complements the scientist who seeks general principles; the former seeks to determine the applicability of general scientific conclusions to specific cases. He or she also gathers data on specific cases in order to make general conclusions about the effectiveness of his or her work with various types of problems and people.

Monitoring the progress of psychotherapy and evaluating its outcome requires a competency that is separate from those associated with the conduct of treatment. First, there are specific areas of knowledge with which the therapist should be familiar. A familiarity with the issues addressed and strategies used in psychotherapy outcome research would be a useful foundation of knowledge to orient the practitioner to the task of evaluating his clinical work. The encyclopedia of psychotherapy research is Bergin and Garfield's *Handbook of Psychotherapy and Behavioral Change*, which is updated every few years. The most recent update is the fifth edition, which was edited by Michael Lambert (2004). There are decisions that have to be made about treatment evaluation strategy: Is the goal to obtain amount of change from pre- to posttherapy vs. simple posttreatment measures that are compared with the published scores of norm groups? Is there an attempt to gather follow-up data and, if so, how long after termination will attempts to obtain this data occur? From what perspective or perspectives will the evaluation data be obtained: the therapist, the patient, family members, employers (Strupp & Hadley, 1977)? Is the primary goal to obtain information about treatment effectiveness or about patient satisfaction with the experience, or both?

Of course, the clinician must be familiar with the available treatment assessment measures or know where to find out about them. The clinician also must have an understanding of psychometric theory as a foundation for evaluating the strength of each measure's psychometric properties. In order to interpret the meaning of pre- to posttreatment change scores, the clinician should be familiar with a convention used by psychotherapy researchers: the notion of *clinically significant* change. This term refers to measured change that exceeds what is possible from chance fluctuations in scores or measurement error, and the posttreatment client scores on the measure of interest are indistinguishable from the scores on a norm group defined as "normal" (Jacobson, Roberts, Berns, & McGlinchey, 1999; Jacobson & Truax, 1991; Lambert, 2010).

An important skill for the clinician to possess is the ability to choose measures that are suitable for assessing those aspects of the patient's functioning that are of interest. Another important skill required for treatment evaluation is the ability to convey clearly to the patient the rationale for taking the time to complete self-report measures or for allowing others with whom the patient interacts to complete measures about the patient's posttreatment functioning. Attitudes that are associated with the evaluation competency include valuing a disciplined approach to gathering data and interpreting the results. The therapist must appreciate the importance of empirical data but balance this attitude with skepticism about the definitive nature of such data. The therapist's future behavior should be influenced by treatment evaluation data that he or she has gathered, but this influence should be tempered with responsiveness to the immediate treatment context.

TREATMENT EVALUATION MEASURES

There are no treatment evaluation measures used in practice or clinical settings that have been developed specifically for psychodynamic therapies. One measure that assesses an area of particular importance to psychodynamic therapists is the Inventory for Interpersonal Problems (IIP; Horowitz, Rosenberg, Baer, Ureno, & Villasenor 1988), which, as the name implies, assesses change in the quality of the patient's interpersonal relationships. There are norms available with which to compare the scores of individual clients.

Psychological and behavior changes are the goals of all types of therapies and there are measures available for common use to capture that information. Measures do vary along several important dimensions. For instance, they vary in terms of their temporal sensitivity to change; the Minnesota Multiphasic Personality Inventory (MMPI-2; Butcher, Dajhlstrom, Graham, Tellegen, & Kaemmer, 1989) is not as sensitive to session-by-session changes as the Outcome Questionaire-45 (OQ-45; Lambert et al., 2004). They both, however, are excellent pre- and posttreatment measures with published norm group scores. Both of these measures also are broad spectrum measures (assessing a broad range of symptom and behavioral functioning). A measure that closely corresponds to the DSM-IV, Axis-II personality disorders is the Millon Multiaxial Inventory (Jankowski, 2002). This widely used assessment tool generates an individual profile composed of scores on 14 personality disorder dimensions. By contrast, there are measures that are suitable for assessing change in specific disorders or symptom clusters, such as the Beck Depression Inventory (BDI) or the Beck Anxiety Inventory (BAI; Beck, Ward, Medelson, Mock, & Erbaugh, 1961). Measures also vary in their complexity and time required to complete and score them. The MMPI-2, MCMI, OQ-45, and the Symptom Check List-90 (SCL-90) (Derogatis, 1983), take a period of time to complete but provide a detailed picture of an individual's symptoms and functioning. The Outcome Rating Scale (ORS; S. Miller, Duncan, Brown, Sparks, & Claud, 2003) is a simple Likert-type rating scale composed of four questions about different broad areas of the patient's life. It takes only a few minutes to complete.

All of the measures discussed so far have a self-report format. There are measures, however, that tap the judgments of the therapist or of independent observers (who may, for example, view the video recordings of an interview). A familiar example of a broad spectrum measure that requires one overall rating, typically made by the interviewing clinician, is the Global Assessment of Functioning Scale (GAF) that is part of the DSM-IV-TR multiaxial diagnosis (American Psychiatric Association, 2000). By contrast, a measure that targets specific symptoms and requires ratings on multiple items is the Hamilton Rating Scale for Depression (HRSD; see Ogles, Lambert, & Masters, 1996).

MONITORING THE COURSE OF THERAPY

In order to be genuinely committed to maximizing the possibility for effective therapy, given the particular circumstances, it is imperative that the therapist have a system for ongoing monitoring of the progress of treatment (or lack thereof). The therapist's subjective impressions of how therapy is going may have fluctuating accuracy, but they are not a scientifically valid way of monitoring treatment. In his programmatic research over the past 20 years, Michael Lambert (2010) has demonstrated that feedback to the therapist of session-by-session status of therapeutic progress can improve outcomes. He also has shown that efficiency in the delivery of treatment can be enhanced by providing regular feedback to the therapist: those treatments that have gone better than expected can be terminated sooner than the therapist had planned, and in those therapies that are going poorly, feedback can prompt the therapist to modify his or her treatment plan or consider referring the patient to another clinician. In either case, the probability of unproductive, wasted sessions is reduced. The savings in healthcare dollars probably is significant.

As is the case with outcome measures, treatment monitoring measures, which usually can be the same, vary in their complexity. For example, the Session Rating Scale (SRS; Duncan et al., 2003) is a four-item, Likert-like scale that is completed at the end of each session. The therapist can use the ratings from one session to modify his or her approach in the subsequent session, or they can be used as an agenda item for discussion about the collaborative work or the state of the therapeutic relationship. The OQ-45, which was discussed as an outcome measure, is sensitive to session-by-session changes on three dimensions: symptomatic distress, interpersonal problems, and social role functioning. Based on thousands of administrations to clinical and nonclinical samples, Lambert (2010) has developed prototypic trajectories of session-by-session progress for different baseline scores on the three dimensions. Consequently, the therapist can compare the patient's actual progress with the expected progress for various norm groups. Lambert has developed sophisticated scoring and interpretive software packages that can be used by therapists to obtain detailed data on the status of their patients. This feedback has been shown to significantly enhance a therapist's management of his or her treatments (Lambert, 2010).

There are other sophisticated monitoring and evaluating systems. The first outcome management system, known by the acronym COM-PASS, is a 68-item scale composed of three subscales: Current Well-Being, Current Symptoms, and Current Life Functioning. The COMPASS system also provides expected trajectories of treatment response (Howard, Moras, Brill, Martinovich, & Lutz, 1996). A simpler package is the Partners for Change Outcome Management System (PCOMS), which is composed of the SRS and the ORS. The package is given to the patient during each session, quickly and easily scored, and can provide immediate feedback that can be discussed in the same session (S. Miller, Duncan, Sorrell, & Brown, 2005).

The other major perspective for evaluating treatment is patient satisfaction. There is one scale with which we are familiar that has established psychometric properties and norms, the Client Satisfaction Questionnaire (CSQ; Atkinson & Greenfield, 2004). The CSQ is available in 3-, 4-, 8-, 18-, and 31-item versions.

The clinician doing psychotherapy in private practice or organizational settings, as well as the trainee at a clinical practicum or internship, has a wide variety of treatment monitoring and outcome evaluation measures from which to choose. We believe it is inevitable that there will be a requirement to monitor treatment progress as well as outcome as a condition for eligibility for reimbursement by public and private payers. We believe that there will be growing use both by clinical training programs and by practitioners of treatment monitoring and evaluation systems like the OQ-45, because these systems allow the therapist to compare the treatment progress of individual patients with expected rates of progress based on large norm groups. This is the technology of the future. Training for competency in treatment monitoring and evaluation already is a criterion for accreditation used by the American Psychological Association Committee on Accreditation when reviewing clinical psychology training programs. Every conscientious psychotherapist should value the achievement of this competency.

9

Planning for Termination and Maintaining Treatment Gains

Termination is unique to the psychotherapy relationship. People do not typically plan to end their relationships, nor do they usually regard this as a positive sign. Yet, ending psychotherapy when a patient feels a greater sense of well-being can be quite hopeful and affirming. Even when unplanned, we hope that the patient can carry forth from the therapeutic work new understandings and experiences that change the course of his or her life for the better. The ending of psychotherapy is necessarily at the forefront of treatment considerations and interventions in any brief treatment, and BDP is no exception. Although BDP does not require a preestablished number of sessions, the model does involve a consistent consideration of time limits. The mind-set is to use time as efficiently as possible, making every minute of therapy count. Also, there is no preconception that enduring change requires a long therapy. BDP is characterized by a "time sensitive" or "time efficient" attitude (Budman & Gurman, 1988).

We intentionally work to establish an interpersonal focus in the form of the CMP early in the treatment. With this clear focus for change, we organize treatment around actively addressing the nature and consequences of maladaptive interpersonal patterns that disrupt the patient's relationships and well-being. When therapy ends, competency in drawing it to a close depends on those fundamental clinical skills highlighted throughout this text, including listening, communicating empathically, reflection-in-action, and basic interpersonal skills.

This chapter addresses three essential clinical competencies associated with termination: preparing for termination, solidifying insight and maintaining treatment gains, and bringing the treatment to a close in a therapeutic way.

Preparing for Termination

This clinical competency involves the ability to prepare the client for termination and bring the treatment to a close in a therapeutic way. Termination is a process that begins with the first session and continues through to the last session. This involves fostering a collaborative, flexible, ongoing approach to termination; respecting the patient's autonomy; and recognizing the impact of termination for the patient.

Solidifying Insight and Maintaining Treatment Gains

This clinical competency involves the ability to prepare patients for termination by reviewing their new awareness of, and shifts in, interpersonal relating and sense of self and helping patients develop and implement a relapse prevention plan to ensure that they will be able to maintain treatment gains.

BRINGING CLOSURE TO TREATMENT

This clinical competency involves the ability to bring the treatment to a close in therapeutic way. At the end of treatment, the therapist can facilitate closure by inviting an explict dialogue about what was helpful in therapy, as well as what the patient may have wished would be different. It is essential, as well, to say goodbye in a way that marks the significance of the therapeutic relationship and process.

TERMINATION IN BDP

Psychotherapy is a work in progress even after patient and therapist part ways. There is no way to be completely finished with reworking entrenched interpersonal schemas that once served a significant function in helping the patient protect herself from painful feelings related to disruptions in self-concept or another's mistreatment. This is work the patient will likely revisit throughout life. And yet, treatment comes to an end; the question is when and how?

Termination in psychotherapy happens as a consequence of therapeutic changes or lack thereof. Ideally, termination occurs at a natural point in treatment when the patient is doing better. In this regard, the patient would evidence greater capacities for healthy relationships, including insight into relational patterns and more flexible ways of relating, and have a more positive sense of self with increased self-awareness and confidence. The patient also may be relating to his therapist differently, perhaps in more egalitarian, more positive, or more genuine ways. Premature termination, however, occurs frequently in practice. It can result from external factors (e.g., a patient's limited resources, restrictions on insurance reimbursement, relocation of either the patient or therapist, or agency restrictions) or as a result of the patient's dissatisfaction, perhaps related to an alliance rupture that has not been identified or that cannot be repaired, or a stagnant/unproductive treatment. It is imperative for the therapist to consider how to make each of these circumstances as therapeutic as possible, planning differently for each.

Although empirical research on termination remains relatively limited, there is some evidence to suggest that the therapeutic significance of termination will vary across patients and across treatments (Knox et al., 2011; Marx & Gelso, 1987; Quintana & Holahan, 1992). The majority of the literature on termination comes from a psychoanalytic or psychodynamic perspective. Psychodynamically oriented clinicians have long regarded the "termination phase" as critical to successful treatment. However, it has been difficult to identify criteria and technical strategies for managing termination as a result of the complexity posed by unique patient–therapist dynamics, treatment processes, and the conditions of termination (Firestein, 1982). This reality has not changed over decades of practice. Nonetheless, what we tend to assume about termination generally comes from descriptions of longer-term treatments, including the expectation that termination will be marked by grief and anxiety over loss of the therapist. However, a review of the literature on termination in time-limited treatment suggests a few distinct, although still tentative assumptions (given the dearth of empirical support), that may guide the BDP therapist.

It appears that termination can be a less psychologically significant event in time-limited compared to longer-term treatments. Empirical investigations specific to brief treatment have indicated that termination may not be a concern at all or may not be painful for patients (Malan, 1963, 1976; Marx & Gelso, 1987; Stewart, 1972). Indeed, Mann's (1973) time-limited treatment approach may be a case in point. Mann emphasized termination as the central focus and strictly limited therapy to 12 sessions in order to mobilize the patient's feelings of loss, which he believed would inevitably emerge. Mann suggested that a patient's concerns regarding ending would become acute in the last four sessions and recommended "relentless" focus on termination to assure a successful outcome. Despite this theoretical proposition, an empirical investigation of Mann's therapy approach found that termination was discussed in an average of 1.3 sessions, sometimes only in passing (M. M. Miller et al., 1983). The authors concluded that perhaps therapist and patient colluded to avoid negative feelings associated with separation, or perhaps Mann overestimated the significance of termination.

On this latter point, there is further evidence to suggest that some patients do not feel especially distressed about ending treatment, and patients can experience successful outcomes without exploring termination issues (Malan, 1963, 1976; Stewart, 1972). In addition, patients can feel quite positive about termination (Marx & Gelso, 1987; Quitana & Holahan, 1992; Roe, Dekel, Harol, Fennig, & Fennig, 2006). If, indeed, treatment goals have been achieved, a patient would be more likely to leave with a sense of accomplishment and security to venture on without therapy. This eventuality is probably more likely to occur for patients who entered treatment with a mature level of functioning and, at least, the capacity to establish an interpersonal support system.

However, we cannot dismiss entirely the significance of termination in brief therapy. Research also has indicated that patients feel greater distress at termination when they have been dissatisfied with the treatment or disappointed by the therapist. Termination may require greater attention when therapy is ending on a poor note, perhaps as a result of a negative outcome or an unresolved alliance rupture. Furthermore, it has been suggested that a mishandled termination can undo what would have otherwise been a successful treatment (Greenberg, 2002; Marx & Gelso, 1987; Strupp & Binder, 1984).

A productive and collaborative dialogue about *all* the feelings and concerns that termination evokes, as well as how the patient has experienced therapy, may play a pivotal role in solidifying treatment gains. The therapist's willingness to discuss the patient's thoughts and feelings about termination, including times when therapist and patient do not agree about ending, is associated with a patient's positive feelings about the treatment. For example, focusing on how much the patient has improved to the exclusion of acknowledging the patient's anxiety or sadness about ending may leave the patient feeling misunderstood. Alternatively, a therapist who focuses on themes of loss and grief rather than recognizing a patient's sense of accomplishment and well-being also may leave the patient feeling misunderstood. Such misunderstanding can overshadow positive gains the patient has experienced in treatment up to that point (Marx & Gelso, 1987; Roe et al., 2006). Generally speaking, acknowledging the particular significance that termination has for the patient is important. The scope and nature of this conversation will depend on the extent to which and on what ways the patient feels affected by the ending.

PREPARING FOR TERMINATION

Make the Ending a Process

A *process* is continuous, systematic, and progressive. *Continuous* suggests that termination is not a moment in time; it is not the goodbye when the patient walks out of the office for the last time, or even the last session. Termination as a process occurs over time. In brief therapy, it may, in fact, begin in the first session since the patient is sensitized to time limits on the treatment. Later in the treatment, processing the ending of therapy is set in motion when the idea to end therapy occurs to one or both participants. *Systematic* suggests an order or plan. There is no protocol for dealing with termination, but we will offer some general guidelines. *Progressive* favors moving forward toward change or improvement, proceeding by steps or degrees. In this regard, termination is a process that involves discussions that can extend and deepen the therapeutic dialogue regarding the patient's experience in psychotherapy, growing insights, changes in relationships, and the meaning of ending for the patient. The termination process will vary in intensity, depth, and duration. For patients who experience termination as an emotionally significant event, the conversation should occur over a number of sessions and should increasingly becoming a dialogue about life without therapy and ways to carry therapeutic gains forward.

Foster a Collaborative, Flexible, Ongoing Approach to Termination

Although there are circumstances that may dictate termination, deciding on how (if not when) to end therapy is best handled as a collaborative and flexible process. In line with our emphasis on inquiry and dialogue, we recommend explicitly discussing termination. This conversation may begin early and continue throughout treatment. In BDP, the reality of limited time is explicit from the start. Some therapists may choose to set the number of sessions or determine an end date at the beginning. Others may leave the end date more indeterminate and rely solely on the mindset of working as efficiently as possible. Always, it is important to discuss openly with the patient the expectation that treatment will be time-limited and focused on identifying and resolving a salient issue or conflict that perpetuates her difficulties. Decisions regarding termination will be guided by advances toward key BDP treatment goals as they are articulated specifically in terms of the patient's presenting concerns. In addition, it is helpful to collaborate with the patient on deciding how to process and mark the ending. There is no uniquely right way, and a therapist's flexibility can foster a more meaningful ending unique to each therapeutic relationship.

Respect and Foster the Patient's Autonomy

Patients often initiate termination and choose to stop for a variety of reasons. Even when it seems countertherapeutic to stop, it is important to respect the patient's autonomy, as well as his or her capacity to make this determination. It is easier to support the decision of a patient who initiates termination because she has achieved her goals than to support this decision for someone who makes it because of dissatisfaction or a disruption in the alliance. Such support, however, may be no less therapeutic. Engaging in a dialogue about the patient's ideas regarding treatment and termination is imperative for conveying respect and affirmation of the patient. This dialogue, of course, will be unique to the patient and the circumstances of termination.

SOLIDIFYING INSIGHT AND MAINTAINING TREATMENT GAINS

Review Growing Awareness of and Changes in Interpersonal Relating

It is helpful to discuss what insights the patient has acquired about her characteristic ways of relating to others that have contributed to her difficulties. This discussion involves not only reviewing a patient's new awareness, but also major shifts in how the patient sees herself, regards others, and experiences interpersonal interactions. In treatments marked by greater dissatisfaction or ruptures in the alliance, this discussion may be uncomfortable and thorny. Nonetheless, even a review of what has not changed and what has been disappointing in the treatment can be helpful. It is one more chance to convey a willingness to listen and an effort to understand what discourages and frustrates the patient. It also is an opportunity to discuss what might have been more helpful. This discussion can lead to some insight regarding the barriers the patient perceives in finding what she most desires and needs in relationships. In the context of a positive alliance and productive therapeutic process, this review would naturally evolve out of the dialogue patient and therapist have shared throughout treatment, as can be seen in the case illustration below.

Case Example: Louise

Louise, a 56-year-old woman introduced in chapter 7, sought psychotherapy because of increasing feelings of loss, loneliness, and isolation related to grief over a number of losses: her mother had died 6 years prior, she had an ongoing conflict with her older sister who stopped talking to her, her four adult children were gone from the home, friends moved out of town, and valued work colleagues left. These losses left Louise feeling "deserted" and "empty." When she was not interacting with people, she felt like there were "holes" in her life. She felt heightened distress when alone and worried that she was "too dependent" on others. She appeared to feel that she had little to offer other people, and her self-confidence was low. Louise was prone to feeling disappointed or disillusioned with herself and others, and her high expectations often left her feeling angry and unhappy. She complained about people who she felt had deserted her: "I need these people, they don't need anybody."

It appeared that Louise wished for smooth, harmonious relationships in which she felt loved and affirmed, yet she struggled with feeling inadequate and "too dependent." As a result, she expected others to abandon her. Poignantly, she said, "People don't reject me, they pass me over." She was reluctant to make demands on others despite great expectations, and as a result of her passivity and disingenuousness with others, she generally felt overlooked and bereft. As a consequence, she found herself often "angry, critical, and frustrated" with others who did not seem to see her for who she was. In turn, she became angry with herself for being so "needy" and cautious in relationships.

In her last session, Louise reviewed events surrounding her daughter's recent wedding with significant emphasis on interactions with her older sister, Beatrice, with whom she had experienced ongoing conflicts since childhood. She noted her sister offered to help with wedding preparations and then seemed to do so begrudgingly, refusing to help clean up after the rehearsal dinner and arriving late to the wedding. Louise was upset by how sour and unhappy her sister was throughout the festivities.

Louise: And we've got a very false kind of relationship and I really don't want any part of it, sister or no sister, I just don't want it. I don't need it. Other people have called me, ya know, Beatrice hasn't called me. And after the wedding, [when everyone came to the house, she was] clearly not enjoying any of it because it didn't center around her, I presume. I don't know what the feeling is there. I think there's a lot of really old stuff.

T: Old jealousies?

Louise: Old jealousy, old sibling rivalry. "I'm the oldest sister and I will tell these two underlings what to do." I think she's got a real problem because she can't tell either one of us what to do. She has no control and I think she can't handle it. We are really out from under her thumb. I feel like I'm more out from under this thumb than I've ever been in my entire life. And I don't know what's going to, how it's going to develop.... I'm less dominated, I'm less bullied, I'm less intimidated. I am more inclined to tell her, "Don't leave me with that mess" (T: uh-huh). I don't feel one minute of guilt.... I made her important. I gave her the power,

I allowed her to start fear in my heart. I felt like I couldn't live without her approval and her goodwill and her whatever she wanted to drop my way every now and then, I thought I couldn't live without it.

Louise developed a new perspective on her relationship with her sister. She discussed her core pain in relationships that she had carried throughout her life. Less afraid of losing her sister's attention, she felt less inclined to submit to her sister's control. As a result, she recognized other possibilities for her life and came away with a more positive sense of herself as good enough. She also was less burdened by a sense of loss and emptiness, recognizing the potential in her relationships and reaching out to others.

Louise: And now I know I can very well live without what she's got to give out on her terms. I don't need it. I have so much love coming my way now, that I don't, I don't know that I can handle it all. I feel pretty relieved about this Beatrice thing.

T: What are you relieved, uh, what are you freed up from, pleasing her, tiptoeing around in order to preserve the relationship?

Louise: Feeling like I have to have it, so I couldn't possibly say or do anything because she'd cut me off so quickly. We're very, very different. Unless she can go with the flow. Unless she can accept me for who I am, I don't need it because I don't need someone to always be trying to put me in their box; their idea of who I should be, what I should be, how I should be. And I think Beatrice has real, very controlling tendencies. I don't need it. You know I don't need it. I was beginning to have a good time. I talk to people everywhere, I smile at people.

T: You're already good enough.

Louise: I'm good enough. I'm good enough to phone people up without waiting for them to phone me and uh, ya know, I began to see how I might shape my life. I see that um, ya know, there are quite a few possibilities for me. Earlier, I couldn't see it, I really couldn't, because everything was just so nailed down, ya know?

At the end of therapy, Louise began to reframe her narrative. She no longer thought of herself as "too dependent." She could own her need for relationships and wanted to be able to assert herself more without being afraid and without being angry.

Louise: I think that, this is a struggle for independence, this struggle for autonomy rather than to be self-sufficient. I think my struggle has been one for independence and one for autonomy rather than self-sufficiency. I don't really want to be without people. I do want people in my life so that is not it. It's being able to be assertive, to be independent, not to lean, not to need to have, you know, 15 people to prop you up to get you off in the morning.

T: Are you saying perhaps that because you feel it is important to have relationships and to be liked by people, you have bent yourself out of shape to achieve that? You have done that perhaps by being too agreeable, not assertive enough. And when you do that, then you also become angry at yourself, and maybe the other person. So that'd be sort of the cycle.

Louise: I'd like to kind of straighten that little crick out of my social skills. I'd like to be able to be a little more assertive, without the anger.

Louise then spoke about what she had learned about herself in therapy.

Louise: I have a lot of problems with this trying to bring perfection into my life. You pointed that out to me a lot, my striving for perfection. Another thing that I think that you made me very aware of, and that is that my continuum is 1, 10. I have left out all of the numbers in between. It's either a 1 or a 10. And I have come to realize that there are degrees. I'm beginning to realize that there are all these steps between 1 and 10. And I think that what's gone on in my head is "Perfection or zero."

Louise was speaking about her growing capacity for tolerating ambivalence and shades of gray. This allowed her to be less critical of herself and others, making it more likely that she would be open to expanding possibilities for her expectations of self and others.

Understand the Interpersonal Impact of Termination for the Patient

Although its significance will vary across patients, termination may offer an opportunity to capitalize on change by reworking dominant interpersonal narrative(s) in connection with leaving the therapist. An astute therapist will attend closely to how a patient's dominant interpersonal concerns influence the treatment process as it comes to a close. Schlesinger (2005) wrote, "In general, the way a patient enters and leaves other significant relationships will be consonant with his way of engaging with the therapist and his way of anticipating separating from the therapist" (p. 17). The ending of treatment may awaken issues of separation and loss in relationships for some patients (Mann, 1973). Alternatively, termination may stir conflicts regarding desires for independence and obligations toward others. In this regard, a patient may be uncertain whether leaving, and feeling good about ending, are acceptable. Other patients may regress to old maladaptive ways of interacting in their relationships as termination draws near. Noticing and addressing the resurgence of more maladaptive modes of relating to others, and to the therapist in particular, is an important aspect of the termination process. Explicitly linking these reactions to termination and to the patient's primary interpersonal concerns and patterns (CMP) may help further solidify a patient's insight and expand possibilities in the patient's mind regarding the potential for healthy and mutually intimate relationships.

Case Example: Carl

Carl, a 37-year-old man, entered therapy feeling increasingly depressed and disillusioned with his relationships. Although Carl yearned for closeness in his relationships, he was highly critical of his desires to feel loved and cared for by others. Because he expected others to reject or ridicule these desires, he inhibited his emotional expressions and instead tended to be intellectualized and pragmatic in his interactions with others. In doing so, he was often critical of others, intolerant of their emotions, and impatient with what he regarded as "frivolities" such as leisurely activities. As a result of his controlled and somewhat critical exterior, others pulled away from him. He was left feeling disregarded, angry, and lonely. Carl was continuously uncertain about how to relate others, but too frightened to take the risk of letting down his guard.[1]

In his last therapy session, Carl started by acknowledging the end: "So, this is the fabled last session," clearly indicating that termination was on his mind. He then spoke of being more angry and disappointed with his wife and business employee since returning from a 10-day overseas trip. His employee apparently did not run the business adequately and his wife did not oversee the employee properly. He described feeling tense and "going through life as a pressure cooker." Carl spoke as though he was aware of having very high standards for himself and for others, an issue he and his therapist explored throughout therapy. He noted, "I assume the worst in my heart and demand the best." He waivered, however, regarding the issue of whether his standards were unrealistically high or whether others were, in fact, inadequate. The therapist noted that Carl was speaking of his wife and employee "in one breath," as though they were the same. This seemed to reflect how Carl perceived and experienced others negatively in a global manner, suggesting a level of rigidity that profoundly interfered with his interpersonal functioning. Although Carl's criticism and hostility had eased over the course of therapy, it appeared that this tendency to be critical and dismissive of others emerged again under the acute stress of termination.

Carl considered that maybe "living on his own" for 10 days made him realize his dissatisfaction, and he spoke of wanting to go off on his own. It is notable that, with his travel schedule, Carl would have had a significant disruption in weekly therapy just prior to the predetermined end of a 25-session therapy.[2] He had been away from all his major relationships and returned disillusioned and disconnected. Although the therapist did not mention this break, he did inquire about the possibility that Carl may have been "underestimating how much this is a reaction to ending. You feel I've used you and am now discarding you as we talked about in the last couple of sessions. Perhaps you are now doing this [to your wife and employee]." Carl promptly denied anger at the therapist. Instead, Carl returned to speaking of wanting to move far away from people; emotionally, it seems, he had already withdrawn. He seemed unaware of his emotional detachment despite speaking of being afraid that he would become like a friend of his who isolated himself after a divorce.

Later in the session, in a matter-of-fact way, Carl described plans to live apart from his wife while simultaneously speaking of plans to seek couples therapy. He dispassionately summed up his complaints with her as "she's not a good roommate," indicating only briefly that she does not clean the house to his satisfaction. Without much apparent regard, he did not imagine this separation would be disruptive or distressing to his 5-year-old son, suggesting that seeing his parents fighting was more troublesome for the child. He noted that, "Something needs to change. I was coasting before. Now, I'm feeling more and I'm unable to deal with it. I'm dissatisfied. Even if this way of coping is wrong, something good will come of it."

The therapist returned to Carl's feelings about ending treatment. The therapist noted that Carl had spoken of wanting to continue but had not broached asking whether this would be possible. He also recognized that Carl was not in a good place—in fact, he was more angry and disillusioned than he had been. The therapist conveyed curiosity that Carl has "so little reaction, so few feelings toward [him]." He suggested, "So much you are saying conveys, 'How can you throw me out at a time like this?'" Carl was reluctant to acknowledge anger toward his therapist even though he seemed to agree that it makes sense. "I have a hard time ... I can see I am acting in a way you'd want to come to my rescue. I am having quite a hard time convincing myself I am angry or disappointed at you. I can't get myself there."

Throughout the session, Carl was really not able to get in touch with feelings he may have had about ending therapy. He continued to speak of withdrawing, saying "only good could come of being apart from [his] wife," speaking of it as an "experiment" as though it was without any consequences. He used similar language speaking of the therapy ending: he feels he "should terminate in order to experience it" and "good could come" of seeing how he did on his own. "Who knows," he said, "maybe I'll find resources in myself." He pushed away the idea of disillusionment with therapy and the therapist, although at one point, he intellectually rationalized that, "Emotionally, it feels right to me that I should be abandoned. That's the natural flow of events."

Toward the end of the hour, the therapist explicitly expressed concern: "I'm concerned about how things are ending. There's a lot of uncertainty in your life." He cautioned Carl to "keep a sharp eye out for [your anger and disappointment] so you don't take it out on someone else." At this point, Carl acknowledged he would miss talking to the therapist if only as a "pressure valve." He then said, "Let me ask, can I continue?" Presumably because time was up, the therapist responded, "I would be happy to meet with you and discuss it." The therapist's concern for the patient became increasingly apparent as he repeated twice that he would like to hear from Carl regardless of whether he decided to continue.

The therapy ended on a sad note, seeming incomplete and unresolved. The therapist believed Carl's current distress and rejection of his wife and employee was connected to his disappointment, hurt, and anger about ending therapy. Carl was willing to consider this link, but he could not emotionally resonate with the idea. The therapist attempted, over several prior sessions, to address how ending therapy may have reactivated Carl's recurrent pattern of becoming dismissive and withdrawn in the face of experiencing rejection. Despite this, he was not able to disrupt the pattern. The therapist, however, did not explicitly link Carl's reactions to ending treatment to his CMP. What might have been the consequence if the therapist had said:

> We have learned about how you hold back expressing your feelings and needs when you feel so disappointed in your relationships. It seems our ending may be stirring your desires for closeness along with your intolerance of your emotional needs. Maybe we're seeing your old guard coming back. You are angry and critical and want to run away from people rather than feel the hurt of being disappointed. You are pushing everyone away, retreating into a pragmatic, intellectualized stance where relationships become an experiment for you to see how well you can function on your own. I'm concerned this will leave you lonely and dissatisfied again. Is there another way this could play out? Perhaps if we can pay attention to how hurt and angry you are that we are ending.

We cannot be sure that spelling out Carl's maladaptive ways of coping with hurt in relationships would have promoted a way to not only consolidate his insight, but also open the door for a new way of relating. Interactions in earlier sessions indicated that Carl had the potential to be receptive to examining his patterns of relating to others. Perhaps, if the therapist could have drawn on this, Carl may have been able to acknowledge the impact of the termination on him.

Anticipate the Reemergence of and Identify Strategies to Manage Difficulties

In order to enhance the patient's capacity to maintain treatment gains, the therapist should initiate relapse prevention planning, although with an interpersonal focus. The natural ambiguity and discontinuities inherent in relationships can fuel anxiety and disappointment. Carl's reaction to termination illustrates a tendency to return to old patterns of relating at times of distress. Therefore, discussing explicitly the maladaptive reactions to ending that the patient needs to be alert for is an important aspect of the termination process. It follows naturally from reviewing the patient's central interpersonal concerns and identifying changes in the patient's ways of relating. This discussion also involves reviewing interpersonal coping strategies the patient has learned in therapy so that she can use them for coping in the future without the therapist's help. Much is written about "internalization of the therapist" as a marker for termination. In this, the patient identifies with and incorporates as her own the therapist's capacities that foster adaptive functioning, such as reflection, inquiry, and hypothesis testing, as well as capacities for intimacy and mutuality in relationships.

Case Example: Louise, Part 2

Louise entered her last session with a different perspective on her relationships, particularly with her sister. She had already begun thinking about new possibilities for how she related with others and felt about herself. The therapist turned their attention to acknowledging the end of therapy and how Louise would maintain her therapeutic gains.

T:	This is our last session. Is that feeling comfortable?
Louise:	Well, I think it will have to. What options do I have? You tell me you're throwing me out there with all those other people. You already said, "Kid, you're on your own." (Laugh.) I'm serious, you told me that, and I'm going to be okay.
T:	Do you want to continue?
Louise:	I have been thinking about it. You said I could call you. I do feel like I need to take a break, like I'm Jonathon Livingston's seagull. I need to get out there. I may not need to return.
T:	You said before, "It feels like I made big changes, but what if they disappear?" as if the changes are magical, as if I am doing something to you. It's as if you are asking, "What if it doesn't sustain?" But my office won't disappear off the face of earth.
Louise:	We can take a break. If I feel I need to return, I will.
T:	How would you know?
Louise:	If I were feeling raw. If I began feeling very uncertain a lot of the time, I would say, "Uh-oh, I'm not functioning as I should."
T:	Yeh, it's a good sign to me that when you were hearing that litany that "no one likes me" and you were able to stop that. Oversimplifying is a real old habit. Talking yourself down, you hear enough of that it feels true.
Louise:	I'm not there yet. I think I've come pretty far. Yes. I'm thinking that I know that I needed to do the kind of, I'm gonna call it wringing out. You know, you can accumulate like in a washer,

you get all of this soap and you get all this water, and you just, before you can complete this thing, hang it out to dry, it's gotta be wrung out. I think I wrung out an awful lot of stuff, and I think that, I'm cleaner as a result. Um, my thought processes are still, the thought processes are still old processes. One thing that I caught just recently was that we had this person coming by our home during the wedding festivities, and he thought I was just great. He even wanted to come back. And I remember that I was preparing for him to come back to visit for another vacation, and I thought, "Oh, my goodness, I can't, you know, I can't go through this. I mean he's gonna discover that I'm dull and, you know, that I've got flaws, that I'm not this perfect person or something. That I might disappoint him in some way." This went through my head just [snapped fingers] like that. Just so automatic. Then, I thought, "And I suppose he doesn't have flaws, and I suppose he never has a dull moment in his life." You know, and it just kinda straightened that thing out. It was the one voice speaking to the other voice. And it's all automatic. And previously, I don't think I would've ever heard that second voice. All I would've heard is the first voice. And I think that's an automatic kinda thing that I'm more aware of, where I put myself down, where I put myself back, where I put myself in a position not in the best of standing, you know, I put myself way down here.

T: It's a habitual, automatic sort of thing. But you are apparently less likely to just listen to that first voice.

Louise: Most assuredly. As a matter of fact, I'm almost looking for that first automatic voice that says, "Oh, no, you're not good enough. Oh no, you can't do this. Oh, no, you're gonna fail. Oh, no, you're inadequate. Oh, yes, you're dull." I'm looking for that.

Louise turned her attention back to her older sister and her regrets at expressing her anger at her sister.

Louise: I find it difficult because I have a tendency to protect people, unless they get to me. I really gave it to her. Then I felt bad about reacting that way. She rubbed me the wrong way. I was ruffled and hated being ruffled.

T: I think you will get better at setting limits in a calmer way. I think with practice, it's going to feel more and more legitimate without having to be angry or upset to do it.

Louise: I knew I lost it and I didn't want to. I wanted to give a calm response. I didn't like my reaction because I was flustered. I don't like that feeling. It's a little out of control feeling. It's a feeling of defense. I didn't want to feel that way.

T: You needed her to hear what you had to say.

Louise: I couldn't get a simple message across. Well, in a way I hate not coming back next week (crying). In a way. I'm not going to see you again (crying). Hey you laugh at my jokes. It's been good, a good experience

T: It's a loss.

Louise: I haven't lost everything. You know, I don't want to be in my doctor's office every single week. I don't want to have to take the car to the shop every week to be fixed. These are professionals that I need from time to time And I feel the same way about you. I don't wanna feel like I must come to see you each and every week. Yet if I need to talk with you to clarify some issue, I want to be able to call you up and come in. And I do know if I need to, I can call and come in.

T: As sad as it is to lose this, because this is a relationship in which you have felt safe and honest and accepted. If you can translate this into other relationships, then it really is okay to lose this.

Louise: Because you can't go shopping with me, have lunch, or come over.

BRINGING CLOSURE TO THERAPY

It is important to say goodbye even when a patient feels ready to end. Carrying out the last session as though it is no different than any other session denies the relationship the patient and therapist have shared. It leaves the therapy unfinished. As we have noted, it is important to actively address termination, leaving time for an extended discussion of the patient's experiences in treatment and expectation of being without therapy. In the following case example, the patient discussed how she had changed over the course of therapy and her greater awareness of her needs and desires in relationships

Case Example: Dana

Dana, a 41-year-old woman, sought therapy for depression, describing that she was frequently crying and experiencing episodes of anxiety. She described feeling lonely and sad, seeing herself as "needy" in her relationships with men, despite valuing independence. She described feeling panicky and overwhelmed, as though she was out of control. She was troubled by times she felt she would "freeze" and her mind would go totally blank, particularly at work. As a result, she became acutely self-conscious and concerned with how others perceived her, believing they thought of her as "stupid" or incompetent. She noted that her increasing insecurity and expectations of negative judgments from others were interfering with her work performance and relationships.

Dana was in a 4-year relationship that she described as nonmonogamous. Initially, she maintained that she preferred a nonmonogamous relationship because it allowed her to have sexual relationships with other men (it turned out these were primarily married men with whom she could feel needed and important). However, Dana experienced significant anxiety when her boyfriend sought other women; she devalued herself in comparison, commenting about one potential rival, "This woman is everything I would like to be and who I think should be with my boyfriend." As Dana acknowledged her feelings of jealousy and self-doubt, she became more attuned to her desires for a stable, committed relationship. Dana described, "I was thinking something was wrong with me because I want more. I realize I am not wrong to want more. He may not want it, but I want it." She ended this relationship around the midpoint of therapy as she acknowledged and accepted as legitimate her disappointment and desire for more. Dana noted that her significant anxiety and sadness disappeared when she ended her relationship. She described feeling "free," as though a barrier were lifted.

In therapy, Dana was able to identify parallels between her relationships with her parents and her boyfriend. She recognized how hard she tried to "get it right" so that her boyfriend would not withdraw. She noted, "I know I wouldn't have walked away from the relationship if I hadn't been looking at how I interacted with people in my life, especially my parents." Initially, she believed she had a "perfect childhood." With time, she realized that she felt her parents' love was always conditional, describing that "on the surface they were very loving, but also very critical." She felt like she was never good enough for her father or mother. She described trying to please her father, but felt "there really wasn't a connection. I guess I was interpreting that as my fault. I wanted it. If I just did the right thing, it would happen. I guess I didn't do the right thing, and it didn't happen." She saw that when her boyfriend would "pull away," she felt the same way, "Next time I'll do it right." She also described feeling very conscious of what she would talk about with him, describing that she "always smiled, never got angry." She maintained her façade, but felt she "was a different person."

In understanding Dana's CMP, it appears that Dana very much wanted acceptance and love from others, but she expected her needs to be rebuffed and neglected. She often felt inadequate and not good enough for others, and ashamed for wanting more than others would give her. As a result, she worked very hard to please others and fulfill what they wanted from her, even at the cost of her own needs. In doing so, she minimized, ridiculed, or outright denied her own needs and desires for attention. She was pleasing to others, always smiling and agreeable; consequently, others continued to pursue their own interests and neglected her. She was left feeling ashamed, lonely, and incompetent as she denied her anger and resentment at always taking care of others without concern for herself.

At termination, Dana arrived to her last session with news that she has gotten back together with her boyfriend. She described feeling oddly "calm" and suggested that she was able to clearly ask for what she needed from the boyfriend, beginning with a monogamous relationship. In reviewing her experiences, Dana genuinely experienced significant change in her ways of relating to her boyfriend and to others. She described a sense of well-being and control that enabled her to get what she needed in relationships.

> I feel calm, in control, not a lot of highs or lows. I appreciate that I feel I can be in control. Everything fell into place. I think it's me. I'm not reacting as much; I'm not afraid. I'm amazed at how calm I am. The sense of security I brought about. I'm not dependent on anyone else.... I just really feel it's like being a new person, something has fallen away, maybe shedding skin and really getting to the core. I really look at it as a sense of calm. Just kind of experiencing things, events, people and not seeing them as a threat.

Dana no longer felt insecure and unworthy. She surrounded herself with a select few relationships that she valued rather than feeling she needed the affirmation of as many people the she could get it from.

I don't need a lot of people around. I have some very close friends. I don't feel like I need people to like me. That's different from before. I'm seeing the world in different way. People are running around out there, chasing something. If you're lucky, you can move away from that. It doesn't mean you're not involved in that but it doesn't really reflect on who you are. Not as much is at stake. I'm there, interacting. My perceptions of it are real important but, others' are not as important, so it frees me up.

Dana was also aware of how she could slip back into former ways of thinking about herself and others, but she was able to "talk [her]self through it." This discussion likely helped solidify her therapeutic gains.

What I did was accept myself. How people interact with me, that's their problem. I really see it that way. Past conditioning—I slip back into that, but can talk myself through that. I see my parents; I appreciate, respect, they did their best. I see how they interact with my daughter and can see how I would have interpreted their behavior. I don't get upset about it. It just is. I don't have any expectations for them. In my relationship, the difference is I have expectations and I'm not afraid to say what I need to have happen. I really try to gauge that and see if my needs are being met. I am fortunate in that he cares enough about me and loves me enough. He worked through things. It's a totally different relationship. [What is different?] I listen to myself and how I feel. I don't try to talk myself out of it. If I'm feeling something, it's not right or wrong, but there. Not that he has to go along with what I want, but at least he has to acknowledge that I am feeling this, just like I do. Then we deal with it, he doesn't have to do what I say.... I needed him to meet a lot of my needs, and then felt guilty because I wanted that. Now, I don't feel needy, I just feel like I am.

The therapist asked Dana about her experience of therapy and the therapist. Dana mused,

It's amazing, in a lot of ways I would feel nothing was happening, it was waste of time. Then, all of sudden, I would come away and it was accumulation of different sessions that I realized where we going with this. I think you really helped me. Almost like a mirror. You didn't give me a lot of advice. I know that, sometimes, I was upset about that. I wanted answers. But you helped me, almost forced me into looking into myself for answers. That was frustrating sometimes.

Dana began to articulate what was helpful in her therapy, but she was amazed that she could change so much with just "short, 50 minute" sessions. She could not recall the specifics of her sessions and felt afraid at times that her depression may once again overtake her.

Dana: It was really being able to look at myself, my actions, and feelings, all those different aspects. It was okay to feel. You encouraged me to look at my feelings. First, to accept them, then to say what does that say about me, to learn about myself? In the short, 50 minutes, it was really amazing. I wish I could remember. [Remember?] I don't recall what we talked about. I remember episodes but not the specifics, actual conversations, the dialogue. I wish I could so I'd have it as a safeguard. I carry this fear. It [her depression] happened so suddenly, I let it happen. Guess I could not let it happen.

T: How did you feel now that it is time to stop?

Dana: It's okay, I think things were kind of dragging. It's probably time. I got back with [boyfriend] so I probably could use a few more sessions. I want to know how much I can fall back on what I learned about myself. [Like a test?] I don't know a test so much as an awareness. I am really aware I am not going to let it happen.... I will be watching for anything that doesn't feel the way I want it to.

Generally speaking, reviewing the patient's experience of therapy offers an opportunity to solidify insight and change. Inviting an explicit dialogue about what was helpful in therapy and how it was helpful can help demystify the therapy process. This can help a patient feel more secure that she will carry forth her stronger sense of self and more adaptive capacities for relationships. For the patient, the end of therapy is also a beginning.

NOTE

1. This case of Carl was discussed at length in Binder (2004).
2. Twenty-five sessions were dictated by the protocol of the Vanderbilt Psychotherapy Research Project of which Carl was a patient/subject.

10

Practicing BDP with Cultural and Ethical Sensitivity

Psychotherapy occurs within personal, relational, and cultural contexts. These contexts inevitably introduce complex, interwoven ethical and diversity considerations that demand a therapist's attention. These contexts also influence how both patient and therapist may approach interpersonal experiences, define what is necessary for a "good life," and view one's obligations and desires. In this chapter, we consider how such personal and contextual dimensions inform and impact a therapist's ethical and culturally competent engagement with patients.

This chapter addresses the essential clinical competencies associated with ethical and cultural sensitivity.

Practicing with Ethical Sensitivity

This clinical competency involves the ability to engage in treatment with caring and respect for patients. Ethically sensitive practice involves the ability to recognize how a therapist's personal and professional values influence ethical and clinical decisions; to use therapeutic power and influence to preserve the patient's welfare, inspire understanding and change, and foster the patient's agency; and to manage therapist self-disclosure and countertransference to prevent nontherapeutic enactments.

Practicing with Cultural Sensitivity

This clinical competency involves recognizing that assumptions about psychological health and development and psychotherapy are culturally embedded; discerning how to convey our values of mental health in a way that is relevant to a patient's worldview and cultural commitments; and accounting for a patient's culture, social and familial contexts, and values when developing a case formulation and when implementing treatment interventions.

THE ETHICS OF PRACTICE: A RELATIONAL–CONTEXTUAL APPROACH

We begin with two assumptions at the heart of a relational–contextual approach to ethics (Betan, 1997):[1] (a) Given the basic objective of psychotherapy as a helping relationship, ethical considerations are inherent to every aspect of clinical practice; and (b) the therapist's moral and personal sensibilities inevitably inform clinical practice and create the context for ethical and cultural considerations in treatment.

First, ethical dilemmas can arise out of any therapeutic circumstance and present a host of complex questions about how to intervene. Furthermore, conflicting obligations often arise as a result of the interpersonal and subjective demands of clinical practice. In psychotherapy, we are dealing with the nuances and ambiguities of developing a particular kind of relationship that involves unique issues around power, influence, intimacy, and mutuality. There are clear examples of ethical violations in our field that appear explicitly in the ethics codes of professional disciplines (e.g., sexual misconduct). However, the subtle ethical nuances of therapeutic engagement require greater attention, as does the fact that therapists make ethical decisions with each clinical intervention. Exploring the particular pulls in psychotherapy around potentially conflicting obligations is fundamental to making ethical decisions and implementing ethical action.

The defining element of professional ethics is that psychotherapists must treat people with caring, dignity, and a sense of mutual respect. Fundamentally, a therapist's ethical sense involves how she defines what is good and necessary in human life and how she applies her assumptions to benefit other persons. It involves the awareness that one's actions and relationships with others carry moral significance. Thus, one's ethical stance reflects sensibilities about how to be connected to and treat others. Furthermore, ethics reflect values and assumptions about human life that are contextual and culturally bound. So, the significance and meaning of ethical considerations are likely to shift with context and changing modes of relating. As such, therapists must develop a moral sense about their own subjective responses to the unique and often difficult and ambiguous relational context of psychotherapy.

ETHICS OF RELATEDNESS, BOUNDARIES, AND INTIMACY IN TREATMENT

As a relational treatment, issues regarding relatedness, boundaries, and intimacy are essential aspects of the responsibilities associated with ethical practice of BDP. *Power and influence, therapist's disclosures in psychotherapy, and countertransference* are aspects of therapist functioning that are significantly influenced by subjective and relational pulls that impact ethical conduct and are apt to present challenging ethical concerns.

Power and Influence in Psychotherapy

When considering dimensions of power in psychotherapy, it is important to keep in mind that psychotherapy involves a necessary hierarchy and asymmetry. First, seeking help from another creates an inevitable asymmetry in the relationship. The patient who brings emotional pain, needs, wishes, and hopes is more vulnerable than the therapist. This asymmetry helps preserve the boundaries of the therapeutic relationship and necessitates the therapist's responsibility above all to provide help to the patient. The therapist must protect the therapeutic frame, paying close attention to boundaries of time and space, roles, and therapeutic objectives, as well as the impact of one's interactions with a patient. Furthermore, the patient must feel secure that the therapist is committed to and capable of handling whatever emerges in the treatment, for the benefit of the patient.

The specialized training of the therapist also contributes to the asymmetry of the therapeutic relationship and the therapist's potential for influence. Therapists often hold capacities that patients have not yet developed, such as the ability to label feelings, make sense of experiences, construct meaning, and see potentials lost to the patient. In the absence of such capacities in the patient, these everyday functions of a therapist are powerful because they can help foster the patient's growth. In this regard, the therapist's power rests in his or her ability to hold a broad vision of the patient's potentials and relate in such a way as to actualize these potentials by encouraging self-expression and deeper knowledge of oneself and others. The struggles that bring patients to therapy result, in part, from difficulties in sustaining a meaningful and full sense of self rooted in secure relational experiences. Thus, embedded in the therapeutic process is a hope and need to find out whether one is acceptable. The ethical obligation of the BDP therapist is to always be negotiating how she uses her influence to make it possible for a patient to develop a vital and capable sense of self and actualize healthy strivings.

Power and influence emerge in subtle and delicate ways in the unique interaction between therapist and client. How a therapist participates in the therapeutic relationship reflects an ethical and clinical stance with regard to the impact she hopes to have on a patient. A therapist may be relatively more distant or overtly friendly, active or quietly involved/passive, directive or collaborative, accepting or judgmental, or timid or forceful in interacting with a patient. How a therapist interacts may be influenced by multiple sources, motivations, and intentions having to do with the therapist's personality style, theoretical orientation, reaction to the patient, or effort to accommodate the patient's relational style and needs at that moment. On a more problematic side, a therapist's use of power and influence may have little to do with the patient's welfare and more to do with the therapist's desires, interests, or needs.

Essential to ethical conduct is engaging the patient in such a way as to preserve the patient's welfare, inspire understanding and change, and foster the patient's agency. It is important always to keep in mind that the therapist holds the potential to dominate and to influence precisely because of the goals of the therapeutic encounter. In this regard, it is important to keep in mind the fact that the therapist inevitably influences a patient's values, and empirical evidence confirms that values are deeply involved in the therapeutic process (Bergin, 1991; Beutler & Bergan, 1991). It is necessary, however, to distinguish between essential therapeutic or mental health values and personal, religious, moral, or cultural values (Strupp, 1980; Tjeltveit, 1986). The therapist must guard against displaying moralistic judgments and imposing her own values in ways that limit a patient's freedom to choose and assert his or her own values. As such, it is incumbent upon therapists to be aware of their own values and distinguish moral values from those of therapeutic relevance in any given context. In addition, therapists need to know how to handle values and value-laden issues that are bound to emerge in treatment.

Therapist Disclosure in Psychotherapy

Recognizing that the therapist is an active participant in the therapeutic relationship with her own worldview, assumptions, needs, and desires, it is inevitable that a therapist will reveal something of himself to the patient. Modern dynamic/interpersonal approaches allow for the use of intentional and planned disclosures as a means of facilitating the treatment process by deepening the patient's awareness of his or her impact on another. Therapist disclosure can involve sharing emotional reactions, motivations, or immediate experience of the patient in the context of an ongoing relationship. This type of disclosure is different from the therapist's disclosure of personal information, whether biographical information, life events, or emotional/psychological experiences. Such disclosures also may serve therapeutic purposes in the appropriate contexts. The intent of therapist disclosure ideally rests with introducing something new to the patient that will enhance exploration, create possibilities for different ways of viewing one's self and others, and advance the therapeutic goals. It is not for the therapist to receive comfort for, recognition of, or relief from her own struggles. We suggest several practice guidelines for a therapist's disclosure:

1. *Ensure that the disclosure is for the patient's benefit, first and foremost.* A therapeutic relationship is defined by the fact that one participant is seeking help from another who offers such help. As with any intervention, therapists must make the decision to disclose while keeping in mind the ethical obligations of preserving a patient's welfare and maintaining a therapeutic focus. In this regard, although disclosing personal struggles could serve to normalize experience or highlight possibilities for change, it is a more risky disclosure. With any disclosure, the therapist's need to be known or validated may override the patient's welfare. For example, noting that one feels ineffectual in the face of the patient's criticism could be more about the therapist's need to get out of the "hot seat" than an effort to explore the patient's immediate concerns. It all depends on the tacit interpersonal message conveyed along with the disclosure.

2. *To increase the likelihood that the therapist's disclosure holds primarily therapeutic benefit, have a clear, well-developed rationale for the disclosure prior to engaging in it.* Impulsive disclosures are often problematic as the therapist may shift or blur boundaries without having time to consider the impact on the patient. However, sometimes therapists spontaneously disclose, evoked by an intense interaction with the patient and the disclosure proves useful. In either case, it is very important to discuss the disclosure, working toward an understanding of its impact on the patient.

Case Example: Dr. Collins

Dr. Collins was experiencing her patient as aloof and withdrawn in a familiar way that typically emerged after the patient shared something meaningful and intimate about himself. Dr. Collins had pointed out this pattern several times. In this session, however, Dr. Collins found herself more disengaged and bored, as well as feeling pessimistic that pointing out the pattern again would have an impact. Pondering her sense of boredom as the patient described his weekly activities in an obsessional manner, Dr. Collins considered that her reaction might be helpful in understanding the patient's chronic sense of alienation from others. She spontaneously elected to tell her patient her thoughts: "We have talked about how you often pull back after you've been more open with me, and I think this is happening again today. You shared your feelings quite openly last session. But, something else is happening that I think would be helpful to share with you. I am also feeling like I have withdrawn from you. This is new for me, and I wonder if it could tell us something about what happens in other relationships when you feel others are so disconnected from you."

In this case example, has Dr. Collins clearly considered a clinical rationale for this intervention, or did it emerge more from her sense of frustration and impotence? While her withdrawal in the face of her patient's detachment triggered the disclosure of her feelings, it is imperative to consider how the patient may feel in response.

3. *Keep in mind that the impact of a disclosure cannot be known in advance.* A patient may have a very different experience of the disclosure than the therapist has, or intended. A patient may experience a therapist's disclosures as intrusive, exploitative, or seductive, for example. It is very important to remain acutely attuned to how a patient receives

and takes in the disclosure. In the example above, Dr. Collins made the judgment that her patient would be open to hearing and be able to tolerate the immediacy of the therapist's experience of him as opposed to speaking of his relationships from a distance. However, the patient may not have been ready for such intimacy and may have experienced Dr. Collins's comments as blaming and rejecting. It would be important for Dr. Collins to ask the patient how he heard her comment, opening up the possibility for exploration and reconciliation.

4. *The therapist should consider whether he would want others to know what and why he disclosed to the patient.* If a therapist is reluctant to reveal the disclosure to colleagues, this is a clear signal that the disclosure may not be in the best interests of the patient or the therapy. In fact, a wish to conceal what was said may point to a pressing need for consultation, ideally prior to the self-disclosure. Shame and anxiety following a disclosure also indicate the importance of gaining clarity about what is occurring in the treatment.

Countertransference: Exploration, Reflection, and Enactments

Maintaining ethical integrity in psychotherapy depends on the careful monitoring of one's responses, pulls, and motivations in interaction with a patient. The interpersonal demands of psychotherapy inevitably trigger the potential for projections, distortions, identifications, and pulls that can threaten the therapist's ethical judgment. The therapist's ability to be aware of, reflect on, and ultimately override personal investments, needs, wishes, and desires is at the basis of ethical conduct. This involves a therapist's capacity and willingness to look honestly at her reactions to patients that inevitably will touch her own deeply rooted fears, meanings, and values.

Facing countertransference feelings can be quite threatening for the therapist. Getting close to one's feelings about a patient may put a therapist in touch with terrible feelings of hate, seductive feelings of love and desire, or overwhelming feelings of dread, despair, and impotence. However, those feelings that remain unknown or disavowed are most likely to disrupt the therapist's ethical stance and capacity to work effectively with a patient. The impact of the therapist's unacknowledged experience can be seen in disruptions of the therapeutic alliance, therapeutic stalemates, or enactments that threaten the therapeutic frame.

Countertransference reactions are both a reflection of the therapist's intrapsychic conflict or unresolved issues, as well as an indication of the relational dynamics between therapist and patient. In this regard, a therapist's reactions can provide hints to understanding the patient's internal experience and how the patient's conflicts influence his or her ways of being and relating with others. Putting her feelings and responses in the context of what is happening with the patient can help promote empathic connection with a patient's experience (Betan & Westen, 2009). Achieving this perspective requires well-developed capacities for reflection and self-awareness.

Reflection and self-awareness—stepping back from immediate experience and thinking about one's beliefs, feelings, and desires that may be motivating one's behaviors at the moment—are critical for regulating strong feelings. In addition, paying attention to triggers and patterns in one's reactions to patients can give hints to what is so troubling or destabilizing. Once the therapist is able to honestly reflect on her reactions, she is more likely to be able to direct the treatment rather than respond unwittingly to personal pressures and interpersonal pulls. The therapist must be open to her experiences and reflect on how her reactions are motivated by both distinctly personal needs and the interpersonal context shared with the patient. This is key to managing countertransference responses ethically.

Therapists have strong reactions toward patients. Patients with personality pathology are more likely to elicit powerful feelings on the part of the therapist that can be quite disruptive and disturbing for the majority of therapists (Betan, Heim, Conklin, & Westen, 2005). Table 10.1 offers clearly delineated, empirically derived descriptions of typical countertransference responses that therapists have toward patients. These descriptions offer a framework for conceptualizing countertransference reactions that can help therapists make sense of what can be disruptive, confusing, and even indiscernible feelings toward patients (Betan & Westen, 2009). Our intent is to promote reflection and self-awareness by normalizing a range of reactions toward and feelings about patients.

Recommendations for Monitoring and Maintaining Ethical Conduct

The discussion so far recognizes the therapist as an active agent in influencing the therapeutic process. We have emphasized the importance of self-monitoring and self-reflection. However, much can still remain outside a therapist's awareness, and enactments are bound to occur. In this regard, we offer the following recommendations for ensuring ethical conduct:

Table 10.1   Categories of Typical Countertransference Reactions

1. *Overwhelmed/Disorganized*: Therapists may experience strong negative feelings, including dread, anger, repulsion, resentment, toward their patients that lead to a desire to avoid or flee the patient, terminate treatment, or enforce rigid boundaries.

2. *Helpless/Inadequate*: Feelings of inadequacy, incompetence, hopelessness, and anxiety are typical reactions among therapists working with patients who have difficulty settling into treatment or building an alliance.

3. *Positive*: Often, therapists enjoy and like a patient and may look forward to sessions, as well as feel excited about and satisfied by their work with a patient.

4. *Special/Overinvolved*: Therapists may feel particularly responsible for a patient, leading to boundary crossings such as increased self-disclosure, extending sessions, feeling guilty or overly concerned about the patient.

5. *Sexualized*: Therapists may experience sexual attraction and arousal, as well as engage in flirtatious behavior with patients.

6. *Disengaged*: Therapists may feel distracted, withdrawn, annoyed, or bored in sessions.

7. *Parental/Protective*: Therapists may wish to protect and nurture the patient in a parental way, above and beyond normal positive feelings toward the patient.

8. *Criticized/Mistreated*: Feeling unappreciated, dismissed, or devalued by the patient is typical for many therapists, as are feelings of anger and judgment in response to feeling mistreated.

Adapted from Betan, Heim, Conklin, and Westen (2005).

1. *Consultation* is at the heart of competent and ethical practice. Every therapist is bound to encounter a patient, clinical situation, or ethical dilemma that arouses one's anxiety, challenges one's ability to perform effectively, or disrupts one's clinical or moral judgment. It is imperative to have a professional support network and seek consultation periodically in one's career, and most importantly, at points of professional uncertainty.

2. *Self-care* involves recognizing and attending to one's vulnerabilities that may disrupt one's ability to provide competent services. The potential for isolation, burnout, or boundary crossings increases as therapists neglect their own emotional, psychological, physical, and

spiritual needs outside of their professional functioning. Self-care may involve proper nutrition, sufficient rest, physical exercise, emotional and spiritual nurturance, leisure activities and hobbies, and preserving connections with family and friends.

3. *Personal psychotherapy* is one avenue of self-care. The competent and mature professional recognizes personal vulnerabilities and proactively addresses distress by seeking psychotherapy. In addition, personal psychotherapy in pursuit of self-exploration will help increase a therapist's awareness of values, biases, needs, and distress that are apt to disrupt professional competence.

PRACTICING WITH CULTURAL SENSITIVITY

The growing diversity of American society and cultural populations is an inevitable consequence of the increasing mobility, technology, and knowledge that have made cross-cultural interchange possible. We cannot assume homogeneity of culture, experience, and value systems and must be prepared to confront diversity and difference in clinical practice. There is an ever-growing need to connect with a broader patient population and establish modes of treatment that fit with what patients most need and value. As therapists interact with individuals whose cultural[2] experiences and expectations differ from their own, there is an ethical obligation to understand diverse meanings of experience in different settings, as well as to reconceptualize treatment and the views of patients and ourselves in this context of diversity.

Assumptions about psychological health and development and psychotherapy are culturally embedded. Although couched in the formality of theory and empiricism, at the foundation, theoretical assumptions reflect values and beliefs about what is necessary and good for human life. Major Western psychological theories and approaches have prioritized selfhood and autonomy, a direct reflection of an individualistic culture (Roland, 1996). Personal achievement and asserting personal needs (Cushman, 1990) become measures of psychological health, and, independence has been identified as a therapeutic value (Strupp, 1980). More collectivist cultures do not share this idea of a highly boundaried self whereby identity is personal and distinct from others. For example, autonomy is a Western ideal and may be irrelevant or relevant in a different way for an Asian or Latino/a patient's sense of self and priorities in life.

Patients may bring very different standards that guide their psychological growth, and bridging this gap is a key to ethical and culturally competent practice. Being sensitive to a patient's differing cultural view highlights the importance of respecting individuals "on and in the terms they themselves define. The critical question is how others wish to be respected" (Meara et al., 1996, p. 44). These fundamentally ethical dimensions of respect and recognition are at the foundation of culturally responsive practice and are apt to emerge in a context of cultural differences between therapist and patient. Yet, even in the context of perceived cultural similarities, therapists must remain aware of how their assumptions may cloud or obscure their ability to fully understand the patient.

In addition, working with patients who do not share the therapist's cultural assumptions may involve negotiating boundaries, goals, and expectations in treatment differently (Frame & Williams, 2005; Hays, 2007). The typical frame of psychotherapy—45 or 50 minute sessions in a professional office with minimal interaction outside of the therapeutic focus—reflects a cultural perspective about what belongs in psychotherapy. Typical boundaries around time and place, fees, extratherapeutic contact, and therapist self-disclosure may be placed into question with patients from diverse cultural backgrounds. For example, the notion of psychotherapy itself, that is, to seek help from a professional outside of the family or community, is fitting to Western culture. However, individuals from many other cultures may rely instead on family or spiritual leaders for help (Comas-Diaz, 2006). Furthermore, the traditional Western mode of psychotherapy does not usually incorporate spiritual or mystical explanations and interventions. Yet, in working with culturally diverse patients, involving the extended family in treatment or consulting a spiritual leader may indeed be fundamental to offering culturally responsive treatment. The therapist's willingness to learn and adapt treatment to what the patient needs is at the core of culturally responsive treatment.

A CULTURALLY SENSITIVE
FORMULATION OF THE CMP

Not only might a therapist's interventions change in working with culturally diverse patients, but also one's understanding of what troubles a patient must incorporate relevant cultural considerations. In developing a culturally sensitive formulation of the CMP, a culturally competent therapist pursues an integrative approach, considering both psychological (intrapsychic) and cultural dimensions in understanding a patient's difficulties. A comprehensive case conceptualization will reflect both cultural and individual dynamics, not as separate dimensions of one's identity and functioning but as interrelated. Appreciating how cultural upbringing and sociopolitical factors (discrimination or oppression, for example) may impact or shape psychological functioning is imperative to culturally and ethically competent practice.

Case Example: Amy

Amy was a 25-year-old, Chinese American, lesbian woman who felt anxious and lonely much of the time and described feeling uncertain about her place in the world. Born in the United States to parents who emigrated from China as adults, Amy straddled two cultural worlds that, in her experience, barely overlapped. Despite being raised in a traditional Chinese home, Amy saw herself as more American than Chinese; however, she struggled with the disconnection from her parents that this had created. Her parents remained relatively isolated from American culture and, as a result, knew very little English. In fact, this language barrier was pivotal to Amy's sense of estrangement from her parents and subsequent sense of guilt and loneliness. Because her parents did not speak English, Amy noted that she could not tell them of her lesbian identity because she literally did not know the words in Chinese to convey this. She effectively had no way to convey a core aspect of her sense of self, leaving her feeling alienated and invisible. Amy wanted her parents to know of this aspect of her identity, but she believed her parents would be unaccepting. Disappointing her parents brought a profound sense of shame that echoed her Chinese values of familial loyalty, obedience, and reflecting well on the family.

This sense of shame and anxiety carried into Amy's interactions with others. She felt inadequate and estranged from others, uncertain of how to bridge her disparate cultural affiliations. She struggled to allow herself to express interest in other women despite being generally open about her sexual identity. She attempted to hide her deep Chinese roots in perfectly articulated English and distinctly American fashion. Still, her physical appearance was not something she could change, and she could not imagine herself as attractive to others.

Cyclical Maladaptive Pattern (CMP)

Amy's key interpersonal challenges revolved around hiding for fear of rejection. She wished to be free to openly identify as a lesbian woman and to feel true to herself. This would have allowed her to pursue a romantic relationship. She also wished to feel a sense of belonging in both her family and the lesbian community. However, Amy expected to be rejected, misunderstood, and shamed. She recognized that there would be little room in her Chinese culture and family for her identity as a lesbian. She could only hope for her parents' tolerance, but only if she could find a way to communicate with them.

As a result of these expectations, in hopes of tempering her sense of loss and disconnection, Amy invested much energy in compartmentalizing her disparate identities, hiding aspects of her self that she believed would invite rejection and shame. With her family, she felt a strong obligation to uphold her cultural values and avoided bringing pain to her parents. In social interactions with others, Amy appeared shy and aloof as she inhibited expressing herself and reaching out to others. Consequently, Amy experienced others as uninterested in her. She experienced other women as bored with her and uninterested in pursuing further contact. At home, Amy felt unknown and experienced her parents' assumptions about her as her parents' efforts to control her. She showed very little of herself to others and, as a result, they treated her as though she was shallow or ineffectual. This left her feeling inadequate, angry, and anxious as she anticipated being alone and estranged, because she believed that her alternatives to hiding—coming out to her parents and pursuing a relationship—would both bring her shame and rejection.

Cultural and social variables are woven into this CMP as they account for the roots of the patient's difficulties. There are a few key points to be highlighted with regard to developing a culturally sensitive case formulation. First, to avoid misunderstanding and mistakenly attributing a patient's beliefs or behaviors to a psychological disturbance, it is helpful to first consider the degree to which cultural expectations may account for the patient's presentation. Names for and the understanding of distress, as well as how to relieve distress, are culturally defined. When faced with behaviors or experiences that may not fit neatly into formal diagnostic constructs, therapists are vulnerable to pathologizing that which they do not recognize or understand. The use of diagnostic constructs may either promote understanding of and empathy for a patient or be used in ways that are condescending, critical, or exploitative of patients. In this regard, working with culturally diverse patients may involve suspending customary diagnostic constructs and focusing instead on culturally relevant explanations of distress (Lewis-Fernandez & Diaz, 2002). For example, as we see in this case example, pronounced deference to others' opinions may not be about dependency as we understand it in the DSM-IV, but rather a reflection of cultural collectivism and familial piety.

Second, attending to a patient's level of acculturation and cultural identities is key to developing a culturally competent case conceptualization. Biculturalism (or multiculturalism), emerging from parallel paths of enculturation or later acculturation, can introduce distinct expectations for and modes of relating. As in the case example, a patient may have multiple, salient cultural identities that differentially influence her interpersonal patterns. We need to appreciate these multiple meanings and the impact on the individual working to balance or integrate diverse cultural pulls.

Finally, we need to appreciate the powerful hold of cultural and familial expectations. Many individuals are strongly rooted in cultural values and mores that bind them to their perceptions and behaviors in interpersonal interactions. What we may see as rigid behaviors or expectations may in fact be a cultural reality. Appreciating the potential for loss and alienation as an individual shifts away from her or his cultural roots is an important facet of culturally responsive case conceptualization and treatment.

NOTES

1. Betan originally referred to this as a "Hermeneutic Model of Ethical Decision Making," which also captured the contextual, emotional, and relational influences on ethical practice. The term *relational-contextual* more clearly communicates the intent of the model.
2. Culture may be thought of in broad terms as reflecting a community's shared background, worldview, and life experiences. Thus, as used here, culture encompasses a broad range of potential identities, including, for example, ethnicity, race, country of origin, socioeconomic class, religion, gender, sexual orientation, disability status, and age.

11

Becoming a Highly Competent and Effective BDP Therapist

Throughout this text, we have developed our narrative of psychotherapy, offering a description of how to begin, cultivate, and end what we hope has been a collaborative process of therapeutic change. At the heart of the therapeutic process in brief dynamic psychotherapy is the therapist's technical skill at developing and maintaining a productive inquiry and dialogue with her patient. This skill is inextricably combined with interpersonal skills as the foundation that supports all of the traditional clinical competencies. Each competency represents an important component of clinical practice, but standing alone would not be sufficient for effective clinical work. Furthermore, therapeutic competence cannot be understood as static or fixed given the contextual and subjective dimensions that influence the therapeutic task.

Psychotherapy is a multifaceted, relationally embedded process that is unique for every patient–therapist dyad. In this regard, although we may think of conducting psychotherapy as a performance domain, it is not a structured performance with clear rules, singular decisions, clearly demarcated actions, or immediately observable outcomes. Consequently, how we understand competent and effective practice cannot simply be defined in terms of adherence to an empirically supported protocol for a specific DSM disorder. Rather, psychotherapy represents a highly complex performance domain that demands an integration of skills, flexibility, and continuous reflection about the clinical encounter and one's reactions to it (Schön, 1983).

Compared to the importance of the topic for clinical practice, there is relatively little research on what constitutes effective training for the skills, knowledge, and attitudes that lead to competent therapist performance (Binder, 2004; Eells, Lombart, Kendjelic, Turner, & Lucas, 2005). We do not know enough about what kinds of instruction, supervision, and experiences in conducting psychotherapy contribute to a therapist's ability to intervene effectively and evaluate her work. However, a growing corpus of research on distinguishing novice from expert clinical performance on competencies such as case conceptualization (e.g., Eells et al., 2005) can help us identify those signposts of growing competency along the path of professional development.

DEFINING AND DEVELOPING COMPETENCY

Competence, as a general construct, refers to an evaluation that the therapist functions at an "average acceptable" level, meeting professional and ethical standards of practice as reflected in knowledge, skills, and attitudes (Kaslow, 2004). Knowledge refers to having a clear understanding of a conceptual foundation to guide one's clinical work. Knowledge is learned through formal training and independent study. Skills refer to abilities to apply basic knowledge, implement specific technical interventions, and select appropriate strategies in addressing clinical problems. Skills are developed through study, observation, formal instruction, deliberate practice, and feedback from supervisors and patients. Attitudes involve the therapeutic values and commitment to one's professional development that facilitate one's clinical work. Exploration of beliefs, values, and reactions that impact one's clinical experiences occurs in coursework, supervision, and life-long reflection.

In BDP, specifically, competence is marked by (a) knowledge of psychodynamic theories and research; (b) the ability to perform specific skills that effectively foster inquiry and dialogue in a manner marked by good judgment and flexibility; and (c) the capacity to function relatively independently, including the ability and willingness to evaluate and adapt one's performance. Highly competent practice in BDP may be distinguished from basic competence by the therapist's capacity and volition to deepen, adapt, and creatively use theoretical understanding and technical skills in ways that meet the unique needs and interpersonal style of the patient. This is similar to how Dreyfus and Dreyfus (1986) characterize the "proficient" practitioner in their model of skill acquisition. They define proficiency in terms of the ability to see the whole picture, distinguish relevant from irrelevant details, and make decisions based on a depth of understanding. The "expert" practitioner is proficient and, in addition, operates with more of an intuitive rather than analytic cognitive style. Her wealth of knowledge is organized in a way that allows relevant information to be rapidly and easily accessible to guide seemingly automatic behavior. The expert therapist is capable not only of being flexible but also of initiating highly creative responses to a fluid clinical context (Dreyfus & Dreyfus, 1986). The following sections provide descriptions and examples of therapists' functioning at different levels of competency in each of the three components of competency: knowledge, skills, and attitudes.

KNOWLEDGE AT DIFFERENT
LEVELS OF PROFICIENCY

We have emphasized the importance of having a well-developed, solid theoretical understanding of personality development, psychopathology, and therapeutic process that serves as a "conceptual map" (Binder, 2004, p. 80) to guide therapeutic understanding and action. Competence, however, is not merely the accumulation of knowledge. To be competent, a therapist must be able to adapt knowledge to address the unique therapeutic context and ultimately be helpful to a particular patient. Adapting knowledge to new clinical situations requires the transformation of declarative knowledge (e.g., the theories and techniques that are learned in texts and courses) into procedural knowledge (i.e., the knowledge of when and how to implement in action these theories, concepts, principles, and rules). If this knowledge transformation does not occur, the student/therapist may have impressive "locker room" knowledge—he or she may have memorized a set of mental rules or procedures to follow—but in actual clinical situations, the student/therapist will not rapidly, smoothly, and easily know what to do or when to do it. No matter how extensive his declarative knowledge, it will remain "inert" (Whitehead, 1929).

 The ability to use one's knowledge to competently guide clinical work requires that the student/therapist go beyond mere familiarity with facts and theories and achieve a sufficiently deep understanding of theoretical concepts that transforms the theory into one's own personal understanding. Making theory one's own in this way involves what we refer to as metabolizing theory (Betan & Binder, 2010). In learning a theory and technical interventions, highly competent therapists do not simply "swallow" knowledge and remain passive in their learning. Instead, they actively assimilate, synthesize, and transform their understanding in order to "bring to life" theoretical ideas and concepts. Metabolizing theory is the process of integrating theoretical concepts and clinical skills with personal style and values so they become an extension of the therapist as she engages in clinical work.

When theory remains detached from one's psychological and interpersonal sensibilities, it can significantly stifle or interfere with, rather than facilitate, clinical understanding and implementation of treatment. Theory that is not metabolized is not automatically available to guide the therapist's understanding and interventions. Instead, in a slow and deliberate manner, the therapist labors to make meaning of the patient's presentation and distress within the framework of a theory. Distracted by their efforts to apply theory, students and novices may fumble in their work with patients, often missing relevant clinical and interpersonal data as well as opportunities to deepen the alliance and enhance the treatment (Binder, 2004).

In contrast to novice and minimally competent clinicians, proficient and expert therapists have a command of theoretical concepts that shapes their understanding of new information. They see patterns in relationships or discrepancies that are not apparent to student/therapists. They can extract a level of meaning from clinical information that is not apparent to student/therapists because their conceptual understanding helps them select and remember relevant details. Deep conceptual understanding allows rapid, fluent access to stored information that is relevant to the immediate clinical context (Donovan, Bransford, & Pellegrino, 1999). The use of theory to deepen understanding of a specific clinical situation, as well as to guide flexible and creative interventions, becomes automatized: in other words, the knowledge becomes proceduralized. The therapist is able to develop more flexible, varied, and nuanced methods for working with a specific patient in a specific set of circumstances. Because so much of her adaptation of theory to the unique circumstances of the moment is automatic, the therapist is in a better position to engage effectively with her patient and to smoothly and rapidly adapt to changing circumstances.

Metabolized theory and clinical knowledge tacitly guide clinical understanding and therapeutic interventions. Under these conditions, the highly competent therapist possesses a conceptual framework to automatically process incoming information from the patient. We see a therapist's theoretical understanding reflected in how she thinks about the patient, the questions she asks the patient, the way she focuses interventions, and what she attends to in the course of treatment. The therapist who has metabolized theory is able to think and speak about a patient or the therapeutic process without getting bogged down in irrelevant details. She is able to apply abstract theoretical concepts in a way that is uniquely meaningful and relevant to each patient. This is not just a matter of how one speaks about the patient and the treatment, but also how one engages the patient in a collaborative process of therapeutic inquiry and dialogue.

Theory is a guide, but the therapist must transform abstract, externally defined concepts and knowledge into a therapeutic narrative that captures something meaningful and immediately felt for each individual patient. The therapist's understanding of the patient comes from the narrative that they have created together. Skills in building a therapeutic alliance and facilitating a therapeutic discourse are paramount, of course, but insufficient in the absence of a coherent and deep conceptual understanding of the patient and of the nature of the encounter between them. Theory needs to be in the background when we are with patients, but never absent.

The consequence of metabolizing theory and concepts for high level clinical performance also addresses the question of how knowledge is transferred from one clinical situation to another. The following vignettes are examples of therapists with different levels of knowledge proficiency.

Frank, a student/therapist with limited command of clinical knowledge interviews a young woman patient for the first time. He does a thorough review of her presenting problems and their history, a thorough developmental history and review of her significant relationships, her history of prior treatments, and a thorough mental status examination. Armed with this abundance of clinical information, including the direct observations that the patient acted in an inappropriately irritable manner and appeared oblivious to her mood or actions, Frank began to review the criteria for personality disorders. Eventually, he was satisfied that the patient met sufficient criteria to meet the diagnosis of borderline personality disorder. Subsequently, Frank interviewed another young woman and did a similar thorough evaluation. He observed that this woman appeared shy and a bit weepy. After the interview, he returned to his DSM-IV-TR and reviewed Axis I disorders of depression and anxiety. Unable to find sufficient criteria for an Axis I diagnosis, Frank reviewed Axis II personality disorders and found sufficient criteria for a diagnosis of borderline personality disorder. These two patients looked symptomatically different, and there was no reason, based on his superficial familiarity with criteria for each personality disorder, for Frank to assume a common diagnosis.

By contrast, Laura is in a better position to rapidly identify parallels between the two patients because she has metabolized major psychodynamic concepts concerning the nature, functioning, and development of a borderline personality disorder. Functioning at a high level of proficiency, Laura evaluates each patient along several personality dimensions, including stability of identity and self-image, maturity level of characteristic character defenses (e.g., intellectualization vs. splitting), stability of reality testing, quality of object relations, superego integration, and degree of trauma in their past, especially childhood. The first patient complained of a series of conflict-ridden relationships in which she continuously felt a sense of "emptiness," while the second woman described long periods of time between romantic relationships, during which she felt lonely and "empty." Laura conceptualized borderline personality disorder as reflecting, among other pathological traits and features, a serious deficit in identity stability, self-esteem regulation, and stable, positive internal object representations. All of these deficiencies can be associated with the sense of "emptiness" reported by the two women, who looked superficially quite different. Consequently, Laura, working with a clear theory of borderline personality disorder, was able to see parallel issues between the two patients that, at least, allowed her to use her experience of the first patient to accelerate the development of her understanding and strategy for intervening with the second patient.

Although we do not fully understand how highly competent therapists metabolize theory, we believe that it is an active, volitional, and effortful process. Reading and learning theory must be paired with actively identifying the applications of the theory in clinical contexts that are meaningful to the student/therapist. Furthermore, the therapist who puts theory into her own words, as well as identifying novel ways the theory may fit her experiences (personal and clinical), is more likely to be able to deeply understand relevant concepts and to be able to transform that understanding into procedural knowledge.

SKILLS AT DIFFERENT LEVELS OF PROFICIENCY

There are a set of interrelated skills necessary for conducting BDP. To provide treatment effectively, a therapist must have well-developed skills that are part of the competencies of assessment, diagnosis, case formulation, intervention, and treatment evaluation. Relationship skills are fundamental and cut across treatment approaches and patient–therapist dyads. Highly competent clinical performance depends on the therapist's capacity to integrate the skills associated with each type of competency.

In chapter 7 on therapeutic intervention, we highlight essential skills in fostering therapeutic inquiry and dialogue, including interpersonal pattern recognition, tracking a therapeutic focus, systematic, incisive questioning, empathic reflections, self-monitoring and self-regulation, and improvising. We have emphasized the therapist's ability to tell the patient's interpersonal story, a story that puts words to what is often implicit in a patient's repetitive interpersonal and symptomatic difficulties. Constructing such a narrative is a collaborative effort that depends on the therapist's success in inviting the patient to share his life experiences, eliciting relevant information, recognizing patterns in the patient's material, and fostering a patient's curiosity about other possibilities. The therapeutic dialogue in BDP involves tracking an overarching theme across a patient's relational stories. It is an essential conversation that not only increases a patient's understanding of his difficulties, but also transforms his feelings, beliefs, and ways of relating.

Skills of the novice therapist are demonstrated by Janice, a graduate student on her first therapy practicum. Janice is only beginning to develop skills in tracking a focused interpersonal story line, and she has a tendency to get distracted by her patient's concerns that are not relevant to this interpersonal pattern. For example, when Josh, a 30-year-old accountant who sought treatment for mild depression, was describing his critical and demanding father, he began to describe feeling distracted and insecure in his work. Janice turned her attention to Josh's difficulties completing his work, inquiring about his work habits and giving him time management advice. In doing so, Janice missed the opportunity to develop a potentially important interpersonal theme around expecting others' criticism and disappointment. With greater interpersonal pattern recognition skills and inquiry skills, Janice may have further explored Josh's experiences of his father and how versions of his expectations may be repeated in his relationships with other authority figures. This may have been a clue to his vulnerability to depression and insecurity. Additionally, Janice may have unwittingly conveyed criticism in her focus on Josh's work habits, thereby recapitulating Josh's maladaptive interpersonal relationships.

Developing skill in selectively attending to (and selectively neglecting) clinical material in terms of whether it is relevant to the patient's main interpersonal difficulties is a priority in achieving competency in BDP. The following vignette illustrates an adequate level of competency in practicing BDP. John, a licensed clinical psychologist who has been practicing for 6 years, was working with Susan, a 19-year-old female college student who presented with significant anxiety following the breakup with a controlling and hostile boyfriend. John invited Susan to speak about her recent relationship, as well as her experience of her early relationships with her parents. Using well-developed interpersonal pattern recognition skills, John was able to track an overarching theme across Susan's stories. He recognized the roots of Susan's anxiety in early insecure attachments that left her feeling uncertain whether she could take care of herself on her own. Drawing on his understanding of how early relational experiences influence later interpersonal and self-functioning, John was able to appreciate the extent of Susan's anxiety and identified salient themes of loss, loneliness, and self-doubt in her narratives. John's ability to recognize that Susan's salient maladaptive interpersonal mode of relating left her feeling insecure and vulnerable to mistreatment by others made it possible for him to connect empathically with her. John could then help Susan develop greater understanding of why her relationship breakup was so frightening for her, as well as help her begin to question her beliefs about her inadequacy and her willingness to tolerate mistreatment in relationships.

Competency in BDP involves skills in eliciting salient relationship episodes, tracking interpersonal patterns across stories, and empathically constructing a meaningful interpersonal narrative about the patient's difficulties. The ability to productively reflect on what guides one's clinical decisions and actions distinguishes highly competent practice (Betan & Binder, 2010; Binder, 2004; Hatano, 1982). Pamela, who has been in practice for decades and has written extensively on psychotherapy process and case conceptualization, illustrates a highly competent therapist. Pamela actively thinks about how theory has informed her case conceptualization by linking specific aspects of the conceptualization to theoretical constructs, even though her case conceptualizations are always jargon-free and highly individualized. Similarly, although Pamela's work with patients looks like a casual conversation to the outside observer, Pamela is tacitly aware of the theory or evidence-based practice guidelines that have informed her choice of therapeutic focus and specific interventions. Over time, highly competent therapists develop a conceptual framework for evaluating what is working and not working with a patient, and why this is so. They devote time to reflecting on a treatment and generating new understandings that guide their interventions. Through years of practice and critically evaluating her own work, Pamela has honed her ability to adapt to novel clinical situations. This has allowed her to be spontaneous and innovative in her interactions with patients. Nonetheless, each unique clinical encounter carries the mark of Pamela's theoretical framework and coherent approach to BDP practice.

ATTITUDES AT DIFFERENT LEVELS OF PROFICIENCY

In our view, highly competent therapists are committed to their professional development, aspiring to move beyond "average acceptable." This ambition is sure to be evident in a desire to continually learn, recognizing that one can expand and develop one's knowledge of clinical process and therapeutic interventions throughout professional life. Keeping up-to-date with and applying empirical and theoretical advances in evidence-based practice are basic to effective practice. Highly competent therapists also are likely to participate in peer supervision and consultation to hone their clinical skills throughout their careers. In addition, the willingness to continually evaluate one's effectiveness as a therapist, as well as acknowledge values and biases that may disrupt one's work, are hallmarks of highly competent practice.

Many student therapists enter training with the desire to help others, commitment to professional development, and capacities for self-awareness and self-reflection. These students are gems for training faculty because they are open to new ideas and also self-determined in their learning. Many other students, however, enter graduate training with an educational history characterized by passively absorbing sufficient information to pass a test rather than pursuing knowledge in order to enhance their understanding of a subject. For example, Justine entered graduate training in clinical psychology immediately following her graduation from college. She was bright and capable of producing high quality academic work as long as she had clear instructions. As a result, Justine stood out early in the program for her intelligence. With time, however, Justine began to struggle with more ambiguous assignments that required her to generate her own knowledge and ideas, such as clinical case formulations, reflective essays on cultural and ethical values that may impact her clinical work, and critical reviews of the literature. Justine was not used to "thinking on her own" or "thinking for herself," and, as a result, she was not invested in seeking knowledge outside of her assignments, did not even appreciate the importance of identifying what she did not know, and seemed to lack basic curiosity. This lack of reflection about her knowledge (thinking about what she knows and does not know) made it difficult for Justine to learn to do psychotherapy. Justine became increasingly anxious about her performance and also indignant about the critical feedback she received from instructors and supervisors. As a result, she began to close herself off from learning from her experiences with patients, becoming more rigid and concrete in her work. Helping Justine develop greater comfort with not knowing and also greater interest in pursuing knowledge on her own became a priority in her training.

Another example of a poor attitude that is not consistent with competent practice comes from a senior clinician who has practiced for decades. Alan worked in both private practice and agency settings and served as a clinic director, supervisor, and faculty member throughout his career. In a supervision setting, Alan remarked that he is no longer surprised by patients because, in 25 years of practice, he has already heard all the stories there are to tell. Alan was clearly bored with his work. He had lost his desire to help his patients, his curiosity in another human being's lived experience, and his personal sense of meaning in his clinical work. If at one time Alan valued his work and was committed to his professional development, he has strayed far away from those attitudes that ensure competent and ethical practice. His negative and nontherapeutic attitude negatively impacted his clinical work, supervision, and teaching.

Todd is an example of a professional who possesses attitudes that support activities that will enhance his competence. He recently finished postdoctoral training, obtained his license, and started seeing psychotherapy patients in private practice. He feels confident about his training, having received intensive supervision for a few years. Yet, Todd is aware he still has much to learn and still more experience to gain to further his knowledge and skills. He knows what he does not know, a sign that he has developed critical thinking skills and can evaluate his own knowledge and skill base. Todd has arranged to join a BDP supervision group in order to sharpen his skills in case conceptualization and intervention. He is looking forward to continuing to have a forum in which to share and reflect upon his work. Todd's approach to furthering his training shows his openness to growth and commitment to ethical practice.

Finally, Evelyn is highly committed to effective and ethical practice. Thirty years in practice and still Evelyn participates in a peer consultation group, presents her clinical work at national and international conferences, and enjoys receiving critical feedback on the way she has understood and approached a patient. Evelyn also relentlessly pushes herself to evaluate her countertransference, personal and cultural biases, and appreciates how these issues may impact her work. Evelyn is a prototype of a highly competent clinician; she holds the essential attitudes and values that reflect her commitment to being at her best as a clinician. She is curious, open to feedback, willing to acknowledge mistakes, respectful of and caring toward her patients, humble, and creative. Evelyn is fueled by her love for her work and the honor she feels when another person entrusts her with his most personal pain.

CONSIDERATIONS FOR TRAINING

A major question for clinical training involves how we can help student therapists develop skills for innovative, flexible, and adaptive use of theory and clinical knowledge in practice. Knowing when and how to adapt treatment emerges from an in-depth understanding of the therapeutic encounter; such understanding comes from learning what to be attuned to in the therapeutic process and having a framework for making sense of what occurs. In other words, clinical sophistication emerges with experience, but only if the therapist can use that experience to enhance her understanding of the work and of herself as she does the work. One main objective in training, therefore, is to enhance a student's capacity to observe how she thinks and processes clinical material, as well as how she evaluates her intervention decisions within a theoretical framework. We have several recommendations for using pedagogic strategies that can facilitate the metabolization of theory and therapeutic procedures. We have found them very helpful in our own teaching of psychotherapy to graduate students.

Facilitating Knowledge Acquisition

1. *Monitor the student's way of thinking.* A student makes sense of new information based on his or her preexisting conceptions about the subject matter. Consequently, in order to maximize the probability that the student acquires an accurate and internally consistent understanding of new theories and procedures, it is essential for the instructor to inquire into and continuously monitor the student's way of thinking about new material. One method for doing this is to encourage active discussions in which all students have the opportunity to raise questions and demonstrate their understanding of the topic being discussed (e.g., the major concepts and principles associated with attachment theory). Frequent formative assessments (e.g., short papers enumerating the main points of a recently presented topic, such as "the role of the therapeutic alliance in different treatment models") are an effective method for remaining attuned to the way students are thinking about the material being presented (Donovan et al., 1999).

2. *Teach the "Big Ideas."* A common pedagogic strategy in graduate training is to assign readings over an extensive area of a subject, based on the assumption that the more students read the more thorough will be their understanding of the subject. In fact, it appears that deep understanding of a subject—such as common factors in psychotherapy process—is most effectively achieved by exposure to a limited number of key concepts in a topic area, presented along with many examples of how the concepts would be used in various clinical situations. This strategy of choosing "Big Ideas" to present to students requires thoughtful choices by the instructor (Binder, 1999; Donovan et al., 1999).

3. *Use real world situations.* The most effective way to store declarative knowledge in memory is to facilitate its transfer into procedural knowledge by presenting declarative knowledge in the context of real world situations where it will be used. This strategy is largely impossible with regard to theories and procedures that are the conceptual foundation of psychotherapy practice. The usual sequence is to take courses in personality, psychopathology, and psychotherapy before seeing patients. However, students can be exposed to increasingly more realistic simulations of actual therapy sessions. The simplest format is to present video recorded segments of

therapy sessions that illustrate specific theoretical points or technical procedures. Students and instructor can discuss the issues while viewing a recorded example of a relevant clinical context. The most sophisticated version of this strategy would be the application of virtual reality computer graphics technology for creating a three-dimensional virtual therapy setting, in which the student interacts with an avatar-patient. This pedagogic strategy is called "anchored instruction"—topics are anchored in a real world context (Barnett & Koslowski, 2002; Bransford, Franks, Vye, & Sherwood, 1989; Brown, 1989; Catrambone & Holyoak, 1989; Cummins, 1992; Gick & Holyoak, 1983; Hatano, 1982; Holyoak, 1991).

Facilitating Skills Acquisition

New therapists have minimal clinical experience, and psychotherapy training typically relies on case examples to expose students to models of case conceptualization and specific interventions. Research in education supports the use of case examples to promote in-depth theoretical understanding and the ability to transfer knowledge to novel problems (Barnett & Koslowski, 2002; Brown, 1989; Catrambone & Holyoak, 1989; Cummins, 1992; Gick & Holyoak, 1983; Hatano, 1982; Holyoak, 1991). We present several recommendations that we believe are effective methods for using case examples to teach clinical theories and therapy procedures:

1. *Compare differences across cases rather than discuss a case in isolation.* Using contrasting cases may help students become more attuned to important distinctions that would demand alternative explanations and interventions (Lin, Schwartz, & Bransford, 2007). Similarly, exposing student therapists to different explanations highlights the importance of adapting theory.

2. *Have students first generate their own opinions about issues in a case or about potential interventions before exposing these students to expert opinions.* Having already made their own observations, students can better appreciate the expert's insights. Students are more likely to dismiss an expert's insights as obvious if they have not already failed to generate such understanding (Lin et al., 2007). Furthermore, in showing how experts think about clinical cases, students may develop greater awareness of how to generate and apply theoretical understanding, as well as hone their abilities to critically evaluate their own knowledge base.

3. *Generate multiple possibilities for understanding and intervening with a patient.* Since psychotherapy is a highly complex, context-specific endeavor, it is imperative that therapists apply their theoretical understanding in a flexible manner to a broad array of possibilities. For each case, students can generate and critique multiple clinical inferences about the patient, ideas for how to engage the patient in treatment, and options for interventions. They can evaluate why a particular understanding, treatment focus, or intervention may be useful or preferable. These exercises will promote critical thinking and may increase students' ability to engage in hypothesis testing.

4. *Videotapes or verbatim transcripts are preferable to written case descriptions.* First, a written case without the context of interpersonal nuances and the dialogue with the patient does not provide students with sufficient clinical information to generate psychological hypotheses and meanings. Second, in a written case conceptualization, often the process of thinking about the patient using a theoretical framework is already completed; this can circumvent the students' process of thinking through and making meaning of a case. Finally, verbatim clinical material is necessary to facilitate students' capacities to track an interpersonal theme across the therapeutic dialogue, recognize the interpersonal nuances of the therapeutic encounter, and learn how to adapt their interventions accordingly.

A Method for Addressing the Problem of "Inert" Knowledge

In psychotherapy training the move from course work to work with actual patients represents the most abrupt transition from acquiring declarative knowledge to needing procedural knowledge of any training in a complex performance of which we are aware. It appears that most novice psychotherapists manage to acquire the procedural knowledge required to conduct psychotherapy, however fumbling, in spite of the pedagogic strategy used by the vast majority of training programs. We worry, however, that students' knowledge of psychotherapy remains inert more frequently than is generally realized. We believe that the transformation of declarative knowledge into procedural knowledge about psychotherapy would be enhanced by the introduction of a new training phase between course work and clinical practica involving work with actual patients. This phase of training would involve an instructional format that consistently applies the principles of "deliberate practice," which has been shown to be a particularly effective method of training for proficiency and expertise in various complex performance domains. This format would involve the student practicing progressively more complex therapy skills in a three-dimensional, virtual reality environment that utilizes patient-avatars. This training environment would provide an opportunity for planned, systematic practice with immediate feedback (Binder, 1999, 2004).

Psychotherapy Supervision

The final phase of psychotherapy training involves conducting supervised treatments. We will end our discussion with some recommendations for conducting supervision which in our combined experiences we have found useful:

1. *Use video recordings.* Put a high value on the use of recordings, preferably video recordings, of students' therapies, in order to scrutinize in detail selected patient–therapist interaction sequences, assumed to be representative of broader themes and processes.
2. *Plan supervision goals and tasks.* Structure the use of recordings by planning specific training tasks during supervision, such as looking for opportunities to examine a type of patient–therapist interaction that has been giving the student particular difficulty.
3. *Attend to the supervisee's experiences and thought processes.* Consistently focus on the student's subjective experiences, mental processes, and personal reactions to the patient during the course of a session. Closely examine her decision-making processes and how she has been using theory to guide her work. The aim is to try to make explicit the student's thinking processes in order to help her be more aware of what is influencing her behavior as a therapist.
4. *Teach Case Conceptualization.* Encourage the student to construct precise case conceptualizations that are anchored in the patient's interpersonal experiences. The case conceptualization should serve as a usable guide to the content of therapist interventions.
5. *Practice identifying the primary theme and evidence of the salient narrative reflecting the case formulation.* Our impression is that incomplete articulation of a patient's personal story line is one of the most common deficiencies in therapist competence. The supervisor should remain alert for material that will further elaborate the patient's narrative and encourage the student to incorporate this material into his or her conception of the patient. Work specifically on helping the super-

visee use the formulation to guide the narrative focus of the treatment. The content of therapist interventions should be consistently relevant to the salient narrative.

6. *Focus early interventions toward inquiry and case conceptualizations.* Students and novice therapists tend to rush to do something for the patient. Work with the student on integrating an initial process of case formulation with early interventions (e.g., questions that have an assessment function but which also can incite the patient to think about his problem in a new way).

7. *Teach the supervisee how to think like a therapist.* As a supervisor, sometimes there is a temptation to become the vicarious therapist, especially when the student is struggling. However, don't forget that the supervisor's most important task is to help the student think like a therapist and, ultimately, to function independently as a competent clinician. In other words, the supervisor should not think for the student.

8. *Evaluate and help sharpen supervisees' interventions.* As the supervisor, be alert to instances where a student makes an intervention that is too general, vague, or incomplete. Work with the student to redo the intervention, at least in a practice session, using more precise wording.

9. *Maintain consistent sensitivity to the therapist's interpersonal stance and specific personal reactions to the patient.* Instruct the student on how to use his personal reactions to the patient as a tool for understanding the immediate patient–therapist dynamics.

10. *Encourage the student to explicate how his conceptual framework guides his understanding of the patient and his decisions about when and how to intervene.* Help the student articulate her conceptual understanding and apply it to patient–therapist interactions and therapist interventions,

11. *Provide explicit, specific feedback.* When providing positive or critical feedback to the student, specify as clearly as possible what the student has done that evoked the feedback, rather than nonspecific compliments or criticisms.

12. *Attend to feelings.* Students tend to shy away from uncomfortable emotions, so be alert for this reaction and discuss instances when it happens, explaining the importance of attending to such feelings.

13. *Attend to a supervisee's reluctance to intervene with patients.* Students also tend to magnify the psychological fragility of their patients, so also be on the alert for this attitude and together evaluate the evidence (or lack of evidence) for it.

14. *Openly discuss supervisee's experiences with multiple supervisors or theoretical approaches.* A student may have more than one supervisor at a time, and there may be inconsistencies, contradictions, and conflicts among the different approaches to treatment promoted by different supervisors. As a supervisor, be alert to this potential source of teaching/learning stress on the student. If this situation arises, discuss its impact on the student, how he is coping with it, and take the situation into consideration when working with the student.

15. *Structure each supervisory session.* It is possible to drift into an overly unstructured way of working in supervision. Consequently, a supervisor should consider sticking to a general structure for each supervisory session. For example: (a) a brief synopsis of the case up to the present time, including how the case formulation has evolved over time, (b) a more detailed discussion about issues that require consideration of the case formulation and treatment model, (c) summarize current clinical issues, (d) conduct a microanalysis of specific recorded therapy segments that illustrate a specific issue or problem encountered by the student.

CONCLUSION

A BDP therapist's development involves harnessing and focusing one's natural curiosity and compassion with well-developed skills in drawing out and making meaning of a patient's pain and struggles. Becoming a highly effective and competent BDP therapist depends primarily on the therapist's commitment to learning: engaging with new ideas; developing skills in listening for interpersonal themes; learning to construct a coherent narrative that captures the patient's primary enduring, negative pattern of engaging in relationships; and honing skills in creating a therapeutic dialogue that leads to a patient's greater awareness of how he unwittingly invites interpersonal experiences that confirm his negative expectations and perpetuate his pain. The competent therapist learns from her patients, and every therapeutic encounter changes the therapist as she assimilates her clinical experience into her growing understanding of human need and human pain. Above all, the therapist's willingness to enter the patient's world and understand the patient's unique experience is at the heart of competent and potent therapeutic practice.

BIBLIOGRAPHY

Abate, F. R. (Ed.). (2002). *Oxford pocket American dictionary of current English*. New York: Oxford University Press.

Achin, J. C., & Pincus, A. L. (2010). Evidence-based interpersonal psychotherapy with personality disorders: Theory, components, and strategies. In J. J. Magnavita (Ed.), *Evidence-based treatment of personality dysfunction: Principles, methods, and processes* (pp. 113–166). Washington, DC: American Psychological Association.

Ackerman, S. J., & Hilsenroth, M. J. (2001). A review of therapist characteristics and techniques negatively impacting the therapeutic alliance. *Psychotherapy: Theory, Research, Practice, Training, 38*, 171–185.

Ackerman, S. J., & Hilsenroth, M. J. (2003). A review of therapist characteristics and techniques positively impacting the therapeutic alliance. *Clinical Psychology Review, 23*, 1–33.

Ackerman, S. J., Hilsenroth, M. J., Baity, M. R., & Blagys, M. D. (2000). Interaction of therapeutic process and alliance during psychological assessment. *Journal of Personality Assessment, 75*, 82–109.

American Psychiatric Association. (2000). *Diagnostic and statistical manual of mental disorders* (4th ed., rev.). Washington, DC: American Psychiatric Association.

American Psychological Association, Presidential Task Force on Evidence-Based Practice. (2006). Evidence-based practice in psychology. *American Psychologist, 61*, 271–285.

Angus, L., & Kagan, F. (2007). Empathic relational bonds and personal agency in psychotherapy: Implications for psychotherapy supervision, practice, and research. *Psychotherapy: Theory, Research, Practice, Training, 44*, 371–377.

Angus, L. E., & Greenberg, L. S. (2011). *Working with narrative in emotion-focused therapy: Changing stories, healing lives*. Washington, DC: American Psychological Association.

Atkisson, C. C., & Greenfield, T. K. (2004). The UCSF Client Satisfaction Scales: 1. The Client Satisfaction Questionaire-8. In M. Maruish (Ed.), *The use of psychological testing for treatment planning and outcome assessment* (3rd. ed. pp. 799–812). Mahwah, NJ: Erlbaum.

Bachelor, A. (1995). Clients' perception of the therapeutic alliance: A qualitative analysis. *Journal of Counseling Psychology, 42*, 323–337.

Bambling, M., & King, R. (2001). Therapeutic alliance and clinical practice. *Psychotherapy in Australia, 81*, 38–43.

Barber, J. P., Connolly, M. B., Crits-Christoph, P., Gladis, L., & Siqueland, L. (2009). Alliance predicts patients' outcome beyond in-treatment change in symptoms. *Personality Disorders: Theory, Research, and Treatment, 1*, 80–89.

Barnett, S. M., & Koslowski, B. (2002). Adaptive expertise: Effects of type of experience and the level of theoretical understanding it generates. *Thinking and Reasoning, 8,* 237–267.

Bateman, A. W., & Fonagy, P. (2006). *Mentalization based treatment for borderline personality disorder: A practical guide.* Oxford, England: Oxford University Press.

Beck, A. T., Ward, C. H., Medelson, M., Mock, J., & Erbaugh, J. (1961). An inventory for measuring depression. *Archives of General Psychiatry, 4,* 561–571.

Beebe, B., & Lachmann, F. (2003). The relational turn in psychoanalysis: A dyadic systems view from infant research. *Contemporary Psychoanalysis, 39*(3), 379–409.

Beebe, B., Lachmann, F., & Jaffe, J. (1997). Mother-infant interaction structures and presymbolic self- and object-representations. *Psychoanalytic Dialogues, 7,* 133–187.

Benjamin, L. S. (2005). Interpersonal theory of personality disorders: The structural analysis of social behavior and interpersonal reconstructive therapy. In M. F. Lenzenweger & J. F. Clarkin (Eds.), *Major theories of personality disorder* (pp. 157–230). New York: Guilford.

Bergin, A. E. (1991). Values and religious issues in psychotherapy and mental health. *American Psychologist, 46,* 394–403.

Betan, E., Heim, A. K., Conklin, C. Z., & Westen, D. (2005). Countertransference phenomena and personality pathology in clinical practice: An empirical investigation. *American Journal of Psychiatry, 162,* 890–898.

Betan, E. J. (1997). Toward a hermeneutic model of ethical decision-making. *Ethics & Behavior, 7,* 347–365.

Betan, E. J., & Binder, J. L. (2010). Clinical expertise in psychotherapy: How expert therapists use theory in generating case conceptualizations and interventions. *Journal of Contemporary Psychotherapy, 40,* 141–152.

Betan, E. J., & Westen, D. (2009). Countertransference and personality pathology: Development and clinical application of the Countertransference Questionnaire. In R. A. Levy & J. S. Ablon (Eds.), *Handbook of evidence-based psychodynamic psychotherapy* (pp. 179–198). New York: Humana Press.

Beutler, L. E., & Bergan, J. (1991). Value change in counseling and psychotherapy: A search for scientific credibility. *Journal of Counseling Psychology, 38,* 16–24.

Beutler, L. E., & Harwood, T. M. (2000). *Prescriptive psychotherapy: A practical guide to systematic treatment selection.* Oxford, UK: Oxford University Press.

Binder, J. L. (1993). Is it time to improve psychotherapy training? *Clinical Psychology Review, 13,* 301–318.

Binder, J. L. (1999). Issues in teaching and learning time-limited psychodynamic psychotherapy. *Clinical Psychology Review, 19,* 705–719.

Binder, J. L. (2004). *Key competencies in brief dynamic psychotherapy: Clinical practice beyond the manual.* New York: Guilford.

Binder, J. L., & Strupp, H. H. (1997). "Negative process": A recurrently discovered and underestimated facet of therapeutic process and outcome in the individual psychotherapy of adults. *Clinical Psychology: Science and Practice, 4,* 121–139.

Binder, J. L., & Wechsler, F. S. (2010). The intervention competency. In M. B. Kenkel & R. L. Peterson (Eds.), *Competency-based education for professional psychology* (pp. 105–124). Washington, DC: American Psychological Association

Björn, P., & Paul A. (2005). An attachment model of personality disorders. In M. F. Lenzenweger & J. F. Clarkin (Eds.), *Major theories of personality disorder* (pp. 231–281). New York: Guilford.

Blatt, S. (2006). A fundamental polarity in psychoanalysis: Implications for personality development, psychopathology, and the therapeutic process. *Psychoanalytic Inquiry, 26,* 494–520.

Blatt, S. J. (2008). *Polarities of experience.* Washington, DC: American Psychological Association.

Blatt, S. J., Auerbach, J. S., & Levy, K. N. (1997). Mental representations in personality development, psychopathology, and the therapeutic process. *Review of General Psychology, 1,* 351–374.

Blatt, S. J., & Levy, K. N. (2003). Attachment theory, psychoanalysis, personality development, and psychopathology. *Psychoanalytic Inquiry, 23,* 102–150.

Bohart, A. C., O'Hara, M., & Leitner, L. M. (1988). Empirically violated treatments: Disenfranchisement of humanistic and other psychotherapies. *Psychotherapy Research, 8,* 141–157.

Book, H. E. (1998). *How to practice brief psychodynamic psychotherapy: The core conflict relationship theme method.* Washington, DC: American Psychological Association.

Bordin, E. S. (1979). The generalizability of the psychoanalytic concept of the working alliance. *Psychotherapy: Theory, Research, and Practice, 16,* 252–260.

Borden, K. A., & McIlvried, E. J. (2010). Applying the competency model to professional psychology education, training, and assessment: Mission Bay and beyond. In M. B. Kenkel & R. L. Peterson (Eds.), *Competency-based education for professional psychology* (pp. 43–54). Washington, DC: American Psychological Association.

Bowlby, J. (1969). *Attachment and loss: Vol. 1. Attachment.* New York: Basic Books.

Bowlby, J. (1988a). *A secure base: Vol. 1. Clinical applications of attachment theory.* London: Routledge.

Bowlby, J. (1988b). *A secure base: Vol. 2. Parent–child attachment and healthy human development.* New York: Basic.

Bransford, J. D., Franks, J. J., Vye, N. J., & Sherwood, R. D. (1989). New approaches to instruction: Because wisdom can't be told. In S. Vosniadou & A. Ortony (Eds.), *Similarity and analogical reasoning* (pp. 470–497). New York: Cambridge University Press.

Breuer, J., & Freud, S. (1893–1895/1955). Studies in hysteria. J. Strachey (Ed. & Trans.), *Standard Edition* (Vol. 2, pp. 1–319). London: Hogarth Press.

Brown, A. L. (1989). Analogical learning and transfer: What develops? In S. Vosniadou & A. Ortony (Eds.), *Similarity and analogical reasoning* (pp. 369–412). Cambridge, England: Cambridge University Press.

Buchanan, B. G., Davis, R., & Feigenbaum, E. A. (2006). Expert systems: A perspective from computer science. In K. A. Ericsson, N. Charness, P. J. Feltovich, &

R. R. Hoffman (Eds.), *The Cambridge handbook of expertise and expert performance* (pp. 87–103). New York: Cambridge University Press.

Budman, H. S., & Gurman, A. S. (1988). *Theory and practice of brief psychotherapy.* New York: Guildford.

Butcher, J. N., Dahlstrom, W. G., Graham, J. R., Tellegen, A., & Kaemmer, B. (1989). *Minnesota Multiphasic Personality Inventory (MMPI-2): Manual for administration and scoring.* Minneapolis: University of Minnesota Press.

Carroll, R. T. (2004). *Becoming a critical thinker* (2nd ed.). New York: Pearson.

Castonguay, L. G., Constantino, M. J., & Holtforth, M. G (2006). The working alliance: Where are we and where should we go? *Psychotherapy: Theory, Research, Practice, Training, 43,* 271–279.

Castonguay, L. G., Goldfried, M. R., Wiser, S., Raue, P. J., & Hayes, A. M. (1996). Predicting the effect of cognitive therapy for depression: A study of unique and common factors. *Journal of Consulting and Clinical Psychology, 64,* 497–504.

Castonguay, L. G., Schut, A. J., Aikins, D., Constantino, M. J., Laurenceau, J. P., Bologh, L., & & Burns, D. D. (2004). Integrative cognitive therapy: A preliminary investigation. *Journal of Psychotherapy Integration, 14,* 4–20.

Catrambone, R., & Holyoak, K. J. (1989). Overcoming contextual limitations on problem-solving transfer. *Journal of Experimental Psychology: Learning, Memory, and Cognition, 15*(6), 1147–1156.

Chi, M. T. H. (2006). Two approaches to the study of experts' characteristics. In K. A. Ericsson, N. Charness, P. J. Feltovich, & R. R. Horrman (Eds.), *The Cambridge handbook of expertise and expert performance* (pp. 21–30). New York: Cambridge University Press

Clarkin, J. F., Lenzenweger, M. F., Yeomans, F. E., Levy, K. N., & Kernberg, O. F. (2007). An object relations model of borderline pathology. *Journal of Personality Disorders, 21,* 474–499.

Clarkin, J. F., Yeomans, F., & Kernberg, O. F. (1999). *Psychotherapy of borderline personality.* New York: Wiley.

Comas-Diaz, L. (2006). Latino healing: The integration of ethnic psychology into psychotherapy. *Psychotherapy: Research, Practice, and Training, 43,* 436–453.

Connolly, M. B., Crits-Christoph, P., Shappell, S., Barber, J. P., Luborsky, L., & Shaffer, C. (1999). Relation of transference interpretations to outcome in the early sessions of brief supportive-expressive psychotherapy. *Psychotherapy Research, 9,* 485–495.

Constantino, M. J., Castonguay, L. G., & Schut, A. J. (2002). The working alliance: A flagship for the "scientist-practitioner" model in psychotherapy. In G. S. Tryon (Ed.), *Counseling based on process research: Applying what we know* (pp. 81–131). Boston, MA: Allyn & Bacon.

Crits-Christoph, P., Connolly Gibbons, M. B., Crits-Christoph, K., Narducci, J., Schamberger, M., & Gallop, R. (2006). Can therapists be trained to improve their alliances? A preliminary study of alliance fostering psychotherapy. *Psychotherapy Research, 16,* 268–281.

Cummings, A. L., Hallberg, E. T., Martin, J., Slemon, A., & Heibert, B. (1990). Implications of counselor conceptualizations for counselor education. *Counselor Education and Supervision, 30,* 120–134.

Cummins, D. (1992). Role of analogical reasoning in the induction of problem categories. *Journal of Experimental Psychology: Learning, Memory, and Cognition, 18*, 1103–1124.

Cushman, P. (1990). Why the self is empty: Toward a historically situated psychology. *American Psychologist, 45*, 599–611.

Daly, K. D., & Mallinckrodt, B. (2009). Experienced therapists' approach to psychotherapy for adults with attachment avoidance or attachment anxiety. *Journal of Counseling Psychology, 56*, 549–563.

Davanloo, H. (1978). *Basic principles and techniques in short-term dynamic psychotherapy.* New York: Spectrum.

deGroot, A. D. (1965). *Thought and choice in chess.* The Hague, the Netherlands: Mouton.

Derogatis, L. R. (1983). *The SCL-90: Administration, scoring, and procedures for the SCL-90.* Baltimore, MD: Clinical Psychometric Research.

Donovan, M. S., Bransford, J. D., & Pellegrino, J. W. (Eds.). (1999). *How people learn: Bridging research and practice.* Washington, DC: National Academy Press.

Dreyfus, H. L., & Dreyfus, S. E. (1986). *Mind over machine: The power of human intuition and expertise in the age of the computer.* Oxford, England: Blackwell.

Duncan, B., Miller, S., Sparks, J., Claud, D., Reynold, L. Brown, J., & Johnson, L. (2003). The session rating scale: Preliminary properties of a "working" alliance measure. *Journal of Brief Therapy, 3*(1), 3–12.

Dunning, D. (2005). *Self-insight: Roadblocks and detours on the path to knowing thyself.* New York: Psychology Press.

Eells, T. D. (2010). The unfolding case formulation: The interplay of description and inference. *Pragmatic Case Studies in Psychotherapy, 6*, 225–254.

Eells, T. D., Lombart, K. G., Kendjelic, E. M., Turner, L. C., & Lucas, C. P. (2005). The quality of psychotherapy case formulations: A comparison of expert, experienced, and novice cognitive-behavioral and psychodynamic therapists. *Journal of Consulting and Clinical Psychology, 73*, 579–589.

Ehrenwald, J. (Ed.). (1991). *The history of psychotherapy.* Northvale, NJ: Jason Aronson.

Ekstein, R., & Wallerstein, R. S. (1972). *The teaching and learning of psychothepay* (rev. ed.). Oxford, UK: International Universities Press.

Ericsson, K. A. (1996). The influence of experience and deliberate practice on the development of superior expert performance. In K. A. Ericsson, N. Charness, P. J. Feltovich, & R. R. Hoffman (Eds.), *The Cambridge handbook of expertise and expert performance* (pp. 683–704). New York: Cambridge University Press.

Ericsson, K. A., & Charness, N. (1999). Expert performance: Its structure and acquisition. In S. J. Ceci & W. M. Williams (Eds.), *The nature-nurture debate: The essential readings* (pp. 199–255). Malden, MA: Blackwell.

Eubanks, C., Muran, J. C., & Safran, J. D. (2010). Alliance ruptures and resolution. In J. C. Muran & J. P. Barber (Eds.), *The therapeutic alliance: An evidence-based guide to practice* (pp. 74–94). New York: Guilford.

Firestein, S. K. (1982). Termination of psychoanalysis: Theoretical, clinical, and pedagogic considerations. *Psychoanalytic Inquiry, 2*, 413–491.

Fonagy, P. (2001). *Attachment theory and psychoanalysis.* New York: Other Press.

Fonagy, P., Gergely, G., Jurist, E., & Target, M. (2002). *Affect regulation, mentalization, and the development of the self.* New York: Other Press.

Foreman, S., & Marmar, R. (1985). Therapist actions that address initially poor therapeutic alliances in psychotherapy. *American Journal of Psychiatry, 142,* 922–926.

Frame, M. W., & Williams, C. B. (2005). A model of ethical decision making from a multicultural perspective. *Counseling and Values, 49,* 165–179.

Freud, S. (1955/1912). The dynamics of transference. In *Standard Edition* (Vol. 12, pp. 99–108). London: Hogarth Press.

Gabbard, G. (2005). *Psychodynamic psychiatry in clinical practice.* Washington, DC: American Psychiatric Press.

Gaston, L., Marmar, C. R., Gallagher, D., & Thompson, L. W. (1989). Impact of confirming patient expectations of change processes in behavioral, cognitive and brief dynamic psychotherapy. *Psychotherapy, 26,* 287–294.

Gelso C. J., & Hayes J. A. (1998). *The psychotherapy relationship: Theory, research, and practice.* New York: Wiley.

Gelso, C. J., & Hayes, J. A. (2007). *Countertransference and the therapist's inner experience.* Mahwah, NJ: Erlbaum

Gick, M. L., & Holyoak, K. J. (1983). Schema induction and analogical transfer. *Cognitive Psychology, 15,* 1–38.

Gill, M. M. (1982). *Analysis of transference* (Vol. 1). New York: International Universities Press.

Goldfried, M. R., Raue, P. J., & Castonguay, L. G. (1996). The therapeutic focus in significant sessions of master therapists: A comparison of cognitive-behavioral and psychodynamic-interpersonal interventions. *Journal of Consulting and Clinical Psychology, 66,* 803–810.

Goncalves, M. M., & Stiles, W. B. (2011). Narratives and psychotherapy: Introduction to the special series. *Psychotherapy Research, 21,* 1–3.

Greenberg, L. S. (2002). Termination of experiential therapy. *Journal of Psychotherapy Integration, 12,* 358–363.

Greenberg, L. S., & Watson, J. C. (2005). *Emotion-focused therapy for depression.* Washington, DC: American Psychological Association Press.

Greenberg, L. S., Watson, J. C., Elliot, R., & Bohart, A. C. (2001). Empathy. *Psychotherapy: Theory, Research, Practice, Training, 38,* 380–384.

Halpern, D. F. (1998). Teaching critical thinking for transfer across domains: Disposition, skills, structure training, and metacognitive monitoring. *American Psychologist, 53,* 449–455.

Halpern, D. F. (2003). *Knowledge and thought: An introduction to critical thinking* (4th ed.). Hillsdale, NJ: Erlbaum.

Hatano, G. (1982). Cognitive consequences of practice in culture specific procedural skills. *The Quarterly Newsletter of the Laboratory of Comparative Human Cognition, 4,* 15–18.

Hatano, G. (1988). Social and motivational bases for mathematical understanding. In G. B. Saxe & M. Gearhart (Eds.), *Children's mathematics* (pp. 55–70). San Francisco, CA: Jossey-Bass.

Hatfield, D. R., & Ogles, M. (2004). The use of outcome measures by psychologists in practice. *Professional Psychology: Research and Practice, 35,* 485–491.

Hays, P. (2007). *Addressing cultural complexities in practice: Assessment, diagnosis, and therapy* (2nd ed.). Washington D.C.: American Psychological Association.

Henry, W. P., Schacht, T. E., & Strupp, H. H. (1986). Structural analysis of social behavior: Application to a study of interpersonal process in differential psychotherapeutic outcome. *Journal of Consulting and Clinical Psychology, 54,* 27–31.

Henry, W. P., Strupp, H. H., Butler, S. F., Schacht, T. E., & Binder, J. L. (1993). The effects of training in time-limited dynamic psychotherapy: Changes in therapist behavior. *Journal of Consulting and Clinical Psychology, 61,* 434–440.

Henry, W. P., Strupp, H. H., & Schacht, T. E. (1990). Patient and therapist introject, interpersonal process, and differential psychotherapy outcome. *Journal of Consulting and Clinical Psychology, 58,* 768–774.

Hill, C. E. (2010). Qualitative studies of negative experiences in psychotherapy. In J. C. Muran & J. P. Barber (Eds.), *The therapeutic alliance. An evidence-based guide to practice* (pp. 63–73). New York: Guildford Press.

Høglend, P. (2003). Long-term effects of brief dynamic psychotherapy. *Psychotherapy Research, 13,* 271–292.

Høglend, P., Amlo, S., Marble, A., Bøgwald, K., Sørbye, Ø., Sjaastad, M. C., & Heyerdahl, O. (2006). Analysis of the patient-therapist relationship in dynamic psychotherapy: An experimental study of transference interpretations. *American Journal of Psychiatry, 163,* 1739–1746.

Høglend, P., Bøgwald, K., Amlo, S., Marble, A., Ulberg, R., Sjaastad, M.C., & Johansson, P. (2008). Transference interpretations in dynamic psychotherapy: Do they really yield sustained effects? *American Journal of Psychiatry, 165,* 763–771.

Høglend, P., Hersoug, A. G., Bøgwald, K., Amlo, S., Marble, A., ... Sørbye, Ø. (2011). Effects of transference work in the context of therapeutic alliance and quality of object relations. *Journal of Consulting and Clinical Psychology, 79,* 697–706.

Høglend, P., Johansson, P., Marble, A., Bøgwald, K-P., & Amlo, S. (2007). Moderators of the effects of transference interpretations in brief dynamic psychotherapy. *Psychotherapy Research, 17,* 162–174.

Holyoak, K. J. (1991). Symbolic connectionism: Toward third-generation theories of expertise. In K. A. Ericsson & J. Smith (Eds.), *Toward a general theory of expertise* (pp. 301–335). New York: Cambridge University Press.

Horowitz, M. J. (1986). *Stress response syndromes* (2nd ed.). Northvale, NJ: Jason Aronson.

Horowitz, L. M., Rosenberg, S. E., Baer, B. A., Ureno, G., & Villasenor, V. S. (1988). Inventory of interpersonal problems: Psychometric properties and clinical applications. *Journal of Consulting and Clinical Psychology, 56,* 885–892.

Horvath, A. O. (2001). The alliance. *Psychotherapy: Theory, Research, Practice, Training, 38,* 365–372.

Horvath, A. O., Del Re, A. C., Flückiger, C., & Symonds, P. (2011). Alliance in individual psychotherapy. *Psychotherapy, 48,* 9–16.

Horvath, A. O., & Luborsky, L. (1993). The role of the therapeutic alliance in psychotherapy. *Journal of Consulting and Clinical Psychology, 61,* 561–573.

Howard, K. I., Moras, K., Brill, P. L., Martinovich, Z., & Lutz, W. (1996). Evaluation of psychotherapy: Efficacy, effectiveness, and patient progress. *American Psychologist, 51,* 1059–1064.

Ivey, G. (2006). A method of teaching psychodynamic case formulation. *Psychotherapy: Theory, Research, Practice, Training, 43,* 322–336.

Jacobson, N. S., Roberts, L. J., Berns, S. B., & McGlinchey, J. B. (1999). A method for defining and determining the clinical significance of treatment effects: Description, application, and alternatives. *Journal of Consulting and Clinical Psychology, 67,* 300–307.

Jacobson, N. S., & Truax, P. (1991). Clinical significance: A statistical approach to defining meaningful change in psychotherapy research. *Journal of Consulting and Clinical Psychology, 59,* 12–19.

James, L., & Beck, A. T. (2005). Cognitive theory of personality disorders. In M. F. Lenzenweger & J. F. Clarkin (Ed.), *Major theories of personality disorder* (pp. 43–113). New York: Guilford.

James, W. (1881). *Principles of psychology* (Vol. 2). Cambridge, MA: Harvard University Press.

Jankowski, D. (2002). *A beginner's guide to the MCMI-III.* Washington, DC: American Psychological Association.

Johansson, P., Høglend, P., Ulberg, R., Amlo, S., Marble, A., Bøwald, K-P., ... Sørbye, Ø. (2010). The mediating role of insight for long-term improvements in psychodynamic therapy. *Journal of Consulting and Clinical Psychology, 78,* 438–448.

Jungbluth, N. J., & Shirk, S. R. (2009). Therapist strategies for building involvement in cognitive–behavioral therapy for adolescent depression. *Journal of Consulting and Clinical Psychology, 77,* 1179–1184.

Kaslow, N. J. (2004). Competencies in professional psychology. *American Psychologist, 59,* 774–781.

Kasper, L. B., Hill, C. E., & Kivlighan, D. M. (2008). Therapist immediacy in brief psychotherapy: Case study I. *Psychotherapy: Theory, Research, Practice, Training, 45,* 281–297.

Kendjelic, E. M., & Eells, T. D. (2007). Generic psychotherapy case formulation training improves formulation quality. *Psychotherapy: Theory, Research, Practice, Training, 44,* 66–77.

Kenkel, M. B., & Peterson, R. S. (Eds.). (2010). *Competency-based education for professional psychology.* Washington, DC: American Psychological Association.

Kernberg, O. F. (1975). *Borderline conditions and pathological narcissism.* New York: Jason Aronson.

Kernberg, O. F. (1984). *Severe personality disorders: Psychotherapeutic strategies.* New Haven, CT: Yale University Press.

Kiesler, D. J. (1996). *Contemporary interpersonal theory and research: Personality, psychopathology, and psychotherapy.* New York: Wiley.

Kivlighan, D. M. (2010). Changes in trainees' intention use and volunteer clients' evaluations of sessions during early skills training. *Psychotherapy: Theory, Research, Practice, Training, 47,* 198–210.

Kivlighan, D. M., Patton, M. J., & Foote, D. (1998). Moderating effects of client attachment on the counselor experience–working alliance relationship. *Journal of Counseling Psychology, 45,* 274–278.

Knox, S., Adrians, N., Everson, E., Hess, S., Hill, C., & Crooks-Lyon, R. (2011). Clients' perspectives on therapy termination. *Psychotherapy Research, 21,* 154–167.

Lambert, M. J. (Ed.). (2004). *Bergin and Garfield's handbook of psychotherapy and behavior change* (5th ed.). New York: Wiley.

Lambert, M. J. (2010). *Prevention of treatment failure: The use of measuring, monitoring, and feedback in clinical practice.* Washington, DC: American Psychological Association.

Lambert, M. J., Morton, J. J., Hatfield, D., Harmon, C., Hamilton, S., Reid, R.C., ... Burlingame, G. M. (2004). *Administration and scoring manual for the Outcome Questionaire-45.* Salt Lake City, UT: OQMeasures.

Lambert, M. J., & Shimokawa, K. (2011). Collecting client feedback. *Psychotherapy, 48,* 72–79.

Lazarus, A. A. (1993). Tailoring the therapeutic relationship, or being an authentic chameleon. *Psychotherapy: Theory, Research, Practice, Training, 30,* 404–407.

Levenson, E. A. (1988). Whatever happened to the cat? *Contemporary Psychoanalysis, 25,* 537–553.

Levenson, H. (1995). *Time-limited dynamic psychotherapy: A guide to clinical practice.* New York: Basic.

Levenson, H. (2010). *Brief dynamic therapy.* Washington, DC: American Psychological Association.

Lewis-Fernandez, R., & Diaz, N. (2002). The cultural formulation: A method for assessing cultural factors affecting the clinical encounter. *Psychiatric Quarterly, 73,* 271–295.

Lin, X., Schwartz, D., & Bransford, J. D. (2007). Intercultural adaptive expertise: Explicit and implicit lessons from Dr. Hatano. *Human Development, 50,* 65–72.

Livesley, W. J. (2003). *Practical management of personality disorder.* New York: Guilford.

Luborsky, L. (1984). *Principles of psychoanalytic psychotherapy: A manual for supportive-expressive treatment.* New York: Basic.

Luborsky, L., & Crits-Christoph, P. (1997). *Understanding transference: The core conflict relationship theme method* (2nd ed.). Washington, DC: American Psychological Association.

Malan, D. H. (1963). *A study of brief psychotherapy.* London: Tavistock.

Malan, D. H. (1976). *The frontier of brief psychotherapy.* New York: Plenum.

Malan, D. H. (1978). Exploring the limits of brief psychotherapy. In H. Davanloo (Ed.), *Basic principle and techniques in short-term dynamic psychotherapy* (pp. 43–70). New York: SP Medical & Scientific.

Mallinckrodt, B. (1991). Clients' representations of childhood emotional bonds with parents, social support, and formation of the working alliance. *Journal of Counseling Psychology, 38,* 401–409.

Mallinckrodt, B., Gantt, D. L., & Coble, H. M. (1995). Attachment patterns in the psychotherapy relationship: Development of the Client Attachment to Therapist Scale. *Journal of Counseling Psychology, 42,* 307–317.

Mallinckrodt, B., Porter, M. J., & Kivlighan, D. M. (2005). Client attachment to therapist, depth of in-session exploration, and object relations in brief psychotherapy. *Psychotherapy: Theory, Research, Practice, Training, 42*, 85–100.

Mann, J. (1973). *Time-limited psychotherapy.* Cambridge, MA: Harvard University Press.

Mann, J., & Goldman, R. (1982). *A casebook in time-limited psychotherapy.* New York: McGraw-Hill.

Marmar, C., Weiss, D. S., & Gaston, L. (1989). Toward the validation of the California Therapeutic Alliance Rating System. *Psychological Assessment, 1*, 46–52.

Martin, D. J., Garske, J. P., & Davis, M. K. (2000). Relation of the therapeutic alliance with outcome and other variables: A meta-analytic review. *Journal of Consulting and Clinical Psychology, 68*, 438–450.

Marx, J. A., & Gelso, C. J. (1987). Termination of individual counseling in a university counseling center. *Journal of Counseling Psychology, 34*, 3–9.

Marziali, E. A. (1984). Prediction of outcome of brief psychotherapy from therapist interpretive interventions. *Archives of General Psychiatry, 41*, 301–304.

McCullough, L., Kuhn, N., Andrews, S., Kaplan, A., Wolf, J., & Lanza, C. (2001). *Treatment of affect phobias: A workbook for short-term dynamic psychotherapy.* New York: Guilford.

McKechnie, J. L. & staff (Eds.). (1976). *Webster's new twentieth century dictionary of the English language* (2nd ed.). New York: Collins.

McWilliams, N. (1999). *Psychoanalytic case formulation.* New York: Guilford.

Meara, N. M., Schmidt, L. D., & Day, J. D. (1996). Principles and virtues: A foundation for ethical decisions, policies, and character. *The Counseling Psychologist, 24*, 4–77.

Meissner, W. W. (2006). The therapeutic alliance—A proteus in disguise. *Psychotherapy: Theory, Research, Practice, Training, 43*, 264–270.

Messer, S. B., & Wolitsky, D. L. (2010). A psychodynamic perspective on the therapeutic alliance: Theory, research, and practice. In J. C. Muran & J. P. Barber (Eds.), *The therapeutic alliance. An evidence-based guide to practice* (pp. 97–122). New York: Guilford.

Meyer, B., & Pilkonis, P. A. (2005). An attachment model of personality disorders. In M. F. Lenzenweger & J. F. Clarkin (Eds.), *Major theories of personality disorder* (pp. 231–281). New York: Guilford.

Meyer, B., Pilkonis, P. A., Krupnick, J. L., Egan, M. K., Simmens, S. J., & Sotsky, S. M. (2002). Treatment expectancies, patient alliance, and outcome: Further analyses from the National Institute of Mental Health Treatment of Depression Collaborative Research Program. *Journal of Consulting and Clinical Psychology, 70*, 1051–1055.

Miller, S., Duncan, B., Brown, J., Sparks, J., & Claud, D. (2003). The outcome rating scale: A preliminary study of the reliability, validity, and feasibility of a brief visual analog measure. *Journal of Brief Therapy, 2*(2), 91–100.

Miller, S., Duncan, B., Sorrell, R., & Brown, G.S. (2005). The partners for change outcome system. *Journal of Clinical Psychology: In Session, 61*, 199–208.

Mitchell, S. A. (1988). *Relational concepts in psychoanalysis: An integration.* Cambridge, MA: Harvard University Press.

Moore, L. (1989, October 22). Ordinary life always went too far. *New York Times*. Retrieved from http://www.nytimes.com/books/97/11/23/home/pritchett-widow.html.

Muran, J. C., & Barber, J. P. (Eds.). (2010). *The therapeutic alliance. An evidence-based guide to practice*. New York: Guilford Press.

Muran, J. C., Segal, Z. V., Samstag, L. W., & Crawford, C. E. (1994). Patient pretreatment interpersonal problems and therapeutic alliance in short-term cognitive therapy. *Journal of Consulting and Clinical Psychology, 62*, 185–190.

National Council of Schools and Programs in Professional Psychology (NCSPP). (2007). *Competency developmental achievement levels of the National Council of Schools and Programs in Professional Psychology*. Retrieved from http://www.ncspp.info/DALof%20NCSPP%209-21-07.pdf

Norcross, J. C., & Wampold, B. E. (2011). Evidence-based therapy relationships: Research conclusions and clinical practice. *Psychotherapy, 48*, 98–102.

Ogles, B. M., Lambert, M. J., & Masters, K. S. (1996). *Assessing outcome in clinical practice*. Boston, MA: Allyn & Bacon.

Ogrodniczuk, J .S., Piper, W. E., Joyce, A. S., & McCallum, M. (1999). Transference interpretations in short-term dynamic psychotherapy. *Journal of Nervous and Mental Disease, 187*, 571–578.

Pachankis, J. E., & Goldfried, M. R. (2007). An integrative, principle-based approach to psychotherapy. In S. G. Hofmann & J. Weinberger (Eds.), *The art and science of psychotherapy* (pp. 49–68). New York: Routledge.

Patterson, G. R., & Forgatch, M. S. (1985). Therapist behavior as a determinant for client noncompliance: A paradox for the behavior modifier. *Journal of Consulting and Clinical Psychology, 53*, 846–851.

Persons, J. B. (2006). Case formulation-driven psychotherapy. *Clinical Psychology: Science and Practice, 13*, 167–170.

Piper, W. E., Joyce, A .S., McCallum, M., Azim, H. F., & Ogrodniczuk, J. D. (2002). *Interpretive and supportive psychotherapies: Matching therapy and patient personality*. Washington, DC: American Psychological Association.

Polanyi, M. (1967). *Personal knowledge*. London: Routledge & Kegan Paul.

Pretzer, J. L., & Beck, A. T. (2005). A cognitive theory of personality disorders. In M. F. Lenzenweger & J. F. Clarkin (Eds.), *Major theories of personality disorder* (pp. 43–113). New York: Guilford.

Quintana, S. M., & Holahan, W. (1992). Termination in short-term counseling: Comparison of successful and unsuccessful cases. *Journal of Counseling Psychology, 39*, 299–305.

Rodolfa, E., Bent, R., Eisman, E., Nelson, P., Rehm, L., & Ritchie, P. (2005). A cube model for competency development: Implications for psychology educators and regulators. *Professional Psychology: Research and Practice, 36*, 347–354.

Roe, D., Dekel, R., Harol, G., Fennig, S., & Fennig, S. (2006). Clients' feelings during termination of psychodynamically oriented psychotherapy. *Bulletin of the Menninger Clinic, 70*, 68–81.

Roland, A. (1996). *Cultural pluralism and psychoanalysis: The Asian and North American experience*. New York: Routledge.

Safran, J. D., & Muran, J. C. (2000). *Negotiating the therapeutic alliance: A relational treatment guide*. New York: Guildford.

Safran, J. D., & Muran, J. C. (2006). Has the concept of therapeutic alliance outlived its usefulness? *Psychotherapy: Theory, Research, Practice, Training, 43*, 286–291.

Safran, J. D., Muran, J. C., & Eubanks-Carter, C. (2011). Repairing alliance ruptures. *Psychotherapy, 48*, 80–87.

Safran, J. D., Muran, J. C., Samstag, L. W., & Stevens, C. (2001). Repairing alliance ruptures. *Psychotherapy: Theory, Research, Practice, Training, 38*, 406–412.

Sandler, J., & Sandler, A. M. (1978). On the development of object relationships and affects. *International Journal of Psychoanalysis, 59*, 285–296.

Satterfield, W. A., & Lyddon, W. J. (1995). Client attachment and perceptions of the working alliance with counselor trainees. *Journal of Counseling Psychology, 42*, 187–189.

Schafer, R. (1992). *Retelling a life: Narration and dialogue in psychoanalysis*. New York: Basic.

Schafer, R. (2004). Narrating, attending, and empathizing. *Literature and Medicine, 23*, 241–251.

Schafer, R. (2005a). *Insight and interpretation: The essential tools of psychoanalysis*. New York: Karnac.

Schafer, R. (2005b). Listening in psychoanalysis. *Narrative, 13*, 271–280.

Scheiber, S. C., Kramer, T. A. M., & Adamowski, S. E. (Eds.). (2003). *Core competencies for psychiatric practice: What clinicians need to know* (A report of the American Board of Psychiatry and Neurology). Arlington, VA: American Psychiatric.

Schlesinger, H. (1982). Resistance as process. In P. L. Wachtel (Ed.), *Resistance: Psychodynamic and behavioral approaches* (pp. 25–43). New York: Plenum.

Schmidt, H. G., & Rikers, R. M. J. P. (2007). How expertise develops in medicine: Knowledge encapsulation and illness script formation. *Medical Education, 41*, 1133–1139.

Schön, D. (1983). *The reflective practitioner: How professionals think in action*. London: Temple Smith.

Sifneos, P. E. (1972). *Short-term psychotherapy and emotional crisis*. Cambridge, MA: Harvard University Press.

Slade, A., Grienenberger, J., Bernbach, E., Levy, D., & Locker, A. (2005). Maternal reflective functioning, attachment, and the transmission gap: A preliminary study. *Attachment & Human Development, 7*, 283–298.

Spence, D. P. (1982). *Narrative truth and historical truth*. New York: Norton.

Sperry, L. (2010a). *Highly effective therapy: Developing essential clinical competencies in counseling and psychotherapy*. New York: Routledge.

Sperry, L. (2010b). *Core competencies in counseling and psychotherapy: Becoming a highly effective therapist*. New York: Routledge.

Stern, D. N. (2002). *The first relationship: Infant and mother*. Cambridge, MA: Harvard University Press.

Sternberg, R. J., & Horvath, J. A. (Eds.). (1999). *Tacit knowledge in professional practice: Researcher and practitioner perspectives*. Mahwah, NJ: Erlbaum.

Stewart, H. (1972). Six-months, fixed-term, once weekly psychotherapy: A report on 20 cases with follow-ups. *British Journal of Psychiatry, 121*, 425–435.

Stiles, W. B., & Goldsmith, J. Z. (2010). The alliance over time. In J. C. Muran & J. P. Barber (Eds.), *The therapeutic alliance. An evidence-based guide to practice* (pp. 44–62). New York: Guilford Press.

Stiles, W. B., Honos-Webb, L., & Surko, M. (1998) Responsiveness in psychotherapy. *Clinical Psychology: Science and Practice, 5,* 439–458.

Stricker, G., & Trierweiler, S. J. (1995). The local clinical scientist. A bridge between science and practice. *American Psychologist, 50,* 995–1002.

Strupp, H. H (1980). Humanism and psychotherapy: A personal statement of the therapist's essential values. *Psychotherapy: Theory, Research, & Practice, 17,* 396–400.

Strupp, H. H. (1993). The Vanderbilt psychotherapy studies: Synopsis. *Journal of Consulting and Clinical Psychology, 61,* 431–433.

Strupp, H. H., & Binder, J. L. (1984). *Psychotherapy in a new key: A guide to time-limited dynamic psychotherapy.* New York: Basic.

Strupp, H. H., & Hadley, S. W. (1977). A tripartite model of mental health and therapeutic outcomes. *American Psychologist, 32,* 187–196.

Summers, R. F., & Barber, J. P. (2010). *Psychodynamic therapy: A guide to evidence-based practice.* New York: Guilford.

Tjeltveit, A. C. (1986). The ethics of value conversion in psychotherapy: Appropriate and inappropriate therapist influence on client values. *Clinical Psychology Review, 6,* 515–537.

van der Kolk, B. A. (2000). Posttraumatic stress disorder and the nature of trauma. *Dialogues in Clinical Neuroscience, 2,* 7–22.

Wachtel, P. L. (1993). *Therapeutic communication: Principles and effective practice.* New York: Guildford.

Wachtel, P. L. (2008). *Relational theory and the practice of psychotherapy.* New York: Guilford.

Wachtel, P. L. (2011). *Therapeutic communication* (2nd ed.). New York: Guilford.

Wallin D. J. (2007). *Attachment in psychotherapy.* New York: Guilford.

Watson, J. C. (2010). Case formulation in EFT. *Journal of Psychotherapy Integration, 20,* 89–100.

Watson, J. C., Goldman, R. N., Greenberg, L. S., (2007). *Case studies in emotion-focused treatment of depression: A comparison of good and poor outcome.* Washington, DC: American Psychological Association.

Watzlawick, P., Beavin, J., & Jackson, D. (1967). *Pragmatics of human communication: A study of interaction patterns, pathologies, and paradoxes.* New York: Newton.

Weiner, J. B., & Bornstein, R. F. (2009). *Principles of psychotherapy* (3rd ed.). Hoboken, NJ: Wiley

Weiss, J., Sampson, J., & the Mount Zion Psychotherapy Research Group. (1986). *The psychoanalytic process: Theory, clinical observations, and empirical research.* New York: Guilford.

Whitehead, A. N. (1929). *The aim of education.* New York: Macmillan.

Winnicott, D. W. (1965). Ego distortions in terms of the true and false self. In *The maturational processes and the facilitating environment* (pp. 140–152). New York: International Universities Press.

Winnicott, D. W. (1975). Through paediatrics to psycho-analysis. *The International Psycho-Analytical Library, 100*, 1–325.

Winnicott, D. W. (1992). *The child, the family and the outside world.* New York: Perseus.

Young, J. E., Klosko, J. S., & Weishaar, M. E. (2003). *Schema therapy: A practitioner's guide.* New York: Guildford.

Zuroff, D. C., Blatt, S. J., Sotsky, S. M., Krupnick, J. L., Martin, D. J., Sanislow, C. A., & Simmens, S. (2000). Relation of therapeutic alliance and perfectionism to outcome in brief outpatient treatment of depression. *Journal of Consulting and Clinical Psychology, 68*, 114–124.

INDEX